21179

Michael Löwy

Georg Lukács –
From Romanticism
to Bolshevism

Translated by Patrick Camiller

Pour une sociologie des intellectuels révolutionnaires – L'evolution politique de Lukács 1908–1929 was first published by Presses Universitaires de France, Paris, 1976
© Presses Universitaires de France

This edition first published 1979
© NLB, 1979
NLB, 7 Carlisle Street, London W1

The translation of Chapter V, 'Lukács and Stalinism', was made by Ann Clafferty and was first published, in slightly different form, in *New Left Review*, 91 (May–June 1975).

Filmset in 'Monophoto' Ehrhardt by
Servis Filmsetting Ltd, Manchester

Printed in Great Britain by
Lowe & Brydone Printers, Thetford, Norfolk

Bound by Kemp Hall Bindery, Oxford

ISBN 86091 003 2

for ILANA
co-author of this work

Contents

Acknowledgements

I would like first of all to express my profound gratitude to Professor Louis-Vincent Thomas of l'Université René-Descartes, supervisor of my doctoral thesis, whose contribution to the direction of my research was of inestimable value.

My thanks are also due to all those who made criticisms or suggestions: Georges Haupt, György Litvan, Sami Naïr, Reginaldo Di Piero, Roberto Schwarz, Charles Urjewicz.

Particular thanks are due to Ilona Duczynska, whose letters were a stimulant and a very great assistance to me, to my friends of the 'Budapest School' – Agnes Heller, Ferenc Feher, and György Markus – whose criticisms, amicable and impassioned as they were, enhanced my understanding of Lukács's work, and to Professor Ernst Bloch, who kindly accorded me an interview.

I would also like to thank the researchers who kindly agreed to share the fruits of their labours with me: Laura Boella (Pisa), Paul Breines (New York), Eva Karadi (Budapest), Leandro Konder (Bonn). Thanks are also due to Martha Dufournaud and Rita Kiss, who translated some of Lukács's Hungarian writings for me.

I am grateful to the personnel of the Lukács Archive of Budapest (in particular Mr Ferenc Janossy, Lukács's executor), the library of the International Institute of Social History in Amsterdam, and the library of the Lelio Basso Foundation of Rome, all of whom allowed me access to their collections.

Finally, I would like to express my debt to the late Lucien Goldmann, who introduced me to the writings of Lukács and whose method has largely inspired my own work.

Introduction

The problem of intellectuals who join the struggle of the proletariat is as old as the workers' movement itself. Marx takes note of it in a famous passage of the *Communist Manifesto*: 'In times when the class struggle nears the decisive hour, the process of dissolution going on within the ruling class, in fact across the whole range of society, assumes such a violent, glaring character, that a small section of the ruling class cuts itself adrift, and joins the revolutionary class, the class that holds the future in its hands. Just as, therefore, at an earlier period, a section of the nobility went over to the bourgeoisie, so now a portion of the bourgeoisie goes over to the proletariat, and in particular, a portion of the bourgeois ideologists, who have raised themselves to the level of comprehending theoretically the historical movement as a whole.'[1]

These lines call for a number of comments. To start with, it is generally a portion of *petty-bourgeois* ideologues, rather than of the bourgeoisie itself, that goes over to the proletariat. The distinction is of great significance. In certain exceptional cases (Friedrich Engels!), individual bourgeois may pass to the side of the proletariat; but they do not constitute a *fraction*, however small, of the dominant class. Next, although it is possible to compare such intellectuals with the nobles who rallied to the Third Estate, we should not overlook the fact that these are *altogether distinct* phenomena. There are two specific reasons for this. First, the enlightened aristocrats of the eighteenth century went over to a class that already occupied positions of economic power, if not actual hegemony, and could provide a whole range of material and social privileges to its various allies or ideologues. Clearly this is not the case for those

---

[1] 'Manifesto of the Communist Party', in Marx, *The Revolutions of 1848*, Harmondsworth, 1978, p. 72 (translation modified).

intellectuals who side with the proletariat. Second, the extent of the shift has become much greater: whole sections of the petty-bourgeois intelligentsia are involved, not just individual 'traitors to their class' such as the nobles who rallied to the assembly of the Third Estate in June 1789. It should further be noted that the phenomenon arises not only when the struggle of the proletariat 'nears the decisive hour' or when the ruling class is 'in dissolution', but also during other stages of the class struggle. As the reaction of intellectuals to the victory of German fascism illustrates, it may even develop after a defeat of the workers' movement. Finally, 'comprehending theoretically the historical movement as a whole' is dialectically related to a politico-ideological commitment that must be explained in sociological terms. It is often the choice of a proletarian class position that makes it possible for intellectuals to attain such theoretical insight.[2]

Few Marxist thinkers other than Gramsci have tried to explain this phenomenon, even though its extent and importance for the workers' movement have grown in the course of the twentieth century. Certainly Lenin, who was himself an illustrious case in point, stressed the crucial role played by revolutionary intellectuals in the ideological struggle against the bourgeoisie and in the construction of a vanguard party. But he made only a few points that are of help in understanding *why* such intellectuals side with the proletariat. The present work is, of course, only a partial and extremely limited contribution to a future Marxist sociology of the revolutionary intelligentsia. It seeks to explain Lukács's political evolution until 1929 within the framework of a study of the radicalized intelligentsia of early-twentieth-century Germany and Hungary – and, in particular, those groups like the Max Weber Circle in Heidelberg and the Budapest 'Sunday Circle', in which Lukács was directly involved. Our twofold aim is to analyse the political ideas of a man often hailed as the greatest twentieth-century Marxist philosopher, and to grasp Lukács's ideological evolution as a case of *exemplary* significance for a sociological understanding of the problem of revolutionary intellectuals.

In studying 'the Lukács phenomenon', then, we shall employ the method of historical materialism – or, to be more precise, an interpretation of the latter which is largely inspired by Lukács's own *History and Class Consciousness*. We could almost say that this is not only a Marxist study of a Marxist thinker, but a Lukácsian analysis of Lukács.

[2] On the relationship between 'science' and 'ideology', 'a class standpoint' and 'objectivity', see M. Löwy, *Dialectique et révolution*, Paris, 1973.

Since our starting point will accordingly be the category of *totality*, we should first spell out the methodological consequences this involves.

1. In its political, aesthetic, and other aspects, the ideology of a given writer can be understood only in relation to his thought *as a whole*; and his thought must in turn be inserted into the *world view* that provides its structure of meaning.

2. Being an aspect of a concrete historical totality, a particular ideology, theory, or world view must be conceived in its dialectical connection with the relations of production, the class-struggle process, political conflict, and other ideological currents. More specifically, it should be understood in its relation to the way in which the various social classes, layers, and categories think and live: their interests, aspirations, desires, and aversions.

3. Dialectical understanding of a historical event – whether it be economic, political, or ideological – involves grasping its role within the social totality, within the *unity* of the historical process. Abstract, isolated 'facts' must be dissolved and conceived as moments of this unitary process.

4. The relationship with the historical, socio-economic, and politico-social totality is not a merely complementary aspect appended from without to the internal analysis of ideological systems and cultural products. This relationship *illuminates from within* the structure of meaning of the political, philosophical, or literary enterprise in question, enabling us to understand processes such as the ideological evolution of the author. It is therefore a key element in interpreting the very *meaning* and content of his work.[3]

5. Research of this kind inevitably goes beyond the traditional compartmentalization of academic disciplines: even when it lends priority to one particular field of investigation (in this case, the sociological field), it involves an approach that is at once economic, sociological, historical, political, philosophical, and so on.

In *History and Class Consciousness* Lukács makes a famous observation on which a great deal of ink has flowed: 'It is not the primacy of economic

---

[3] See L. Goldmann, *Recherches dialectiques*, Paris, 1969, p. 42.

motives in historical explanation that constitutes the decisive difference between Marxism and bourgeois thought, but the point of view of totality. . . . The primacy of the category of totality is the bearer of the principle of revolution in science.'[4] Contrary to the claims of sundry 'materialist' critics of Lukács, this statement does not deny the role of the economy in the historical process: it was intended simply to bring out what makes Marxism a *revolutionary* science. It in no way prevents Lukács from explicitly recognizing 'the objective economic foundations of social institutions'.[5] Our analysis of anti-capitalist intellectuals and of Lukács's own thought will therefore be situated within the framework of Marx's thesis concerning *economic determination in the last instance*. However, this thesis is itself the object of so much misunderstanding that it needs to be clarified in several respects.

First, the decisive role of the economic 'infrastructure' asserts itself with regard to ideological phenomena through a series of *mediations*, the most important of which is *the field of class struggle*.

Second, to explain a cultural creation by reference to the economy is not at all the same as to offer a psychological explanation in terms of a given individual's 'economic interests'. Far from being reducible to vulgar Benthamite utilitarianism, the method of Marxism focuses on the objective interests of social classes – on the economy as the *objective precondition* of social life.

Third, in the life and social activity of individuals, groups, and even social classes, the *principal role* may be played by political or ideological factors throughout a given historical situation or period. Nevertheless, it is the relations of production within the concrete social formation that *account for the precise role* and, in certain cases, *the predominance of such factors*. Marx acknowledges the weight of religion and politics in the Middle Ages and Antiquity respectively: 'The Middle Ages could not live on Catholicism, nor could the ancient world on politics. On the contrary, it is the manner in which they gained their livelihood which explains why in one case politics, in the other case Catholicism, played the chief part (*die Hauptrolle spielte*).'[6]

Fourth, every concrete analysis must take account of the *relative autonomy* enjoyed by the sphere of ideology; it is quite evident that thinking also evolves according to a set of internal exigencies of

[4] G. Lukács, *History and Class Consciousness*, London, 1971, p. 27.
[5] Ibid., p. 57.
[6] Marx, *Capital*, vol. i, Harmondsworth, 1976, p. 176.

systematization, coherence, rationality, and so on. Nothing could be more sterile than to approach the entire content of a literary, philosophical, or political undertaking with nothing else in mind than to discover its 'foundation in the economy'. This would be to ignore the rules of continuity specific to the history of ideologies, to ignore the peculiarities of each ideological sphere (art, morality, etc.) or the requirements of the internal logic of a given enterprise (or even the author's personal traits considered as a psychologically determined personality). This concept of relative autonomy (in the original sense of the Greek *auto-nomos*: 'specific rules') allows us to go beyond the eternal polemic between, on the one hand, that idealist history of thought for which ideological systems completely detached from socio-historical 'contingency' float freely in the pure air of the Absolute, and on the other hand, that vulgar, pseudo-Marxist economism that reduces the entire universe of thought to an unmediated reflection of the 'infrastructure'.[7]

In the light of these methodological presuppositions, it seems to us that the evolution of Lukács's thought should be related to an analysis of those socio-economic, political, and other historical conditions under which an anti-capitalist and/or revolutionary ideology took shape in the German and Hungarian intelligentsia at the turn of the century. This is not the same as a traditional, academic study of a writer's 'milieu' or 'influences'. What is of interest to us is not Lukács's 'milieu' in the vague and superficial, or anecdotal, sense of the term, but the radicalized sector of a clearly-defined social category such as it existed during a precise historical period and in a complex relationship to certain social classes. Rather than 'explain' Lukács's thought by the influence of Weber or Dostoevsky, we shall seek to explain *why* he was influenced by a particular author at a given stage in his development. For the way in which a doctrine is 'received' is itself a social fact to be understood in relation to a concrete historical totality.

It is impossible to understand the 'metamorphoses' of Lukács's philosophical and political thought without studying sociologically how sections of the German and Hungarian intelligentsia came to oppose

[7] See the writings of Lucien Goldmann: *The Human Sciences and Philosophy*, London 1969; *Recherches dialectiques*, and others. We cannot, of course, in the scope of this introduction, go into the key questions of historical materialism. The above remarks are intended simply as a set of 'programmatic' theses laying down the methodological guidelines of this study.

capitalism; how some of them were then attracted to the workers' movement; and how, above all in Hungary, they were finally integrated into the revolutionary vanguard of the proletariat. There are a number of reasons why the 'case' of Lukács is to a certain extent *paradigmatic*, throwing an especially clear light on the general problem of the revolutionary intelligentsia.

1. After Marx, Lukács is probably the *most important* 'traditional' intellectual to have passed into the ranks of the proletariat – 'traditional' being understood with all its academic and/or cultural connotations. (In this sense, of course, such political leaders as Lenin or Rosa Luxemburg were far from typical 'traditional' intellectuals.)

2. Unlike the majority of revolutionary thinkers, who came to socialism during their early youth, Lukács embraced militant Marxism at quite an advanced age. It is thus possible to study systematically all the stages of his ideological evolution. In other words, the road Lukács travelled in ten years was covered by most Marxist intellectuals in a much shorter space of time, often before they were eighteen years old. Hence the richness and interest of his 'long march' towards Marx and Lenin.

3. In the breadth of his thought, which is rooted in two cultures at once and yet goes beyond them towards a global intellectual horizon, Lukács is an essentially *universal* figure – his opponents would say 'cosmopolitan'.

4. The social bases of Lukács's ideological evolution are also universal in character, inasmuch as they combine the problematic of an industrially advanced social formation (Germany) with that of a relatively 'backward' and dependent society (Hungary).

5. Lukács possessed in the highest degree that virtue of *Gründlichkeit* which is attributed, rightly or wrongly, to German thought as a whole. At each stage of his intellectual development, he drew out the final conclusions of his positions, always operating with a profound, systematic, and rigorous consistency. In studying Lukács's work through all its stages, we can thus gain a better understanding of a number of twentieth-century cultural and political phenomena: neo-romanticism, the tragic view of the world (and, in Goldman's opinion, existentialism), 'ultra-leftism', Bolshevism and Stalinism.

I
Towards a Sociology of the Anti-Capitalist Intelligentsia

1. Intellectuals as a Social Category

What is an intellectual, that indisputably strange being so difficult to classify? The first obvious point is that the intellectual may be recruited in every class and layer of society; he may be an aristocrat (Tolstoy), an industrialist (Owen), a professor (Hegel), or a craftsman (Proudhon). Intellectuals are not a class but a *social category*, defined not by their place in the production process, but by their relation to non-economic instances of the social structure. Just as bureaucrats and military men are defined by their relationship to politics, so are intellectuals to be situated in relation to the ideological superstructure. Thus, intellectuals are a social category defined by their ideological role: they are the *direct producers* of the ideological sphere, the creators of *ideologico-cultural products.* Their specific place in what we may call the process of ideological production is the place of the immediate producer, as distinct from that of the entrepreneur, administrator, or distributor of cultural goods. Defined in this way, intellectuals comprise such groups as writers, artists, poets, philosophers, scientists, research workers, publicists, theologians, certain kinds of journalist, teacher and student, and so on. They make up the 'creative' sector of a broader mass of 'intellectual' (as opposed to 'manual') workers – a mass that includes the liberal professions, office workers, technicians, and others. Intellectuals are therefore the section of this mass furthest removed from economic production.

Although the behaviour of intellectuals is to some extent determined by individual class origin, it is more potently influenced by membership in a common social category. Similarly, except in times of crisis, the bureaucrat and the military man behave first of all as members of their respective category.

Being the most distant from the process of material production, the social category of intellectuals enjoys a certain autonomy from classes, which is expressed in its instability and in various shifts and fluctuations. This is why Alfred Weber and Karl Mannheim bestowed upon them the epithet *Freischwebend*, or 'free-floating'. However, there is no really 'neutral' or supra-class intelligentsia – contrary to what Mannheim suggests with his tendency to make such autonomy absolute. The floating of intellectuals, like that of the hot-air balloons on St John's Night, is a provisional state; in general, they eventually yield to the law of gravity and are attracted either by one of the great social classes in conflict (the bourgeoisie, the proletariat, sometimes the peasantry) or by the class nearest to themselves: *the petty bourgeoisie*.

In fact, although the label 'petty-bourgeois intellectual' is often employed as a term of abuse, it contains a large measure of truth. Between the intelligentsia and the petty bourgeoisie there is a relationship of affinity, closeness, or complicity which can be sociologically explained as follows. First, the majority of the intelligentsia is recruited from the petty bourgeoisie, or to be more precise, from the sector of 'intellectual workers' as opposed to other members of that class such as small traders and small peasants. We should therefore neither ignore nor overestimate the bond of social origin that undeniably links a major fraction of this social category to the petty bourgeoisie. Second, the intellectual professions of writer, teacher, artist, and others, as well as the means of labour and subsistence offered to intellectuals, have traditionally fallen by their very nature to the petty bourgeoisie, and in particular to members of the liberal professions. (Of course, a minority of intellectuals have nevertheless belonged, by occupation and social position, to the bourgeoisie, the aristocracy, and even the working class.)

2. The Anti-Capitalist Radicalization of Intellectuals

In an article written in 1920, Lukács argued that the intelligentsia as a social class was not revolutionary, and that intellectuals can become revolutionaries only *as individuals*.[1] What Lukács seemed to forget, however, was that when a veritable mass of individuals (intellectuals)

---

[1] Lukács, 'Zur Organisationsfrage der Intellektuellen', *Kommunismus*, vol. 1, no. 3, 1920, pp. 17–18.

become revolutionary, we are dealing no longer with a 'personal' case or a psychological matter, but with a *social phemonenon* requiring a sociological explanation.

Now, it is obvious that Lukács was by no means an isolated case. A large part of his own circle and a great number of intellectuals of diverse backgrounds joined the Hungarian Communist Party between 1918 and 1919. And as Lukács himself recognized in 1969, many more supported Béla Kún's Commune in one way or another: 'Although this was not true of the entire Hungarian intelligentsia, the leading stratum of Hungarian culture was disposed, from the very first, to collaborate with the soviet regime. Consequently, the government's cultural policy acquired a very broad social base.'[2]

In point of fact, Lukács and his Hungarian comrades are just one example of a much more widespread experience. Ever since Marx's time, countless intellectuals have joined the political ranks of the proletariat, especially its revolutionary vanguard; and yet the sociological foundations of this indisputable and well-known fact have not been adequately studied. We shall now attempt to formulate a number of general hypotheses on this subject, basing ourselves on the highly exemplary case of Lukács. The problem we must confront is this: why do a significant number of intellectuals become radically opposed to capitalism, and why do they end up embracing the workers' movement and the Marxist *Weltanschauung*? The causes appear to be very different from those that lead the proletariat towards socialism. For the path of the proletariat involves the direct experience of exploitation, and its principal driving force is of a directly socio-economic order.

How, then, does an intellectual become *anti-capitalist*? How does the intelligentsia become *radicalized*?[3] What, in particular, were the causes of this phenomenon during Lukács's youth? Two distinct kinds of sociological process must be analysed: that characteristic of the petty bourgeoisie as a whole, and that which is of an ethico-cultural nature and specific to intellectuals. Given the deep affinity between petty bourgeoisie and intelligentsia, the 'mechanisms' whereby the former is radicalized necessarily have repercussions upon the latter. The causes that produce an

---

[2] Lukács, 'La politique culturelle de la Commune de Budapest' (1969), in *Action Poétique*, no. 49, 1972, p. 29.

[3] *'Radical.* Adj. which seeks to act on the underlying cause of the effects one wishes to change', *Petit Robert* dictionary, p. 1447. [Cf. the definition given by the *Shorter Oxford Dictionary*: 'going to the root or origin . . . esp. *radical change, radical cure*' – translator's note.]

anti-capitalist mentality within the petty bourgeoisie are therefore largely operative upon intellectuals. However, tendencies that become diluted within the class as a whole assume a much more concentrated and intense form in the social category whose social function is precisely ideological elaboration.

As regards the petty bourgeoisie, considered as a social class defined by its position in the relations of production, these causes are essentially socio-economic and socio-political.

1. The 'pre-capitalist' character of labour within the petty bourgeoisie. For the artisan, the peasant with a small plot, the member of a liberal profession, or the traditional intellectual, there is no separation between the producer and the product of his labour, between individual and production process, or between the labourer's personality and his creation. The development of capitalism, which begins to split, dissociate, and tear apart this unity, is felt by the petty bourgeois as a process inimical to his way of life, his very mode of being.

2. Proletarianization of the petty bourgeoisie and of intellectuals. This takes various forms: unemployment or under-employment, falling living standards, reduction to the lot of the wage labourers. Frequently, but not necessarily, the fact that the petty bourgeois thus draws objectively closer to the proletarian condition results in a bitter and virulent revolt against a capitalism held responsible for such brutal 'downgrading'.[4]

3. Politically, the Jacobinism of the left wing of the petty bourgeoisie – a specific combination of plebeian democracy and romantic moralism (Rousseau) – tends to come into conflict with the ideology and liberal-individualist practice of the big bourgeoisie. In countries in which the bourgeoisie is playing a revolutionary role, this contradiction is more or less neutralized: the petty bourgeoisie and intellectuals tend to gravitate towards the bourgeoisie, as happened in eighteenth-century France. By contrast, in 'backward' countries in the nineteenth century (Germany) and twentieth century (Russia), where the bourgeoisie is no longer revolutionary and, fearing the popular masses, capitulates to the monarchy, the feudalists, and the conservatives, petty-bourgeois Jacobinism tends to become radical and to clash with a bourgeoisie accused of betraying democratic principles. Where the petty bourgeoisie and intelligentsia are at the height of a struggle for freedom and democracy, such radicalization

---

[4] Such revolt, of course, does not always lead to socialism, and may even lead to fascism.

may even lead a fraction to break violently with the bourgeoisie and become socialist. Two classical examples are that of Marx and a number of German intellectuals before 1848, and that of the Russian intelligentsia after the end of the nineteenth century. In Russia between 1917 and 1919, not only the intellectuals but also considerable sections of the urban and, above all, rural petty bourgeoisie gave their support to the Bolsheviks, who seemed the only force capable of realizing the tasks of the democratic revolution.

It remains to examine the specific causes of the anti-capitalist radicaliz-ation of intellectuals *as intellectuals* – that is to say, abstracted from the features they have in common with the petty bourgeoisie. Since intellectuals are defined as a distinct social category by their relation to the ideological superstructure, it is understandable that their evolution towards socialism should pass through certain ethico-cultural and politico-moral mediations.

First, intellectuals, writers, poets, artists, theologians, scientists, and others *live in a universe governed by qualitative values*: the living and the dead, the beautiful and the ugly, truth and error, good and evil, the just and the unjust, and so on. Thus, many intellectuals find themselves, so to speak, naturally, spontaneously, and organically in contradiction with the capitalist universe – one rigorously governed by *quantitative values*, exchange-values. For an artist, a painting is above all else beautiful, luminous, expressive, or disturbing; for capitalism, it is first and foremost an object worth 50,000 francs. Here there is an opposition between two fundamentally *heterogeneous* worlds; and between the intellectual and capitalism there is frequently a relation of antipathy, in the old alchemist's sense of 'lack of affinity between two substances'. The two substances are qualitative and quantitative values; ethical or aesthetic culture and money. Nor is this a static relationship, for the quantitative universe is constantly expanding, threatening to absorb and denature qualitative values, to dissolve and digest them, to reduce them to their exchange-value.[5] The intellectual tends to resist this constant threat of the transformation of every material or cultural good, every feeling, moral principle, or aesthetic emotion, into a commodity-'thing' to be brought to market and sold for a fair price. And to the extent that he resists, he cannot fail to become instinctively anti-capitalist in his very marrow. Only insofar as he

[5] Cf. Lucien Goldmann, *Towards a Sociology of the Novel*, London, 1975, p. 11.

capitulates, accepting the domination of exchange-value over the qualitative values of his ideologico-cultural universe, only to this extent can he be integrated by capitalism. This customary distinction between two types of intellectual sometimes takes the form of a violent break.[6] But, of course, there are also intermediate cases in which an eclectic attempt is made to reconcile the two demands.

(The choice of resistance is clearly expressed in the romantic anti-capitalism and ideological counterposition of 'Culture' and 'Civilization' that marked the Central European intelligentsia in the late nineteenth and early twentieth centuries. One of Lukács's greatest merits is to have reformulated, in the Marxist terms of the theory of reification, the confused, romantic critique directed by intellectuals against the inexorable process of quantification characteristic of the capitalist mode of production.)

Second, since intellectuals are so far removed from material production, and above all since their very social category is defined by its ideological role, they constitute the group in society for which ideologies and values have the greatest significance and the most crucial weight. Thus, no one 'takes more seriously' than intellectuals the principles, values, and ideals of bourgeois humanism – from the Renaissance through the Enlightenment to classical German idealism. Now, Lukács shows that the bourgeoisie, once in power, was forced to act in contradiction with its own ideology, to deny, degrade, and in practice to abandon the values it had never ceased to claim as its own.[7] It is therefore in the name of such humanist principles that the intelligentsia turns against capitalism and the bourgeoisie, in some cases discovering the proletariat as the class capable of genuinely realizing the ideals of freedom, equality and fraternity. For intellectuals, 'Marxist humanism therefore becomes the inheritor of the highest achievements of bourgeois thinkers, and the workers' movement should become the practical executor of ideas that have hitherto been supported only in theory'.[8]

---

[6] Thus, Salvador Dali was expelled from the group of surrealists, who gave him the dishonourable nickname 'Avida Dollars' ['dollar-greedy'].

[7] Lukács calls this 'the moral crisis of the internal lie [of] the bourgeoisie'. ('The Old Culture and the New Culture', in Lukács, *Marxism and Human Liberation*, New York, 1978, p. 10.)

[8] J.-M. Brohm, 'Introduction' to F. Jakubowsky, *Les superstructures idéologiques dans la conception matérialiste de l'histoire*, Paris, 1971, p. 60. It should be added, however, that Marxist humanism is not merely the continuation but the dialectical *Aufhebung* of bourgeois humanism.

For Lukács and his generation, the outbreak of world war in 1914 was probably the most vivid demonstration of the gulf between the humanist traditions of classical culture and the concrete reality of bourgeois society and the capitalist world. The 'politicization' he and many other intellectuals experienced after 1914 is, to some extent, an expression of this ethico-cultural trauma.

Of course, intellectuals did not react to this contradiction in a homogeneous manner. In relation to the World War, for example, three broad tendencies may be distinguished: 1) an attempt to deny the conflict between the reality of capitalism and its humanist ideology, such that the 1914–18 war is presented either as a struggle of German civilization against Russian barbarism or as a struggle of western democracy against Germanic barbarism; 2) a critique of the war based precisely upon the liberal-democratic ideology of peace, brotherhood among peoples, and the democratic rights of nations – a critique, however, which may grow more radical, assuming a globally anti-imperialist and anti-capitalist character and leading to: 3) the discovery of the proletariat as the sole bearer of democratic and humanist values against generalized bourgeois barbarity.

The latter two variants are possible because of the very nature of the social category – the specific weight of values within the intellectuals' way of life. Whether they choose the second or the third variant depends not only on the degree to which they are *repelled* by capitalism, but also on the strength of the *attraction* exercised by the proletarian camp.

Such attraction is above all ideological or theoretical. *Marxism*, being a consistently scientific and revolutionary system, appears to many radicalized intellectuals as the only theory that explains and uncovers the true origins of reification, the only theory that identifies capitalism as the root cause of the crushing sway of the quantitative – of the depersonalization of life, the degradation of values, and the existence of war. Marxism attracts intellectuals not only by virtue of its scientific rigour and the universal character of its world view, but also because it seeks to radically abolish the hegemony of exchange-value over social life, and because it points to a real social force striving towards that goal: the revolutionary proletariat. Many radicalized intellectuals discover the proletariat as subject of history and gravedigger of capitalism only through the mediation of Marxism as a theoretical system. Thus, whether intellectuals side with the proletariat politically, or whether their revolt remains instead purely ethico-cultural, depends to some extent on the existence of a Marxist tradition and the accessibility of Marxist literature in their country.

Sometimes, a radical and consistent rejection of capitalism may by itself lead intellectuals to discover Marxism and pass into the ranks of the proletariat. But for a large section, an external event like the 1917 Russian Revolution must first act as a catalyst, crystallizing their diffuse and amorphous anti-capitalism and attracting them to the side of the proletariat. This was true especially of intellectuals who, like Lukács, reached an extreme degree of violent ethico-cultural opposition to capitalism and were not at all attracted by a Social Democratic workers' movement under reformist, parliamentarian hegemony, whether in its revisionist or Kautskyist variant. Only with the massive irruption of the revolutionary proletariat onto the stage of history (in 1918–19) did this 'extremist' fringe of the intelligentsia rally to the working class by joining its most radical wing: the Communist Party.

3. The Anti-Capitalism of Intellectuals in Germany

Why is it that the phenomenon of an anti-capitalist intelligentsia, more or less universal in Europe at the turn of the century, reached an especially high pitch in Germany? One reason was undoubtedly the tradition of romantic anti-capitalism which had been strongly implanted among German intellectuals since the early nineteenth century.

According to Lukács, 'the romantic ideology, despite a temporary retreat in the mid nineteenth century, had the greatest influence of all over German intellectuals. And this was no accident, since its forms best corresponded to the situation of intellectuals amid German wretchedness. . . .'[9] In fact, their social situation and way of life closely bound intellectuals to the pre-capitalist sectors of German society, the petty bourgeoisie in particular. For while German romanticism was an ideology common to the social layers and classes whose interests and way of life were being shaken by the development of capitalism, the traditional petty bourgeoisie formed the most important social base of the movement, furnishing its main literary, philosophical and political spokesmen.[10]

[9] Lukács, *Brève histoire de la littérature allemande*, Paris, 1949, p. 94.

[10] Within this class a particularly important role was played by a social category absent in Catholic countries like France: the scions of Protestant pastors. 'It is especially the son of the Protestant parson in whom the Enlightenment stirs doubts of the traditional religion, but who does not therefore succumb to the opposite extreme of an abstract rationalism. He experiences a transformation of his religious attitude. All his traditional habits of thought and emotional reactions which were fostered by the religious life in the parsonage survive the

In romantic ideology, opposition to the Enlightenment, the French Revolution and the Napoleonic Code combined with an anti-capitalist rejection of the bourgeois social universe, of economic liberalism and even industrialization. Faced with the development of capitalism, which progressively reduces man to an abstract, calculable quantity and establishes a rigorously quantitative system of reasoning, romanticism passionately defended the concrete, qualitative and intuitive forms of living and thinking, and the personal and concrete human relations which still lived on amongst the pre-capitalist layers (peasantry, petty bourgeoisie, nobility). Old traditions, life-styles and social attitudes, now spurned by abstract capitalist rationalism, were thus ideologically rehabilitated and refurbished by the romantics.[11] Against the abstract conception of property and freedom propagated by the liberal bourgeoisie, romantic doctrine developed the traditional, qualitative view of property and freedom as concrete, personal relations. For example, feudal property – inalienable, non-quantifiable, and organically tied to the owner – was counterposed to the venality of the modern capitalist relationship. For Adam Müller, 'all the capital which past centuries accumulated and rightly immobilized has been commercialized and drawn into the process of universal depreciation'. 'Everything that can be turned into money is stripped from landed property, as if the whole world had to be surrendered to the caprice of loveless exploiters. The valueless corpse of an age-old suzerainty is abandoned for a song . . . the whole of the present-day money economy is but the outward sign of that anti-social mentality, that proud egotism, that immoral infatuation with Enlightenment rationalism which

---

impact of the Enlightenment. Deprived of their positive content, they are directed with redoubled strength against the rationalist atmosphere of the time.' (K. Mannheim, 'Conservative Thought', in *Essays on Sociology and Social Psychology*, London, 1953, p. 123.) See also R. Aron, *German Sociology*, London, 1957, p. 114: 'German philosophers, especially in the nineteenth century, came largely from a background of officials, particularly church officials; the clergyman's son is the typical representative. . . . Even if they have lost their religious faith they retain a certain feeling for religion as the highest form of spiritual aspiration. . . . This kind of religion without God leads to a recognition of the role of the emotions, which cannot be reduced to reason, and frequently inspires a protest against capitalist, rationalized society.'

[11] Mannheim, pp. 87–90. In Mannheim's view there is a certain affinity between conservative and proletarian thought: 'Although deriving from entirely different basic aims, this affinity nevertheless unites the two modes of thought in opposition to the aims of the bourgeois capitalist world, and the abstractness of its thought.' (Ibid., p. 92.) In the section on Hungarian intellectuals, we shall return to Mannheim's essay and examine its relationship to Lukács's thought.

gave rise to the hideous revolutions through which we have been living for thirty years now.'[12] Adam Müller categorically rejected the economic doctrine of Adam Smith, on the grounds that it 'hands over the State bound hand and foot to industry, transforms every dealing into a commercial transaction, every service into wage-labour, and recognizes only one form of human relations, namely, the market'.[13]

Paradoxically, because of its conservative anti-capitalist standpoint, romanticism was able to afford the luxury of a vision of class contradictions within industrial society more lucid than that of liberal-bourgeois ideology, blinded by the myth of 'pre-established harmony'. 'Since we have undertaken to build a world on egotism,' wrote Müller, 'since we have undertaken to build a rational edifice that excludes God and Revelation, a money system that knows nothing of free, mutual services, a private property not balanced by communal goods, in short a State without a Church – why should we be surprised that, in such a world, only two classes are left confronting each other: the small class of owners and the infinitely large one of those who own nothing?'[14]

The last phrase inevitably recalls certain formulations of the *Communist Manifesto*. Marx, however, had nothing but contempt for what he called 'feudal socialism'. While recognizing that 'at times, by its bitter, witty and incisive criticism, [it] strikes the bourgeoisie to the very heart's core', he stressed that it is 'always ludicrous in its effect, through total incapacity to comprehend the march of modern history'.[15] He was no less critical of the other variant of mid-century neo-romanticism: that 'German socialism' or 'true socialism' which was the politico-ideological expression of the pre-capitalist petty bourgeoisie.[16] In fact, Marx's socialism had nothing in

---

[12] Adam Müller, *Deutsche Staatsanzeigen*, 1816, quoted here from J. Droz, *Le romantisme politique en Allemagne*, Paris, 1963, pp. 98–9.

[13] Ibid., p. 95.

[14] Ibid., pp. 165–6.

[15] 'Manifesto of the Communist Party', in Marx, *The Revolutions of 1848*, Harmondsworth, 1978, p. 88.

[16] Ibid., p. 92: 'While this "true" socialism thus served the governments as a weapon for fighting the German bourgeoisie, it, at the same time, directly represented a reactionary interest, the interest of the German philistines. In Germany the petty-bourgeois class, a relic of the sixteenth century, and since then constantly cropping up again under various forms, is the real social basis of the existing state of things. To preserve this class is to preserve the existing state of things in Germany. The industrial and political supremacy of the bourgeoisie threatens it with certain destruction – on the one hand, from the concentration of capital; on the other, from the rise of a revolutionary proletariat. "True" socialism appeared to kill these two birds with one stone. It spread like an epidemic.'

common, either socially or ideologically, with anti-capitalist romanticism. Its roots lay in a quite different section of the petty bourgeoisie – the Jacobin, enlightened, revolutionary-democratic, anti-feudal and 'Francophile' section, whose brilliant literary representative was Heinrich Heine, an intransigent enemy of romanticism. Originating in the most advanced and most 'bourgeois' regions of Germany (the Rhineland and Westphalia), this 1793-type 'republican', and often Jewish, intelligentsia was profoundly disappointed by the political 'cowardice' of the German liberal bourgeoisie, by its incapacity to wage a consistent revolutionary-democratic struggle against the feudal monarchy. Some of them therefore broke with the bourgeoisie and sought another class ally against the established regime. On his arrival in Paris in late 1843, Marx found a clear and coherent solution, imposing itself with irrefutable clarity: the proletariat would play this revolutionary role by achieving both the political (anti-feudal) and the universal human (socialist) emancipation of Germany.[17] To some degree, Schopenhauer and especially Nietzsche served as links between early-nineteenth-century romanticism and its refurbished version of 1880 to 1918. But Nietzsche's social and political ideology both stood near and ran counter to the anti-capitalist current of romanticism. He largely shared Adam Müller's basic positions: hatred of the French Revolution ('for then the last political nobleness Europe had known, that of seventeenth- and eighteenth-century France, collapsed under the weight of vindictive popular instincts'[18]) and hatred of the 'French ideas', 'modern ideas', or 'eighteenth-century ideas' rooted in English 'plebeian commonness'.[19] And yet he saw in Napoleon, that arch-enemy of conservative Romantics, not only 'a synthesis of the *inhuman* and the *super-human*', but even the *embodiment* of 'the ancient classical ideal . . . the noble ideal *par excellence*'.[20]

The same contradictions may be found in Nietzsche's attitude to capitalism. Like the romantics, he violently criticized machine-production, the modern division of labour, the abolition of small craft-production, the depersonalization of individuals, and the growth of large industrial towns – all phenomena that he intuitively associated with the cultural decline of European society. And, again like the romantics, he

[17] 'Introduction to the Critique of Hegel's Philosophy of Right', in Marx, *Early Writings*, Harmondsworth, 1975, pp. 255–7.
[18] Nietzsche, *The Genealogy of Morals*, New York, 1956, pp. 186–7 (translation modified).
[19] Nietzsche, *Beyond Good and Evil*, Chicago, 1955, pp. 190–1.
[20] Nietzsche, *The Genealogy of Morals*, p. 187.

counterposed to the uncultured industrial epoch ('the twilight of the arts') an idealized vision of the lofty culture of pre-capitalist societies. According to Lukács, 'the romantic critique of capitalist civilization is at the heart of Nietzsche's philosophy and hence of his aesthetics'.[21] Nevertheless, in his passionate and ferocious hostility to the Christian religion, the Church, and the clergy (*'Ecrasez l'infâme!'*), in his brutally individualist ethic of the superman and visceral anti-collectivism (hatred of 'the herd') Nietzsche sharply diverged from the romantic current and brought a new dimension to 'the German ideology'. It is beyond the scope of this work to enter the heated debate on Nietzsche's 'legacy': was he the harbinger and prophet of imperialism and fascist barbarism (as Lukács alleged), or was he rather a forerunner of the libertarian mentality?[22] Suffice it to say that when romantic anti-capitalism developed in certain literary and academic circles at the turn of the century, it often passed through the ideological mediation of Nietzsche's thought.

Now, during this period in Germany, the cultural critique of capitalism found root among intellectuals in general, and especially among writers and poets. But it was in university circles that it reached its most intense, systematic, and consistent expression. Why did the universities become such centres of romantic anti-capitalist ideology?

German academics in general – and above all the *Geisteswissenschaften* sector of classical scholars, philosophers, legal scientists, historians and social scientists – enjoyed an especially privileged social position during the nineteenth century. A relatively homogeneous and well-integrated community, marked by singular prestige, influence and status, these 'mandarins' held a dominant position in Germany's system of stratifi-

---

[21] Lukács, 'Nietzsche als Vorläufer der faschistischen Asthetik' (1934), in F. Mehring, G. Lukács, *Friedrich Nietzsche*, Berlin, 1957, p. 57. See also p. 48: 'In his attitude to the cultural effects of capitalist development, Nietzsche begins from the positions of romantic anti-capitalism – from its critique of the culture-destroying results of the "machine-age".' Lukács quotes the following passage as a typical example of Nietzsche's approach: 'Soldiers and leaders always have a much higher relationship to one another than worker and employer. For the present, at least, all civilization based on a military foundation stands high above all so-called industrial civilization; the latter in its present form is in general the lowest form of existence known up to the present time.' (Ibid., p. 55.)

[22] The anarchist Rudolf Rocker quotes approvingly the following words of Nietzsche: 'Culture and the state . . . are antagonists. . . . The one prospers at the expense of the other. All great periods of culture are periods of political decline. Whatever is great in a cultured sense is non-political, is even antipolitical.' (R. Rocker, 'The Ideology of Anarchism', in I.L. Horowitz (ed.), *The Anarchists*, New York, 1964, pp. 191–2.) The link is clear between this position and Thomas Mann's views in his 1918 *Reflections of an Unpolitical Man*.

:ation. In fact, their pre-eminence corresponded to a precise stage in the development of the German social formation – one in which the feudal mode of production was losing its dominance, but industrial capitalism had not yet established its final hegemony. 'At that intermediate stage, the ownership of significant amounts of liquid capital has not yet become either widespread or widely accepted as a qualification for social status, and hereditary titles based on landholdings, while still relevant, are no longer absolute prerequisites. In this situation, educational background and professional status may well become the only important bases for claims upon social standing that can rival the traditional prestige of the aristocracy.'[23]

The state form corresponding in Germany to this socio-economic transition – namely, a highly bureaucratized traditional monarchy – inevitably furthered the social, political and cultural power of the mandarins. It was university professors who controlled the entire system of qualification, articled service, examination, selection and ideological formation required for the recruitment of personnel to the bureaucracy. They therefore held a strategically crucial position vis-à-vis the political-administrative structure of the state. Max Weber, comparing the German university system to the Chinese mandarinate, stressed the importance of general cultural training for access to the bureaucratic state apparatus: in Germany as in China, 'such an education, until recently and almost exclusively, was a prerequisite for the official career leading to positions of command in civil and military administration'.[24]

Thus, insofar as higher education was crucial to the stratification system in Imperial Germany, academics occupied an extraordinarily privileged and influential position during the nineteenth century. The university mandarinate was the exponent and most prestigious representative of a

[23] F. Ringer, *The Decline of the German Mandarins: The German Academic Community, 890–1933*, Cambridge, Massachusetts, 1969, p. 7. According to Ringer, 'if industrialization s slow and state-controlled, if the traditional social organization persists for a long time, then burgher intellectuals are more likely to concentrate attention exclusively upon the rights of the learned. They will seek to constitute a kind of nobility of the educated to supersede the "merely traditional" ruling class . . .' (ibid., p. 7).
[24] *From Max Weber, Essays in Sociology* (ed. Gerth and Mills), London, 1967, p. 427. Weber's preceding remarks on China can be almost literally applied to the German mandarins of the nineteenth century: 'Social rank in China has been determined more by qualification for office than by wealth. This qualification, in turn, has been determined by education, and especially by examinations. . . . The increasingly bureaucratic structure of Chinese politics and of their carriers has given to the whole literary tradition of China its characteristic stamp.' (Ibid., p. 416.)

whole 'cultured elite' stretching into the liberal professions, the bureaucracy, the army, and so on.

For the neo-Kantian philosopher and academic Friedrich Paulsen, writing in 1902 about the German universities, 'those who have a university education form a kind of intellectual aristocracy. . . . They constitute a kind of official nobility, and as a matter of fact, they all really take part in the government and administration. . . . On the whole, those who follow these callings constitute a homogeneous social stratum; they recognize each other, because of their academic training, as social equals. . . . On the other hand, a person in Germany who has no academic education is without something for which wealth and noble birth cannot offer a complete recompense. The merchant, the banker, the wealthy manufacturer or even the large landowner will occasionally become sensible of the lack of such an education. . . .'[25]

In reality, the German academic mandarinate was already in decline when Paulsen's book was published. The profound changes affecting the socio-economic formation towards the end of the century had seriously undermined the foundations of mandarin power. Between 1870 and 1914 Germany was transformed into a highly industrialized nation, thanks to the unification of the domestic market, the abolition of economic partitioning, and other favourable conditions resulting from national unification. This industrialization was rapid, intensive, even ruthless. In steel production, Germany lagged behind France and far behind England in 1860; yet by 1910 it was producing more steel than France and England combined. Around the turn of the century, Germany completed the transition from a 'poor', semi-feudal country to the second industrial power in the world, surpassed only by the United States.

Foreign trade increased at a similar pace: from 2.5 thousand million marks in 1875 to 10.1 thousand million in 1913. German capital invested abroad rose from 5 thousand million marks in 1880 to 35 thousand million in 1913. The mighty concentration of capital and the formation of cartels in the textile, coal, steel, chemical, electrical and other industries were further signs of a process of accelerated industrial growth *without precedent in history*. Through this process Germany passed directly from the level of backward capitalism to the stage of imperialism.[26]

This sudden, overwhelming rise of industrial capitalism did serious

[25] F. Paulsen, *The German Universities and University Study*, London, 1908, pp. 119–20.
[26] Sources: P. Guillen, *L'Allemagne de 1848 à nos jours*, Paris, 1970, pp. 58–60; and Ringer, pp. 42–3.

damage to the economic position, life-style, and socio-cultural values of all pre-capitalist layers, and in particular to those of the university man-darins. Not only were their traditional cultural values marginalized, degraded, and engulfed by the commodity world of exchange-value with its purely quantitative criteria, but the academic elite's own fief, the German university, was itself progressively brought under the command of the capitalist mode of production. It was none other than Max Weber who, with bitter insight, analysed this tendency in his famous speech of 1919, 'Science as a Vocation'. 'We can observe distinctly', he wrote, 'that the German universities in the broad fields of science develop in the direction of the American system. The large institutes of medicine or natural science are "state capitalist" enterprises, which cannot be managed without very considerable funds. Here we encounter the same condition that is found wherever capitalist enterprise comes into oper-ation: the "separation of the worker from his means of production". The worker, that is, the assistant, is dependent upon the implements that the state puts at his disposal. . . . Thus the assistant's position is often as precarious as is that of any "quasi-proletarian" existence and just as precarious as the position of the assistant in the American university.

'In very important respects German university life is being Americanized, as is German life in general. This development, I am convinced, will engulf those disciplines in which the craftsman personally owns the tools, essentially the library, as is still the case to a large extent in my own field. This development corresponds entirely to what happened to the artisan of the past and it is now fully under way. . . . An extraordinarily wide gulf, externally and internally, exists between the chief of these large, capitalist, university enterprises and the usual full professor of the old style.'[27]

Weber's outstanding analysis allows us a better grasp of the affinity – despite all the points of social and cultural divergence – between the academic mandarinate on the one hand and the craftsmen, small traders, small allotment farmers, and all the other petty-bourgeois layers shaken by the ever more crushing hegemony of the capitalist mode of production on the other hand. How, then, did the mandarins respond to the sudden advent of the industrial epoch, which tended to reduce them to a marginal and powerless position in society?[28]

[27] 'Science as a Vocation', in *From Max Weber*, p. 131.
[28] Cf. Ringer, pp. 12–13: 'As full industrialization and urbanization is approached,

Traumatized by the social and cultural effects of capitalist domination, the academic intelligentsia reacted 'with such desperate intensity that the spectre of a "soulless" modern age came to haunt everything they said and wrote, no matter what the subject; all their thinking was marked by 'their horror of a streamlined and, they will say, shallow and materialistic age'.[29]

Thus, towards the end of the century a new version of anti-capitalist romanticism made its appearance, above all in academic circles, the *leitmotiv* of which was the opposition between *Kultur* and *Zivilisation*. According to this view of things, the realm of *Kultur* was characterized by ethical, aesthetic, and political values, an individual way of living, and an 'internal', 'natural', 'organic', and typically German spiritual universe; whereas *Zivilisation* referred to the originally Anglo-French, 'external', 'mechanical', or 'artificial' phenomenon of material and technical-economic progress. This problematic, strongly tinged with conservative romanticism, was later developed by Tönnies, Julius Langbehn, and Alfred Weber, achieving its most popular, but not most profound, expression in Oswald Spengler's *Decline of the West* (1918). It should be added that a similar 'neo-romantic' current arose among non-academic German intellectuals, especially writers, who shared in their own way the social and cultural preoccupations of the mandarins. The principal figures of this current, to which we shall return later, included Theodor Storm, Stefan George, Paul Ernst, and even Thomas Mann to some degree.

Now, although *fin de siècle* academic anti-capitalism revived a number of themes of the romantic movement, its distinguishing feature was a certain 'mood of resignation'. Even after the defeat of Napoleon, Adam Müller could still harbour the illusion that capitalist rationalism might be held in check: 'The most poisonous fruits fell from this tree at Leipzig and Waterloo, but the stem will continue to flourish and bear fruit until a hero's arm hacks it down or heavenly thunderbolts topple it once and for all.'[30] But the most lucid mandarins of 1890–1914 already saw clearly that the rise of industrial capitalism was an irreversible and inevitable process; they knew for a fact that no Teutonic hero could every slay the *Deutsche*

---

wealthy entrepreneurs and industrial workers are likely to challenge the leadership of the cultured elite. . . . Struggle as they will, the mandarins are likely to find their influence upon public affairs reduced. Party leaders, capitalists, and technicians will usurp their leadership. . . . The traditional schooling of the elite, designed to turn out true mandarins, heroes, and symbols of a broad and mildly esoteric culture, will no longer seem practical enough to modernists.'

[29] Ibid., pp. 3, 13.

[30] Adam Müller, *Deutsche Staatsanzeigen*, quoted from J. Droz, p. 99.

Bank, and that no thunderbolt would strike down the all-powerful *Allgemeine Elektrizität Gesellschaft.*

This academic anti-capitalism took on two main forms: a reactionary, traditionalist 'orthodoxy' characteristic of the least articulate sectors of the German university establishment – those with the least political sophistication and intellectual significance; and an 'enlightened' or 'modernist' conservatism, more realist and sophisticated, whose chief representatives were recruited among social scientists.[31] However, the two currents were not always very clearly demarcated from each other, and they may often be found together in such partially anti-capitalist movements as the *Verein für Sozialpolitik* (Social Policy Association).

The *Verein* was founded in 1872 by a group of eminent academics, most of them economists: Gustav Schmoller, Adolph Wagner, Lujo Brentano; towards the end of the century, Tönnies and Max Weber began to take part in its activities. Although it was the ideological centre of that well-known *Kathedersozialismus* (academic socialism), the group embraced a doctrine that showed little trace of socialism in the Marxist or proletarian sense of the term. Rather they issued a critique of the bourgeois individualism, materialist utilitarianism, economic *laissez-faire*, and crude egotism of capitalist entrepreneurs; their aim was to equate Marxism and Manchester liberalism, while appealing to supreme ethical values: national grandeur, social harmony, and the Germanic cultural tradition.

Their concrete social programme looked to an 'ethical-social re-orientation of the economy' through such measures of state intervention and social reform as factory inspection, social security, and progressive taxation. However, the *Verein für Sozialpolitik* was by no means ideologically homogeneous: at the conservative pole Wagner defended the interests of rural Germany against industry, campaigned for an increase in agricultural tariffs, and fervently conducted propaganda for nationalism and economic autarky; at the opposite pole Lujo Brentano waged a struggle against the big landowners, took part in the campaign against higher grain prices, and sought to give the labour unions a role within an 'ethically oriented' social policy. Between the two stood Schmoller, an enthusiastic supporter of the monarchy and the Prussian bureaucracy ('the only neutral elements in the social class war'), and an advocate of paternalist government on the grounds that it could curb the worst effects of the struggle between workers and entrepreneurs by introducing a

[31] Cf. Ringer, pp. 130–4.

number of social reforms.[32] We cannot understand the collaboration of figures with such apparently diverse views, unless we grasp that their positions were but variants of a single romantically anti-capitalist problematic, itself the ideological product of the aspirations and anxieties of an academic mandarinate in crisis.

The 'modernist' anti-capitalist current represented by Brentano found its most coherent, profound, and lucid expression in the academic sociology of the late nineteenth and early twentieth centuries: 'Modern German sociology was a true child of mandarin modernism; it cannot be understood apart from this ancestry. It reflected the mandarins' characteristically pessimistic attitude toward modern social conditions. It dealt with the destructive effects of capitalism upon precapitalist forms of social organization. It traced the disturbing results of this process in political and cultural life, and it raised some troubling questions about relations between men in modern society. Indeed, German sociology echoed anxieties and concerns which had been thematic in the social and political theories of Romantic conservatism. But it differed from those older philosophies in several important respects. . . . It was not agrarian or feudal in orientation, because it had no social connection with the landed aristocracy. . . . A sense of resignation was typical of all accommodationist social theory. The modernists, unlike their orthodox colleagues, realized that there was no total escape from modernity. They proposed to face facts, to accept some facets of modern life as inevitable. . . .'[33]

In criticizing the evils of capitalism, however, the German sociologists, like many early-twentieth-century romantics, continued to share the socio-economic concerns of those traditional petty-bourgeois sectors to which they were bound by countless family and social ties, as well as by the 'craft' nature of their life-style. (This was also true of artists, writers, poets, and other groups.) The most typical example of such ideological affinity between academic social science and pre-capitalist middle layers is the work of the true founder of modern German sociology: Ferdinand Tönnies.

Born in 1855 into a family of small Schleswig-Holstein farmers, Tönnies spent his childhood in the countryside and, after his father retired, in the small coastal town of Husum, located in the same region. Tönnies's mother came from a family of Protestant pastors, his father

[32] Cf. Ringer, ibid., pp. 146–51.
[33] Ringer, ibid., pp. 162–3.

from the age-old Friesian clan of independent peasants, who had never been subjected to feudal serfdom.[34] The post-1870 rise of capitalism also hit traditional agricultural regions like Schleswig-Holstein, where the old form of small peasant production began to be replaced by a capitalist agriculture that gradually dissolved and destroyed the previous social structures.

In *Gemeinschaft und Gesellschaft*, the work of 1887 that would inspire the whole of German sociology down to the 1930s, Tönnies abstractly counterposed two socio-economic universes as types of socio-cultural relations: one of these he called 'Community' (*Gemeinschaft*), the other 'Society' (*Gesellschaft*). He thereby left out of account the objective (economic) base of the social structure, substituting for it the subjective principle of *will*: 'essential' (*Wesenwille*) in the case of Community, 'arbitrary' (*Kürwille*) in that of Society. For Tönnies the community universe of family, village, and traditional small town is regulated by customs, manners, and rites; labour is motivated by pleasure and love of producing – a feature expressed in household economy, agriculture, and the crafts; social relations are marked by mutual aid and trust, and the whole system is crowned by the reign of *Kultur* (religion, art, morals, philosophy). By contrast, the societal world of large towns, nation-states, and so forth is animated by calculation, speculation, and profit; personal gain is the sole purpose of labour, reduced in modern commerce and industry to the level of a mere instrument; social life is torn by egotism and Hobbes's war of all against all, set against the constant, irreversible development of *Zivilisation* (technical-industrial progress). Despite his striving for objectivity, Tönnies's work is permeated with deep nostalgia for the traditional agrarian *Gemeinschaft* (of which his Schleswig-Holstein is implicitly the archetype): 'All praise of rural life has pointed out that the *Gemeinschaft* (community) among people is stronger there and more alive; it is the lasting and genuine form of living together. In contrast to *Gemeinschaft*, *Gesellschaft* (society) is transitory and superficial. Accordingly, *Gemeinschaft* should be understood as a living organism, *Gesellschaft* as a mechanical aggregate and artifact.'[35]

With the keenest regret Tönnies took note of the development of

[34] Cf. W.J. Calmann, R, Heberle, 'Introduction' to Tönnies, *On Sociology: Pure, Applied, and Empirical*, Chicago 1971, p. xv. These commentators argue that Tönnies always remained 'emotionally tied . . . to land and folk in Schleswig-Holstein', and that despite his scholarly life, 'he had an easy way with the common people'.

[35] F. Tönnies, *Gemeinschaft und Gesellschaft* (English translation), London, 1955, p. 39.

capitalism in the rural economy: 'The axiom "profit is the sole end of trade" thus finds its application, and to this oldest and most real "economy" ... [which is thereby] degraded from the rank of mother of all regular work to a branch of national or world industry.'[36]

Clearly this entire problematic – especially the opposition between traditional 'organicity' and modern 'artificiality' – owes a great deal to romanticism; we may therefore unhesitatingly locate its sociological doctrine within the mental universe of romantic anti-capitalism. *Gesellschaft*, in Tönnies's thought, evidently refers to capitalist society viewed in a critical light, whereas *Gemeinschaft* embraces the whole field of pre-capitalism, involving an idealization of the 'living', 'natural' societies of the past as against the 'mechanical', impersonal, and anti-cultural character of modern industrial society.[37] For him, as for the romantics, the contradiction between concrete, qualitative values on the one hand and the process of market quantification on the other lies at the very heart of all reflection about society: 'From the standpoint of morality, Tönnies's theory once again leads to the conclusion that calculation and speculation kill all life and therefore dry up the very well-spring of morality. Whereas the value of labour used to consist entirely in the domination of matter by concrete and palpable human energy, it becomes in capitalist society no more than an abstract, mathematical quantity to be bought by means of paper money; and the same is true of every genuine and sincere community value.'[38]

Nevertheless, as we have already pointed out, both Tönnies and the other German sociologists sharply diverged from the romantic *Weltanschauung*, clearly understanding that the advent of capitalism was inevitable, and that it was impossible to return to the 'organic' past. The contradiction between *Kultur* and *Zivilisation* therefore became a *tragic* and insoluble conflict.[39] Tönnies's only remaining hope was that, through the trade unions and consumer co-operatives, structures of a community

[36] Ibid., p. 102.

[37] Cf. Lukács, *Die Zerstörung der Vernunft*, Berlin, 1955, p. 468.

[38] J. Leif, 'Introduction' to Tönnies, *Communauté et société*, Paris, 1944, p. xvii. Cf. Tönnies, *Gemeinschaft und Gesellschaft*, p. 90: 'The more widespread and freer trade becomes, the more probable it is that the pure laws of exchange trade prevail and that these other, non-commercial qualities that relate men and things may be ignored.'

[39] Lukács, *Die Zerstörung der Vernunft*, p. 469. Cf. Ringer, p. 168: 'Tönnies never abandoned his conviction that the whole course of modern culture was profoundly tragic; but he resisted the temptation to escape from pessimism into what seemed to him obscurantist illusion.' We shall return to this tragic dimension of the world view of the German intelligentsia.

type might be kept alive within modern industrial society. Hence his affinities with the reformist wing of Social Democracy; hence, too, his decision to join the SPD in 1932 as an act of protest against the rise of Nazism.

The problematic underlying Tönnies's sociological system re-appears at the heart of the work of certain of his contemporaries – in particular, his favourite poet, Theodor Storm, who lived in the same town of Husum. Storm's writings are deeply imbued with the cult of traditional 'organic' values, now decomposed by modern individualism. As one of his biographers argues, Storm 'was out of tune with an epoch that tends to weaken social bonds and destroys the communities that arose through organic growth. . . . In his work, he therefore laid increasing stress on the vital value of the community.'[40]

In *Soul and Form*, published in 1910, the young Lukács himself provides a remarkable analysis of Theodor Storm's work and of its social foundations. He argues that the cornerstone of Storm's aesthetics is the craftsman's know-how, itself inseparably linked to a certain bourgeois-artisan form of life (*Lebensgestaltung*).[41] Lukács's own comments shed much light on our problematic: 'The process of work was decisive, not the result. Here the nineteenth-century artist's outlook is deeply and genuinely related to the outlook of the Middle Ages, that golden age of the romantic nostalgia for craftsmanship.' He goes on to make a surprising, near-Marxist characterization of the 'infrastructure' of Storm's work: 'Many developments, especially economic ones, occurred in Germany later than in other countries, and many old social forms and ways of living were preserved there longer than elsewhere. In the middle of the nineteenth century there still existed in Germany, especially near the borders of German territory, towns where the old bourgeoisie was still as strong and lively as ever, that bourgeoisie which is so utterly different from the bourgeoisie of today. These writers sprang from the womb of that

[40] F. Stuckert, *Theodor Storm, der Dichter in seinem Werk*, Tübingen, 1952, pp. 44, 127. Cf. p. 49: 'As a man and a poet, Storm essentially remained within the realm of the private or within the circle of narrow, organically evolved communities. His verse . . . penetrated this world and preserved crucial life-values of our people that either found themselves threatened with destruction by political and economic development, or else could find no place in the modern formation.' Stuckert discusses the importance in Storm's work of the family, the 'clan' (*Stam*), the local community (*Wohngemeinschaft*), the village commune (*Dorfgemeinde*), and so on (pp. 47, 127, 128). We need hardly mention the strict homology with Tönnies's social doctrines.

[41] Lukács, *Soul and Form*, London, 1974, pp. 61–2. The word 'bourgeois' should here be understood above all in the original sense of 'burgher'.

bourgeoisie, they are its true and great representatives . . . homeland, family, class were for them the experience which determined everything else.'[42] Storm's poetic universe is therefore dominated by 'the strength of renunciation, of resignation, the strength of the old bourgeoisie in face of the new life', its observation of its own decay 'with a quiet certainty which accepts the inevitable while weeping over it', a sense of history which 'bestows on everything the melancholy yet ungrieving reflections of ineluctable decay'.[43] The parallel with Tönnies is striking indeed, and it shows us how one and the same 'mental structure' (to use a concept dear to Lucien Goldmann) may be expressed in constellations of meaning as diverse as lyrical poetry and academic sociology.

Contrasting Storm with Thomas Mann, Lukács argues that 'the atmosphere of decay which engulfs his world is not yet strong and conscious enough to become monumental once more, as is the case with Thomas Mann's *Buddenbrooks*'.[44] Thomas Mann himself, after reading *Soul and Form*, described it as 'a beautiful and profound book by the young Hungarian writer'; and in his 1918 *Reflections of an Unpolitical Man*, he showed the most lively interest in this 'brilliant, extremely fine and truthful' study. Not without reason, he believed that his own literary work had partially inspired Lukács: 'I find myself in the position of a father who, with a smile on his face, allows himself to be taught by his educated son.' Mann therefore recognized his close relationship (*Stammesverwandschaft*) with Storm – his link, as a descendant of the old patriarchal bourgeoisie, with 'the representatives of German artistic craftsmanship', Storm and Meyer. Indeed, he felt drawn towards them by a bond of 'human and social attraction'.[45] With regard to *Buddenbrooks* (1901), Mann expressed his agreement with Lukács's interpretation of the novel as a permanent record of the spirit of decadence surrounding Storm's world. Returning, in the last chapter of his *Reflections*, to the significance of his first great novel, he argued that the story of the Buddenbrooks' fall ultimately referred to the development of 'Civilization' in Germany. By this he meant western-type progress, democratization, 'improvement' (the ironic quotation marks being his own), a 'moral-political-biological' process which disgusted Mann and to which he opposed the concept of 'Life' understood as a Nietzschean

[42] Ibid., pp. 62–3. Cf. *Die Seele und die Formen*, Neuwied, 1971, p. 93.
[43] Ibid., pp. 63, 64, 70.
[44] Ibid., p. 76.
[45] Thomas Mann, *Betrachtungen eines Unpolitischen* (1918), Berlin, 1925, pp. 75–9.

'conservative concept'.[46] Lukács was therefore right in 1953 when he stressed that, in the *Reflections*, a legitimate critique of bourgeois democracy is 'still covered over and distorted by a German form of romantic anti-capitalism'.[47] Thomas Mann's real, albeit highly complex and ambivalent, affinity with the conservative anti-capitalist problematic emerges again in his enthusiasm for Adam Müller and Nietzsche. Thus, he argues that Müller's 'considerations on statecraft are perhaps among the most witty and truthful ever written on the subject'; and he clearly shares Nietzsche's 'deep repugnance' for 'French ideas', eighteenth-century ideas, and 'the noisy chatter of the bourgeois democrat'. In Mann's eyes, the person who best represents this loathsome mentality of 'doleful revolutionary philanthropy' is Giuseppe Mazzini, that Latin *carbonaro* and freemason who produced such unbearable rhetoric about progress.[48] Any similarity with a certain Settembrini is purely coincidental.

Thomas Mann's cultural-romantic anti-capitalism, like that of many other German writers, merged with nationalism in justifying the First World War as a conflict between German *Kultur* ('the soul, freedom, art') and Anglo-French *Zivilisation* ('society', 'suffrage rights', 'literature').[49] As we shall see, the fact that soon after he disowned *Reflections of an Unpolitical Man* and supported the Weimar Republic does not necessarily imply that he made a clean break with the problematic of romanticism. However, it would be quite one-sided, not to say false, to reduce Mann's rich, subtle, and multiform *Weltanschauung* to this anti-capitalist dimension alone.

In Heidelberg, the main centre of sociological thought in early-twentieth-century Germany, a pleiad of intellectuals and academics came together around Max Weber. The list of regular or occasional participants in Max Weber's famous 'Heidelberg Circle' between 1906 and 1918 included: the sociologists Ferdinand Tönnies, Werner Sombart, Georg Simmel, Alfred Weber (a sociologist of culture and Max's brother), Arthur Salz (a member of the *Verein für Sozialpolitik* of '*Kathedersozialisten*'), Robert Michels (then a 'revolutionary syndicalist'),

[46] Ibid., pp. 79, 626–7. The 'biological' aspect of decay appears for Mann in the dizzying fall of German birth-rates after 1900.
[47] Lukács, *Die Zerstörung der Vernunft*, p. 58. For Mann himself, writing in 1930, this work was 'the last great retreat action, fought not without gallantry, of a romantic bourgeoisie in face of the triumphant "new"'. (*A Sketch of My Life*, London, 1961, p. 52.)
[48] Mann, *Betrachtungen eines Unpolitischen*, pp. 51, 245, 395, 558.
[49] Ibid., p. xxxvi.

Ernst Troeltsch (a sociologist of religion, himself of a 'social Christian' orientation), and Paul Honigsheim (then a young student); the neo-Kantian philosophers Wilhelm Windelband, Hugo Münsterberg, and Emil Lask; the neo-Hegelians Ehrenberg (a Jew become Christian mystic) and Rosenzweig; the legal scientist Georg Jellinek; the aesthetician and friend of Stefan George Friedrich Gundolf; the pacifist poet Ernst Toller; the psychiatrist and future Kierkegaardian philosopher Karl Jaspers; the Dostoevsky specialist Nikolai von Bubnov and the two young Dostoevskian eschatologists Ernst Bloch and Georg von Lukács.

Of course, one cannot speak of a single ideology shared by this motley group of people; but undoubtedly there was a strong romantically anti-capitalist current among them. In a highly illuminating testimony, Honigsheim has written: 'Even before the war, from more than one quarter there had been a trend away from the bourgeois way of life, city culture, instrumental rationality, quantification, scientific specialization, and everything else then considered abhorrent phenomena. . . . Lukács and Bloch, Ehrenberg and Rozenzweig were part of this trend. This neo-romanticism, if one may call it that, was connected to the older romanticism by means of many, if concealed, little streams of influence; we can cite only examples: Schopenhauer, Nietzsche, and later Schelling, Constantin Franz . . . and the Youth Movement. . . . Neo-romanticism in its various forms was also represented at Heidelberg . . . and its adherents knew on whose door they should knock: Max Weber's door.'⁵⁰ One expression of this state of mind was the curious revival of religious feeling, a form of radical abandonment of bourgeois rationalism. Again according to Honigsheim: 'It was a time when religion was coming into fashion – in the cafés and drawing-rooms – when one would quite naturally read the mystics and quite spontaneously sympathize with Catholicism; it was a time when it sounded good to look with contempt on the eighteenth century . . . so that one could then rail against liberalism to one's heart's content.' This tendency also made itself felt in the Max Weber Circle: Bloch and Lukács, among others, then enjoyed voicing 'rapturous praise for Catholicism'.⁵¹

More than the Catholic Church, however, it was Russian mysticism and Russian literature that welded the Heidelberg Circle together, providing a further mode of rejecting western capitalist civilization. At the Sunday

⁵⁰ P. Honigsheim, *On Max Weber*, New York, 1968, p. 79.
⁵¹ P. Honigsheim, 'Der Max-Weber-Kreis in Heidelberg', *Kölner Vierteljahrschrift für Soziologie*, 1926, p. 284; and Honigsheim, *On Max Weber*, p. 91.

meetings, held in Weber's home, this slavophilia was encouraged by two
figures in particular: Nikolai von Bubnov, a professor in the history of
mysticism at Heidelberg University and author of various publications on
Russian religious philosophy, especially on Dostoevsky; and the writer
Fyodor Stepun, who had introduced to the German public the work of the
theoretician of Russian mysticism, Vladimir Solovyev.[52] As a result, the
writings of Tolstoy and Dostoevsky were at the centre of debate in the
Max Weber Circle – especially that aspect which concerns the contradiction between the radical, uncompromising Absolute Ethic preached by the
Russian writers, and an ethic of responsibility with its implication that the
individual should, like Dostoevsky's Grand Inquisitor, assume the burden
of sin on his own shoulders.[53] This problematic was still haunting Max
Weber when he gave his famous 1919 talk to students on the vocation of
politics; for he then explicitly mentioned Dostoevsky's Grand Inquisitor
as the most striking expression of this contradiction.[54] We shall see that
Lukács's ethico-political dilemmas of 1918–19 bear an astonishing
resemblance to Weber's preoccupations, and that they have a common
source in Dostoevsky and Tolstoy.[55]

---

[52] Lukács wrote a review of Solovyev's work in 1915, describing him as 'the most
significant intellectual representative of Russia's aversion for materialism and positivism'.
(Lukács, 'Solovjeff, Vladimir, *Ausgewählte Werke*, Bd. 1', *Archiv für Sozialwissenschaft und
Sozialpolitik*, vol. 39, Tübingen, 1915, p. 572.)

[53] Cf. Honigsheim, *On Max Weber*, pp. 80–1: 'Much more significant for the discussions
in the Weber house was the fact that Tolstoy and Dostoevsky were, so to speak, actually
present. . . . I don't remember a single Sunday conversation in which the name of Dostoevsky
did not occur. Perhaps even more pressing, even inflaming, was the necessity of coming to
grips with Tolstoy.'

[54] Weber, 'Politics as a Vocation', in *From Max Weber*, p. 122: 'The proponent of an ethic
of absolute ends cannot stand up under the ethical irrationality of the world. He is a cosmic-
ethical "rationalist". Those of you who know Dostoevsky will remember the scene of the
Grand Inquisitor, where the problem is poignantly unfolded. If one makes any concessions at
all to the principle that the end justifies the means, it is not possible to bring an ethic of
ultimate ends and an ethic of responsibility under one roof or to decree ethically which end
should justify which means.' See also pp. 125–6: 'Whoever wants to engage in politics at all,
and especially in politics as a vocation, has to realize these ethical paradoxes. . . . I repeat, he
lets himself in for the diabolic forces lurking in all violence. The great *virtuosi* of a cosmic love
of humanity and goodness, whether stemming from Nazareth or Assisi or from Indian royal
castles, have not operated with the political means of violence. . . . The figures of Platon
Karatayev and the saints of Dostoevsky still remain their most adequate reconstructions.'
Referring to both 'the fatherland' and 'the future of socialism', Weber argues before his
young, left-wing audience that 'everything that is striven for through political action
operating with violent means and following an ethic of responsibility endangers the
"salvation of the soul"'.

[55] Lukács was later to reach the same conclusion as Weber: the future of socialism
inevitably requires compromise with 'the diabolic forces lurking in all violence'.

The Max Weber Circle also maintained relations with a much more esoteric and self-enclosed Heidelberg group: the Stefan George Circle, which brought together friends and almost religious admirers of the famous poet. At least one member of this group, the art critic Friedrich Gundolf, also took part in the activities of the Weber Circle; and Weber himself read George's poetry with great interest. In 1908 Lukács devoted an essay to George, and later republished it in *Soul and Form*. Here he stressed the 'deeply aristocratic' character of the poet's inspiration – his tendency to keep out 'every lachrymose banality, every cheap sentiment'. However, the essay did not please those initiated into the mystical circle of George's admirers, since it failed to recognize the poet's supposedly supernatural power of prophesy.[56] Many years later, in 1946, Lukács returned to the significance of Stefan George's work, pointing out the 'aristocratic-aesthetical non-fraternity present in his world view'. And Lukács added: 'George ardently spurns the social life of his epoch. All he sees in it is a soul-destroying prose, ruination incarnate. . . . The consequences of the German shade of romantic anti-capitalism are here plain to see. George's "prophesying" came into being through hatred of the world of contemporary capitalism and democracy. . . .'[57] We are immediately struck by the similarity between this outlook and the neo-romantic current within Max Weber's circle.

Now, Max Weber himself cannot properly be classified as a neo-romantic; in fact, his politico-ideological position is very hard to define. Was he a 'liberal', as Merleau-Ponty would have us believe? Was he 'an active representative of the policies of monopoly capital', as the Soviet Academy of Sciences argues? Or was he a Nietzschean aristocrat, as Jean-Marie Vincent has suggested? Was he for or against parliamentary democracy, militarism, and Social Democracy? Without in any way wishing to foreclose the debate, let us simply draw attention to the 'freely-

[56] Lukács, *Soul and Form*, p. 89; and Lukács, 'Methodischer Zweifel', *Der Monat*, April 1966, p. 95.
[57] Lukács, *Brève histoire de la littérature allemande*, pp. 198–9, 202. Lukács stresses the political consequences of the 'prophesying' through which George 'became the spiritual leader of rising reaction'. 'Not content with hurling passionate accusations against the contemporary world, he more and more virulently announced its necessary downfall and the advent of a new world, a "new Reich", which would save us from wickedness and ugliness. . . . On the basis of such poems, fascism would claim George as one of its own. This was not altogether justified: George wanted nothing to do with Hitlerism and died in self-imposed exile. . . . Yet the fact remains that in certain essential respects objective links did exist' (ibid., p. 201).

consented relationship' which, despite significant differences, exists between Weber's sociology and his romantic anti-capitalism. Vincent rightly characterizes Weber's ideology as 'a kind of precarious humanism, alien to such basic trends of social development as bureaucratization and disenchantment' – a pessimism, that is, which stubbornly rejects certain features of the evolution of the modern world.[58] In this respect, Weber was doubtless profoundly influenced by Tönnies; he often takes over the latter's categories and analyses, including his critique of capitalism, yet tries to go beyond them towards a more objective vision of modern socio-economic reality.[59]

The rise of industrial (bourgeois) society evokes a more pronounced resignation in Weber than in Tönnies. Capitalism has to be accepted not because it seems 'better than the older forms of social organization', but because it seems 'to be practically inevitable'.[60] Still, this idea does not prevent him from nostalgically looking back to the 'enchanted' pre-capitalist world and its ethico-cultural values: 'The fate of our times is characterized by rationalization and intellectualization and, above all, by the "disenchantment of the world". Precisely the ultimate and most sublime values have retreated from public life either into the trans-cendental realm of mystic life or into the brotherliness of direct and personal human relations.'[61] Above all, it does not prevent him from formulating a lucidly pessimistic, if elitist, critique of the growing hold exerted over men by the bureaucratic apparatus, the cold, 'rational', impersonal, and inhuman machine: 'Imagine the consequences of the kind of bureaucratization and general rationalization which we are now approaching. Already today, the principle of rational calculation (*Rechenhaftigkeit*) makes itself felt at every stage, in every enterprise of big

[58] J.-M. Vincent, 'Aux sources de la pensée de Max Weber', in *Fétichisme et société*, Paris, 1974, pp. 134, 143. Vincent also points out that Weber's 1895 inaugural lecture at Marburg University proposed a concept of the state 'very largely drawn from German conservative or romantic thought' (ibid., p. 120).

[59] Cf. W. Heise, *Die deutsche Philosophie von 1895 bis 1917*, East Berlin, 1962, p. 69: 'The sociological conceptions of both Tönnies and Weber contain elements of romantic anti-capitalism, albeit in very different forms. In Tönnies it is expressed in his analysis and prognosis of society, in Weber in his notion of the inevitable advance of rationalism, bureaucratization, and so on. Both lay stress on the individual's growing impotence faced with the process of social development, the existing social powers and institutions, the state, the bureaucracy and the giant firms, and the domination of the producers by machines.'

[60] '"Objectivity" in Social Science', in Max Weber, *The Methodology of the Social Sciences*, New York, 1964, p. 62.

[61] 'Science as a Vocation', in *From Max Weber*, p. 155.

private industry as well as in all other economic enterprises run along modern lines. Through such calculation, the output of each individual worker is mathematically measured, and each man becomes a mere cog in the machine . . . it is horrible to think that the world will one day be filled only with these cogs, only with small men clinging to small jobs and seeking to find bigger ones – a state of affairs which . . . plays a more and more important role in the thinking of our present administrative system. . . . This passion for bureaucracy . . . is enough to bring us to the point of despair. . . . The key question is not how to further and stimulate this tendency, but how to oppose this machine-mentality and keep a part of humanity free from such fragmentation of the soul, from ultimate domination by the bureaucratic form of life.'[62]

The very way in which Weber defines the spirit of capitalism is close to that of the neo-romantics, even though he carefully avoids any explicit value judgment: 'Man is dominated by the making of money, by acquisition as the ultimate purpose of his life. Economic acquisition is no longer subordinated to man as the means for the satisfaction of his material needs. This reversal of what we should call the natural relationship, so irrational from a naïve point of view, is evidently as definitely a leading principle of capitalism as it is foreign to all peoples not under capitalistic influence.'[63]

Unless we grasp this anti-capitalist dimension, which is of course only one aspect of a complex, refined, and sometimes contradictory theoretical system, we shall have difficulty in understanding such phenomena as Weber's sympathy for labour unions: 'They alone within the Social Democratic Party have not humbled themselves and have maintained their idealism in the face of the party's spirit of platitude. . . . Under the conditions existing in Germany, the trade unions are and will remain the only refuge for idealistic activity and convictions within the Social Democratic Party.'[64] Can we explain this sympathy, following Jean-Marie Vincent, by the fact that 'the trade-union movement went much further [than the party] in discarding revolutionary ideology', on account of its leaders' pragmatic realism?[65] Rather it would seem that Weber's thinking tended *in the opposite direction*; how else can one understand his

[62] Max Weber, *Gesammelte Aufsätze zur Soziologie und Sozialpolitik*, Tübingen, 1924, p. 412.
[63] Max Weber, *The Protestant Ethic and the Spirit of Capitalism*, London, 1967, p. 53.
[64] Weber, *Gesammelte Aufsätze*, pp. 398–9.
[65] J.-M. Vincent, *Fétichisme et société*, p. 127.

emphasis on trade-union 'idealism' as opposed to Social Democratic 'platitude'? According to Eduard Baumgarten, Weber saw the unions precisely as a counterweight to the *embourgeoisement* and bureaucratization of the party[66] – an attitude drawing the eminent Heidelberg sociologist closer to his 'revolutionary syndicalist' disciple Robert Michels. Indeed, Michels has stated that Weber was interested in his ideas, and that the pages of the *Archiv für Sozialwissenschaft* were open to the syndicalist current.[67] (Hubert Lagardelle, Arturo Labriola, and Enrico Leone were among those who had articles published in the journal.) Finally, in his always revealing and penetrating account, Paul Honigsheim argues that Weber's *Weltanschauung* brought him 'into the vicinity of the anarchists and, above all, the Bergsonian syndicalists'.[68] Only in this light is it possible to understand Lukács's surprising remark to his Heidelberg friends: 'Max Weber [is] the man who could get socialism out of the miserable relativism brought about by the work of Franck and his consorts.'[69] The judgement was wrong in every respect, yet it was based on illusions that can be explained only by taking into account the *sui generis* anti-capitalist dimension of Weber's thought.

Probably the most important and influential 'visitor' to Weber's circle was Georg Simmel, under whom Lukács, Bloch, and Karl Mannheim studied in Berlin.[70] For Lukács, writing in 1953, Simmel's thought should also be viewed as an expression of the anti-capitalist discontent of intellectuals, and as located within the general tendency to develop an anti-capitalist critique of culture.[71] It is no accident, then, that the *leitmotiv* of one of Simmel's major works, *The Philosophy of Money* (1900),

---

[66] E. Baumgarten, *Max Weber, Werk und Person*, Tübingen, 1964, p. 608.

[67] R. Michels, 'Eine syndikalistische gerichtete Unterströmung im deutschen Sozialismus (1903–1907)', in *Festschrift für Carl Grünberg*, Leipzig, 1932, pp. 357–9.

[68] Honigsheim, *On Max Weber*, p. 132.

[69] Quoted in Honigsheim, p. 27.

[70] In a 1919 article dedicated to the memory of Simmel, Lukács gave an enthusiastic appreciation of his work: 'He exerted so great a power of attraction over anyone in the younger generation with philosophical inclinations, that virtually none escaped the magic of his thought, at least for a time' (Lukács, 'Georg Simmel' in *Pester Lloyd* No. 230, 2 October 1918).

[71] Lukács, *Die Zerstörung der Vernunft*, p. 361. We are interested in Lukács's assessment of his various contemporaries for two evident reasons: 1) the socio-historical depth of his analyses, however one-sided they may sometimes be; and 2) the connection between thinkers like Max Weber, Tönnies, and Simmel, and Lukács's own work. Even if his views about them in 1953 differ greatly from his views of 1910–19, they nevertheless help to clarify a number of important questions.

is the growing preponderance of quantity over quality, the tendency to dissolve the latter into the former and to replace every specific, individual, and qualitative determination by simple numerical determination.[72] The most striking expression of this tendency is the fact that money more and more overwhelmingly dominates the life of society. By virtue of such universal venality, it is not only all material objects that become commodities with a 'market price', but also such theoretically un-quantifiable values as honour and conviction, talent and virtue, beauty and salvation of the soul.[73] Prostitution, being the ultimate form of the market's sway over human values, expresses the fundamental nature of money: its cold impersonality, its reduction of human beings to the level of a mere means to an end.[74] Capitalism, Simmel argues, is grounded on the transformation of human labour itself into an object-commodity alien and opposed to the workers and with its own laws of motion. The whole realm of capitalist production appears as a universe governed by inner laws independent of the will of individuals. Although these analyses naturally recall the Marxist problematic of commodity fetishism, Simmel regards the phenomenon studied by Marx as only a 'particular case' of the more general 'tragedy of culture': the estrangement of objective from subjective culture, the rise of the culture of things and the decline of the culture of persons.[75] In this way of thinking, Marx's concrete, historically de-

---

[72] In a 228-page unpublished manuscript written in 1933–4, Lukács refers to both the social context and the historical importance of Simmel's work. Towards the end of the century in Germany, he argues, 'the problems of the capitalist division of labour and the capitalist hypostatization or reification of human relations (Simmel's *Philosophy of Money*) came to be posed much more forcefully and centrally than they had been a few decades earlier, when capitalism appeared as *Kulturkritik* only as an alien power destructive of organic links' (Lukács, *Zur Entstehungsgeschichte der faschistischen Philosophie in Deutschland*, manuscript, Lukács Archivum, p. 33).

[73] G. Simmel, *The Philosophy of Money*, London, 1978, pp. 256, 277.

[74] Cf. Simmel, p. 377: 'We experience in the nature of money itself something of the essence of prostitution. The indifference as to its use, the lack of attachment to any individual because it is unrelated to any of them, the objectivity inherent in money as a mere means which excludes any emotional relationship – all this produces an ominous analogy between money and prostitution.'

[75] Ibid., pp. 456–69. The section from p. 448 to p. 452 bears the heading: 'The increase in material culture and the lag in individual culture'. This theme is further developed in Simmel's important article of 1912, 'Der Begriff und die Tragödie der Kultur' (*Logos*, vol. 2, 1911–12, p. 20): 'The "fetishistic character" which Marx ascribed to economic objects in the epoch of commodity production is only one distinct case of the universal fate of the contents of our culture. These contents are exposed to the following paradox: they are created by subjects for subjects, and yet pass through the transitional form of objectivity (*Zwischenform der Objektivität*) . . . an immanent development logic which alienates (*entfremdet*) them from

terminate economic analysis is transformed, or rather dissolved, into a tragic view of the world, an ahistorical social psychology, a philosophy of culture with deeply *metaphysical* overtones.[76]

It is impossible to discuss the metaphysical tragic vision without at once referring to the poet and playwright Paul Ernst. In fact, Ernst used often to visit Simmel between 1895 and 1897, and it is to him that Lukács would dedicate his famous 1910 essay 'The Metaphysics of Tragedy'.[77] Alongside his neo-classical tragedies on themes either medieval (*Canossa*, 1907) or Teutonic (*Brunhild*, 1908), which won Lukács's interest and affection, Ernst also wrote a large number of aesthetic and literary essays in which the whole problematic of romantic anti-capitalism is unfolded: the decomposition of community values, the growing depersonalization and mechanization of modern life, and so on.[78] The central topic is once again the opposition between *Kultur* and *Zivilisation*: 'We must free ourselves from the link between our conceptions of culture and the conquests of civilization. Barbarians can use electricity and navigate the skies; but only cultured men (*Gebildete*) have deep feelings and lofty thoughts. Science, too, is now subordinated to the course of economics. But it is the poet and priest, not the *homo oeconomicus*, who can decide whether a people has culture or not.'[79]

From the late nineteenth century to his death in 1933, Paul Ernst underwent a strange ideological evolution which expressed, in a fairly characteristic way, the ambiguities of the romantic anti-capitalism then widespread among German intellectuals. Thus, about 1888 he joined the Social Democratic Party and began an exchange of letters on political and literary questions with Friedrich Engels. (Engels's letter to Ernst of 5 June

---

their origin and their goal. . . . This is the real tragedy of culture. . . . We shall designate as a tragic fatality the fact that forces aimed at the destruction of a being first appear on the ground of that very being itself.'

[76] In the preface to *The Philosophy of Money* (p. 56), Simmel explicitly defined his methodological relationship to Marxism: 'The attempt is made to construct a new storey beneath historical materialism such that the explanatory value of the incorporation of economic life into the causes of intellectual culture is preserved, while these economic forms themselves are recognized as the result of more profound valuations and currents of psychological or even metaphysical preconditions.'

[77] Lukács, 'The Metaphysics of Tragedy', in *Soul and Form*.

[78] Cf. Karl August Kutzbach, 'Nachwort des Herausgebers', in Paul Ernst, *Gedanken zur Weltliteratur* (*Aufsätze*), Gutersloh, 1959, p. 415. See also Paul Ernst, ibid., p. 388: 'When Schiller was writing his poems, no one knew anything about the present-day *embourgeoisement* and mechanization of the world; but Schiller had already foreseen it.'

[79] Ernst, p. 34.

1890 on the sociology of Ibsen's works is very well known.) In 1891 he joined a left, semi-anarchistic wing of the SPD, one known as *die Jünger* ('the young ones') and composed mainly of intellectuals – 'a revolt by students and *littérateurs*', Engels would call it.[80] Having eventually left the party, Ernst began in 1892 to collaborate with the 'agrarian socialist' Rudolf Meyer on a work entitled *Der Kapitalismus fin de siècle*. But he soon left politics to dedicate himself to literary activity. Between about 1908 and 1911 he wrote his neo-classical tragedies; and having made friends with Lukács, he engaged in a fertile correspondence with him which lasted from 1911 until 1926.[81] Finally, after 1917 he moved more and more towards a politico-literary ideology of a nationalist and ultra-conservative character – an ideology whose consummate expression is *Kaiserbuch*, that hymn to the glory of the medieval German Reich upon which Ernst worked between 1923 and 1928.[82]

Even during this reactionary phase, however, anti-capitalism remained at the heart of Ernst's thought: in an essay written in 1926, he nostalgically looked back to the 'organic' world destroyed by capitalism and industry, denouncing the world dominated by capital as an 'absurd barbarism' (*sinnlose Barbarei*). It is interesting to note that this article was the subject of Lukács's last letter to Ernst, written in 1926 or perhaps 1927; and that the Bolshevik militant still found some common ground with the conservative poet. 'However much our ideas may differ,' wrote Lukács, 'discussion is possible so long as our judgments of capitalism are similar. I believe that you are mistaken on nearly every question, but you are not on the other side of the barricades.'[83]

Ambiguity, ideological hermaphroditism, a surprising tendency to move from one extreme to the other, the obvious incoherence of romantic anti-capitalism – no one better expresses these features than Robert Michels, the 'syndicalist' sociologist of the Max Weber Circle. In 1903,

[80] Cf. F. Mehring, *Geschichte der deutschen Sozial-demokratie*, Berlin, p. 678. One of these 'littérateurs' was the outstanding utopian-anarchist writer Gustav Landauer, a future leader of the Bavarian Soviet Republic who was murdered by the counter-revolution in 1919.

[81] Cf. 'Letters from Lukács to Paul Ernst', *The New Hungarian Quarterly*, No. 47, Autumn 1972, pp. 88–99; and *Paul Ernst und Georg Lukács, Dokumente einer Freundschaft*, Emsdetten, 1974.

[82] Curiously enough, although Lukács dispenses the term 'precursor of fascism' right and left in his 1944 history of German literature (applying it, for example, to Rainer Maria Rilke), he carefully avoids mentioning Paul Ernst in this regard. Did he overlook him? Or does the explanation lie in Lukács's embarrassment or indulgence towards his former friend?

[83] *Paul Ernst und Georg Lukács*, pp. 198, 202.

when he was living in the university town of Marburg, Michels began to organize what he would later call 'an underground, syndicalist-oriented current within German socialism'; this current was composed essentially of students and academics, and its ideology was a mixture of Kant, Marx, and Tolstoy in unequal proportions.[84] Michels and his friends passionately condemned the mediocre, routinist parliamentarism of German Social Democracy, its lack of energy and political virility. In Michels's racy image, the SPD was 'a giant which, despite the size of its organs, could not make a virgin pregnant'. The young sociologist therefore sought alternative points of political reference, eventually establishing personal and political ties with syndicalists in Italy (Arturo Labriola, Enrico Leone) and France (Georges Sorel, Hubert Lagardelle, Edouard Berth, Paul Delesalle, and others). He also took part in the Max Weber Circle in Heidelberg, where he enjoyed the friendship and benevolent protection of Werner Sombart and Max Weber.[85] The 'social Christian' leader Friedrich Naumann, who was a friend of Max Weber, described Michels about 1911 as an 'idealist' and 'romantic revolutionary . . . boldly wandering about in the territory between Social Democracy and anarchism'.[86]

In 1907, Michels attended the Stuttgart Congress of the Second International as a delegate from the syndicalist faction of the Italian section. There he met a number of syndicalist friends whom he later described as follows: 'The philosopher Edouard Berth, who was Sorel's favourite disciple. . . . Hubert Lagardelle from Toulouse, accompanied by his beautiful wife Sinaya, who came from a Russian noble family related to the Hohenzollerns; Gustav Hervé, a university lecturer . . . together with his Russian friend Dr Boris Kritschevski and the outstanding socialist deputy Ettore Ciccotti, former professor of history at Messina University. It really was select company, enjoying great powers of wit and Europe-wide renown.'[87] But this academic homogeneity concealed an important

---

[84] Cf. Michels, 'Eine syndikalistisch gerichtete Unterströmung im deutschen Sozialismus', in *Festschrift für Carl Grünberg*, p. 346. According to Michels himself, Marburg was 'a small, non-industrial town, in a small and middle-peasant environment' (p. 343). It was also the centre of a neo-Kantian current known as the 'Marburg School'. Among its members were Herman Cohen, Paul Natorp, and Ernst Cassirer.

[85] Michels emphasizes the close relationship between his and Weber's thought in 1911. He adds: 'Max Weber later fought on the side of democracy. But his concept of democracy had fascist overtones: we might say that his ultimate political ideal was charismatic' (p. 358).

[86] In Michels, p. 365.

[87] Ibid., p. 364. Michels also quotes the remark made by Sombart, who had hurried to

difference: German 'revolutionary syndicalism', unlike its Italian or French counterparts, had virtually no links with the workers' movement; an essentially intellectual – or rather, university-based – current, it was in the last analysis a highly marginal expression of academic anti-capitalism.

In 1907 Michels broke his last ties with the socialist movement, and in 1911 he published his famous work on the sociology of political parties: *Zur Soziologie des Parteiwesens in der modernen Demokratie: Untersuchung über die oligarchischen Tendenzen des Gruppenslebens.*[88] Michels's book – and this is its undeniable merit – was one of the first serious attempts to analyse the phenomenon of bureaucracy within the workers' movement. At first sight, it appears to be a *linksradikale* (far-left) critique of the anti-democratic and conservative SPD bureaucracy. But in reality it is inspired by the elitist ideology of Pareto and Mosca: oligarchic power within the party is 'an inexorable social law', the result of 'the objective immaturity of the masses'; 'leadership is a necessary phenomenon in every form of social life', and hence 'the ideal government would doubtless be that of an aristocracy of persons at once morally good and technically efficient'.[89]

Michels reached a new stage in his ideological evolution when a series of his essays on Italian syndicalism was published in the 1912 *Archiv für Sozialwissenschaft.* There he argued for a 'proletarian imperialism' in Italy, such as that preached by the 'national syndicalists' (and direct precursors of fascism) Enrico Corradini, Arturo Labriola, and Paolo Orano. The road was open whereby Michels would enter the fascist university establishment, becoming professor of sociology at Perugia University in response to an invitation from Mussolini himself.[90]

An analysis of intellectuals close to French revolutionary syndicalism would go beyond the scope of this work. So let us simply note that the group around the review *Mouvement Socialiste* (Sorel, Lagardelle, Berth, et al.), which temporarily had some common ground with the CGT (General Confederation of Labour), also displayed a romantically anti-capitalist ideology. (Before 1914, the CGT organized primarily a skilled-craft proletariat whose way of life and social survival were threatened by

---

Stuttgart to meet the 'revolutionaries': 'They were likeable people, refined and well-educated; cultured people with clean clothing, good manners, and elegant wives – the sort one would gladly talk with on an equal footing.' Is the irony intentional?

[88] R. Michels, *Political Parties*, New York, 1959.

[89] Ibid., pp. 389, 400, 404, 407.

[90] E. Santarelli, 'Le socialisme national en Italie: précédents et origines', *Le Mouvement Social*, No. 50, January-March 1965, pp. 62–3.

the modern industrial development and concentration of capital under
way in France at the turn of the century.) Moved by hostility to parliament
and democracy, an irrationalist, Bergsonian idealism, and an attachment
to traditional moral values, one portion of this group of intellectuals
eventually joined *Action Française* about 1910; later still, following a path
very similar to that of Robert Michels, some would become fascist
(Lagardelle, for example) or would at least be attracted by Mussolini's
prowess (Sorel). For their part, the CGT workers would rally in large
numbers to the young Communist Party. But we should not lose sight of
the profound ambivalence of this ideology, later characterized by Edouard
Berth as 'a tragic conception of the world developed under the auspices of
Proudhon, Nietzsche, Marx, Bergson, and Sorel'.[91] Its very ambivalence
explains Berth's own pro-communist tendencies after the war (his
involvement in the *Clarté* movement together with Barbusse and
Raymond Lefevre), as well as Sorel's bizarre and confusionist 'defence of
Lenin' in 1919.

In Germany, too, fascism (or reaction) was not necessarily the end-
result of the romantic anti-capitalism of intellectuals, writers, and
academics. If we take as our reference-point the Max Weber Circle in
Heidelberg – one of the main radiating centres of this current – we can
certainly find a 'left wing' that became Marxist, revolutionary, and
Bolshevik after the First World War. This 'Heidelberg Left' contributed
to the communist movement: a great Marxist, utopian-messianic philosopher, Ernst Bloch; a poet, playwright, and Red Army commander under
the 1919 Bavarian Soviet Republic, Ernst Toller; and the greatest
twentieth-century Marxist philosopher, people's commisar during the
1919 Hungarian Soviet Republic— György Lukács.

Toller represents the revolutionary-expressionist evolution of romantic
anti-capitalism. In an autobiographical novel, *Eine Jugend in Deutschland*
(1933), he pays the following tribute to Max Weber, from whom he had
received his earliest political education, about 1916 or 1917: 'It was to Max
Weber that the youth of the day turned, profoundly attracted by his
intellectual honesty . . . [His] fighting temperament had often shown itself
in our evening conversations. With words which endangered life and
freedom he laid bare the Reich and exposed its evils. The greatest evil
seemed to him the Kaiser. . . .'[92] Toller later came under the influence

[91] E. Berth, 'Avant-propos' to *Les méfaits des intellectuels*, Paris, 1926, p. 28.
[92] E. Toller, *I Was a German* (*Ein Jugend in Deutschland*), London, 1934, pp. 89, 91.

of the great anarcho-syndicalist thinker Gustav Landauer, described by
his friend Martin Buber as a 'revolutionary conservative'. Landauer
wanted the basic unit of society to be not the capitalist town but a rural
Gemeinschaft – a socialist village at once agricultural and industrial, based
on the conservation, refurbishing and development of peasant community traditions.[93] Landauer's 1915 *Summons to Socialism* made 'a
decisive and determining impression' on Toller, who began corresponding
with him in 1917. At first simply a pacifist revolted by the war (of which he
had personal experience as a draftee), the young poet rapidly evolved
towards an anti-capitalist position: 'The politicians had deceived
themselves just as they had deceived the people; they called their interests
ideals, and for these ideals – for gold, land, mines, oil, for dead things – for
such ideals man must die and hunger and despair. The question of war-
guilt pales before the guilt of capitalism.' In the name of this burning
pacifism, Toller therefore rebelled against the capitalist economy and the
capitalist state: those Golems or false idols which claim unlimited
sacrifices in human life.[94]

Arrested on a Munich workers' demonstration against the war, Toller
wrote in prison between 1917 and 1918 a romantic-expressionist drama
that would make him famous. This play, *Die Wandlung*, contains grand
visions of an idealist and messianic character:

> Now open themselves, born of the world's womb
> The high arched doors of Humanity's cathedral.
> The youth of every people strides flaming
> To the glowing crystal shrine they sensed in the night.[95]

Toller later joined the USPD [*Unabhängige Sozialdemokratische Partei
Deutschlands* – the Independent Social Democratic Party, a left split from
the SDP founded in 1917] and became friends with its leader Kurt Eisner,
a neo-Kantian socialist and president of the left-wing government of
Bavaria. After Eisner was assassinated by a reactionary aristocrat, Toller

[93] Cf. M. Buber, *Pfade in Utopia*, Heidelberg, 1950, ch. 6: 'Landauer'. We should bear in
mind that in 1891 Landauer had been involved in the 'Jünger' group along with Paul Ernst.

[94] Toller, pp. 98, 101, 107–8.

[95] Quoted by John Willett in *Expressionism*, London, 1970, p. 156. The following is
another quite characteristic passage: 'Stride on, oh youth, stride on, oh fruitful
youth,/Fruitful eternally amidst a barren (*erstarrtes*) world/Within your breast/You bear the
life divine (*gluterfüllt vom Geist*).' (E. Toller, 'The Transfiguration' ['Die Wandlung'], in
Seven Plays, London, 1935, p. 77.)

himself became one of the leaders of the fleeting Bavarian Soviet Republic. His participation in the April 1919 'Munich Commune', together with Gustav Landauer and the expressionist poet Erich Musahm, shows to what extent such expressionist and neo-romantic currents could assume a genuinely revolutionary dimension, in spite of their ideological confusion and limitations.

In a famous essay on *The Grandeur and the Decadence of Expressionism* (1934), Lukács highlights the close relationship between this artistic current and romantic anti-capitalism, especially the cultural critique of capitalism to be found in, for instance, Simmel's *The Philosophy of Money*. At the same time, Lukács tries to trace the links between expressionism and USDP ideology, mentioning as a typical example of their unity precisely Toller's experience in Munich. Quite speciously and one-sidedly, however, he sees in the political and artistic movements only 'the vacillation of the petty bourgeoisie when faced with imminent proletarian revolution . . . its fear of the "chaos" of revolution'. And he concludes with a ferocious remark, in which one senses an after-taste of the Comintern's 'Third Period' sectarianism: 'The harsh struggles of the early re-volutionary years, the first defeats suffered in Germany, broke down ever more clearly the spurious differences between revolutionary rhetoric and the moaning of capitulators. It is not by chance that, at the time of the dissolution of the USPD, expressionism also ceased to exist as the dominant literary current in Germany.'[96]

Lukács here passes in silence over the fact that the USPD disappeared in 1920 when a majority of delegates at the Halle Congress *decided to fuse with the German Communist Party*; and that Ernst Toller himself, along with many other expressionist writers, joined the Communist Party after spending several years in prison for his actions at the head of the Bavarian Soviet Republic and Red Army.

Lukács's schematism is even more striking when he alleges that 'expressionism was undoubtedly one of the diverse bourgeois ideological currents that would later result in fascism; its ideological role in paving the way was neither greater nor smaller than that played by various other currents of the time'.[97] Three years after this essay appeared, the Nazis organized their infamous exhibition of *Degenerate Art*, which contained works by nearly every well-known expressionist painter. In a note added

[96] Lukács, 'Grösse und Verfall des Expressionismus' (1934), in *Essays über Realismus*, Neuwied, 1971, p. 136.
[97] Ibid., p. 120.

to the article in 1953, Lukács remained quite unperturbed: 'The fact that the National Socialists later rejected expressionism as a form of "degenerate art" in no way affects the historical truth of the analysis set out below.'[98] But although we have no wish to deny the ideological ambiguity of this current, any historical analysis that disregards the revolutionary dimension of expressionism and reduces it to a forerunner of Nazi ideology is, to say the least, far from 'precise'.

The other notable representative of the 'Heidelberg Left' was Ernst Bloch, a writer whose work, closely linked in style and content to the expressionist current, was the most coherent example of revolutionary romanticism and the most unshakeable proof that it is possible to evolve towards Marxist communism from a world view of romantic anti-capitalism. In this respect, Bloch is the living refutation of the 'elder' Lukács's one-sided and schematic argument concerning the inevitably poisoned (i.e., reactionary, if not actually fascist) character of the fruits of this ideological tree.

Bloch's highly original thought has its roots in late-nineteenth- and early-twentieth-century German sociology. He took his first steps in Simmel's Berlin seminar, becoming one of the professor's favourite pupils. Later, in his own works, he developed the Simmelian problematic of the tragedy of culture: the opposition between soul and its objectified forms. In *Geist der Utopie*, for example, he employed the following suggestive metaphor: 'All human alienation [*alles menschlich Entfremdete*] is ultimately valueless, since God . . . at the last judgement recognizes only the ethical as a gold-value: all formal externalizations . . . while seemingly objective in themselves, . . . have for God only the value of Assignats.'[99]

About 1912 Bloch left Berlin for Heidelberg, where Lukács introduced him to the Max Weber Circle. According to Paul Honigsheim, Bloch's *Weltanschauung* was then 'a combination of Catholic, gnostic, apocalyptic, and collectivist economic elements'.[100] Max Weber's wife, who did not like Bloch, described him as 'a new Jewish philosopher . . . a young man . . . who evidently regarded himself as the precursor of a new Messiah', and

[98] Ibid., p. 149.

[99] E. Bloch, *Geist der Utopie* (1918), Frankfurt, 1971, p. 434. Lukács was clearly struck by this image, since he writes in a 1915 letter to his friend Paul Ernst: 'We must always emphasize that our soul is the only essence, and that all *a priori* eternal objectifications of the soul are (in the words of Ernst Bloch's fine metaphor) only paper-money whose value depends on their convertibility into gold' (*Paul Ernst und Georg Lukács*, p. 66).

[100] P. Honigsheim, *On Max Weber*, p. 28.

whose thought was characterized by soaring 'apocalyptic speculations'.[101] Once the First World War broke out, Bloch became 'politicized' and drew close to Marxism, although without abandoning that messianism which would inspire the famous last chapter of *Geist der Utopie*: 'Karl Marx, Death, and the Apocalypse'. In that chapter he denounced the war as a product of capitalism – 'an unadorned businessman's war' (*nackten Unternehmerkrieg*) – and saw in anti-capitalist revolution the only way 'to tear the paper of life from the mouth of the Golem of European militarism'.[102] Consequently, it was with great hope and an almost religious fervour that he hailed the start of the Russian Revolution. (The book was finished in May 1917, before the October Revolution.) Above all, he hailed the 'workers and soldiers soviet' as a force seeking to destroy 'money economy and business morality: the acme of everything base in man'. However, his view of events in Russia was still deeply impregnated with the religious-spiritual universe of Tolstoy and Dostoevsky – a universe, indeed, which was one of the main ideological reference-points for romantically anti-capitalist German intellectuals of the epoch. This mystical 'Russophilia' underlies the truly bizarre passage of *Geist der Utopie* in which Bloch explains that Marx's works crossed the German frontier into Russia in the hands of 'praetorians who, with the Russian Revolution, are for the first time installing Christ as Emperor'.[103]

Bloch's support for the Russian workers and soldiers soviet clearly placed him in the revolutionary proletarian camp despite his mysticism and demarcated him from all the reactionary or conservative currents and thinkers who emerged from literary or sociological neo-romanticism. As Iring Fetscher has acutely observed of *Geist der Utopie*: 'The artist, for Bloch, cannot close his eyes to the degradation of art and the decline of creative powers introduced by the generalization of the market and the transformation of every object into a commodity. Moreover, since Bloch understood that regret for the loss of quality and purity remains impotent and reactionary if not linked to a will to change things, he rallied to the

[101] Marianne Weber, *Max Weber: A Biography*, New York, 1975, pp. 468–9. Although Bloch is not mentioned by name in this passage, all indications are that Marianne Weber is referring to him.

[102] Bloch, *Geist der Utopie* (1918), p. 396. Bloch is referring to the monster of Jewish mythology – a being who was created by a Prague rabbi and whose vitality came from a piece of paper stuck in its mouth (*piktat ha hai'im*) bearing the 'explicit name' (*ha shem hamephorash*) of the Lord.

[103] Ibid., pp. 298–9. See the interview with Bloch contained in the French edition of the present work.

revolutionary workers' movement – in his own thinking – and placed his hopes for the future in it.'[104] Nevertheless, in 1918 Bloch still displayed that nostalgia for a pre-capitalist past and certain social and religious values of the Middle Ages which he would bring to the heart of his utopian-messianic vision of the future. Thus, at one point in *Geist der Utopie* he writes: 'The totality of Utopia presents the picture of a hierarchy which is no longer economically profitable, which has at its base only peasants and artisans, and which is perhaps distinguished at the top by honour and glory, a nobility (*Adel*) without serfs and wars, a new breed of chivalrous (*ritterliche*) and pious men, and the authority of a spiritual aristocracy.'[105] In an interview he granted me, Bloch explained this approach (apparently shared by Lukács) in terms of an inverted hierarchy inspired by Catholic doctrine, a hierarchy in which ascetic discipline and trials and tribulations (but not privileges) increase as one approaches the top of the ladder.[106] In any case, in the second edition of *Geist der Utopie* (1923) this 'medieval' problematic disappears and the passage quoted above is replaced by the following: 'The distant totality of Utopia presents the picture of an edifice (*Bau*) without a single economically profitable part; with everyone producing what he can, everyone consuming what he needs.'[107] We need hardly stress that the difference between the two formulations is the difference between neo-romanticism and Marxism: the very reworking of the book testifies to Bloch's ideological evolution in the period from 1918 to 1923.

However, although Bloch's philosophy increasingly appropriated Marx's thought, it always maintained a (revolutionary) romantic dimension. This explains both his deep affinity with Lukács before 1918 and the progressive separation of the two thinkers after that date. It is clear from the interview he gave me that Bloch regarded Lukács's post-war positions as a kind of betrayal of the ideas they had shared during their youth. The famous polemic on expressionism between these friends-opponents during the 1930s was merely the result of the basic divergence between a Marxism with neo-romantic overtones and a rigorously 'neo-classical' Marxism. Still more significant is the difference in their political analyses and attitudes concerning fascism in Germany. Lukács vehemently

[104] I. Fetscher, 'Ein grosser Einzelganger', in *Uber Ernst Bloch*, Frankfurt, 1969, p. 108.
[105] Bloch, p. 410.
[106] See the interview with Bloch mentioned in note 103.
[107] Bloch, *Geist der Utopie* (1923), Frankfurt, 1973, p. 306. English translation in Bloch, *Man on His Own: Essays in the Philosophy of Religion*, New York, 1970, p. 40.

denounced late-nineteenth- and early-twentieth-century romantic thought as the ideological taproot of fascism, and looked for salvation in a politico-cultural alliance with the enlightened democratic bourgeoisie embodied, in his view, in the figure of Thomas Mann; whereas Bloch, in *Erbschaft dieser Zeit* (The Legacy of our Epoch, 1933) sought to analyse the torn, contradictory cultural world of the German petty bourgeoisie by distinguishing genuine hope and revolt from their reactionary context. Bloch considered the irrationalism and anti-mechanicism of this layer not as a mere 'destruction of reason', but as an unthinking reaction to the sufferings inflicted on the petty bourgeoisie by industrial development and capitalist irrationality. His conclusion was that the task of politically winning the impoverished middle layers and stimulating their contradictions with capitalism was as important for Germany as the conquest of the peasantry had been for the revolution in Russia.[108]

One specific aspect of neo-romanticism that would continue to mark Bloch's thought deeply was the religious-atheist, 'ecclesiastical', and revolutionary-messianic dimension. In *Thomas Münzer: Theologian of Revolution* (1921) – a work which Bloch himself has described as 'revolutionary-romantic' – he invokes an age-old subterranean tradition of mysticism and heresy: 'The Brothers of the Valley, the Cathari, the Waldensians, the Albigensians, Joachim of Floris, Francis and his disciples, the Brothers of Good Will, of Communal Life, of the Free Spirit, Meister Eckhardt, the Hussites, Münzer and the Baptists, Sebastian Franck, the Enlightenment philosophers, Rousseau and Kant's humanist mysticism, Weitling, Baader, Tolstoy – all these come together in a vast tradition whose moral consciousness is again knocking at the door in order to put an end to . . . the state and every kind of inhuman power.'[109]

Beyond heresies, however, Bloch was also interested in Catholicism and the church. In the 1918 edition of *Geist der Utopie*, he set forth a rather

---

[108] Bloch, *Erbschaft dieser Zeit* (1933), Frankfurt, 1969, passim. Cf. Fetscher, p. 109. From the standpoint of revolutionary strategy, Bloch's position is much better-founded than that of Lukács. But neither puts his finger on the main error of the German Communist Party (with which they were connected at the time); for it was the other currents of the workers' movement – the SDP and the left socialist SAP – that should then have been regarded as the major potential allies. The workers' united front against fascism, advocated by the Comintern Left Opposition, was the only realistic and revolutionary answer to the rising Nazi danger; it was also the necessary precondition for an alliance with anti-capitalist sections of the petty bourgeoisie.

[109] Bloch, *Thomas Münzer als Theologe der Revolution*, Munich, 1921, pp. 295–6.

amazing vision of the future: socialism, by freeing man from material worries, only intensifies the socially irresolvable (*sozial unaufhebbare*) problem of the Soul – a problem that should be related to 'the superhuman and supra-terrestrial means of grace at the disposal of a church that will necessarily, and whatever else happens, be established after [the advent] of socialism'.[110] This theme also appears in the 1923 edition: 'A changed Church is the carrier of widely visible goals . . . it is the conceivable realm of the flow of traditions and a nexus with the end; and no order, however successful, can do without this last link in the relational series between the collective "we" and the problem of a final purpose (*Wozu-Problem*).'[111] Even his work on Münzer, while severely criticizing the church's compromises with the world, contains this nostalgic reference to an 'authentic' church: 'Beyond the existing church, how can we stop ourselves thinking of that much deeper one about which so many heretics dreamt even inside – a church that would retain something of its original demands and experience a real tension with existence itself.'[112]

In his mysterious and sibylline alchemist's combination, then, Bloch managed to reconcile, or rather to fuse, Karl Marx and the Apocalypse, Meister Eckhardt and the October Revolution, scientific socialism and the Christian church. This bold association of seemingly contradictory elements irresistibly calls to mind a certain communist Jesuit who fervently supported both proletarian revolution and the Catholic church and is often seen as a representation of Lukács, sometimes of Bloch, or yet again as a *sui generis* synthesis of the two. I am, of course, referring to 'Leo Naphta', Thomas Mann's peculiar literary creation in *The Magic Mountain*.

Very rarely has a character in a novel aroused such heated political discussion and literary controversy. Is he a fascist, as Lukács claims, or a Bolshevik in priest's clothing, as Yvon Bourdet has argued? Is he not Lukács himself, as Maurice Colleville, Pierre-Paul Sagave, Nicolas Baudy, and, more recently, Yvon Bourdet have all maintained? As we shall try to explain, these contradictory theses and hypotheses are all both true and false.

According to Lukács, 'the Jesuit Naphta' is quite simply 'the spokesman of the reactionary, fascist, anti-democratic *Weltanschauung*', or

[110] Bloch, *Geist der Utopie* (1918), p. 410.
[111] Bloch, *Geist der Utopie* (1923), p. 307. English translation in Bloch, *Man on his Own*, p. 41.
[112] Bloch, *Thomas Münzer*, p. 234.

'the spokesman of a Catholicizing, pre-fascist ideology'.[113] In the inflammatory revolutionary-proletarian declarations repeatedly made by the (Jewish) intellectual Naphta, Lukács sees only the reactionary anti-capitalist demagogy characteristic of fascism. He further emphasizes the similarity between this character's morbid way of thinking and the apologia for sickness to be found in Novalis. Thus, Lukács is in no doubt that the axis of Mann's novel is 'the ideological struggle between life and death, health and sickness, reaction and democracy', the struggle of democratic and fascist ideologies, personified by Settembrini and Naphta respectively, 'over the soul of an average German bourgeois', represented by Hans Castorp.[114] He even goes so far as to acclaim the prophetic vision of Thomas Mann, who 'nearly ten years before the victory of fascism', 'showed with literary means that anti-capitalist demagogy is the most powerful propaganda weapon available to fascism'.[115]

However, Lukács does point out that the novel 'ends in stalemate'. He then presents two reasons why this is so. First, Thomas Mann had 'an instinctive understanding of the immediate post-war relationship of forces'. (This argument is highly debatable, given that the period in question was none other than the 'golden age' of the Weimar Republic, when Social Democracy took part in the exercise of power.) Second, Thomas Mann never wrote a tendential 'novel with a message': 'he perfectly balances the strengths and weaknesses of the two sides, having a particularly keen sense of the weakness of the old democratic outlook under attack from romantic anti-capitalism.' Lukács therefore is forced to admit that Mann used the character of Naphta to bring out 'the seductive (even spiritually and morally seductive) character of romantic anti-capitalism' and 'the correctness of certain elements of its critique of present-day social life'. But he persists in seeing Naphta's seductiveness as nothing more than 'reactionary demagogy' heralding the emergence of fascism.[116]

<hr>

[113] Lukács, *Essays on Thomas Mann*, London, 1964, pp. 33, 35.
[114] Ibid., pp. 34, 35.
[115] Lukács, 'Die deutsche Literatur im Zeitalter des Imperialismus', *International Literatur* (Moscow), 1945 (translated here from Lukács, *Thomas Mann*, Paris 1967, p. 212); and Lukács, 'Thomas Mann und das heutige öffentliche Leben', *Ungarische Rundschau*, 1955 (translated here from Lukács, *Thomas Mann*, p. 224). See also *Essays on Thomas Mann*, p. 161: '[Mann] was one of the first writers to recognize the danger of the new, emerging type of reaction, fascism, and to take issue with it courageously at the highest level. This ideological struggle forms the axis of his novel *The Magic Mountain*.'
[116] Lukács, 'Die verbrannte Poesie', *Internationale Literatur*, 1942, and 'Über

We should add that it was only in 1942, soon after the Nazi invasion of the USSR, that Lukács 'discovered' the hidden fascist lurking behind the refined, ironical mask of Leo Naphta. Does Naphta's ideology really fall under the category of 'fascist' or 'precursor of fascism'? Let us closely examine one of the little Jewish Jesuit's main 'programmatic' tirades, if that is what we should call them. 'The Fathers of the Church called mine and thine pernicious words, and private property usurpation and robbery. . . . It was not the tradesman or the industrialist, but the labourer and the tiller of the soil, who were honourable in their eyes. For they were in favour of making production dependent upon necessity, and held mass production in abhorrence. Now, then: after centuries of disfavour these principles and standards are being resurrected by the modern movement of communism. The similarity is complete, even to the claim for world-domination made by international labour as against international industry and finance; the world-proletariat, which is today asserting the ideals of the *Civitas Dei* in opposition to the discredited and decadent standards of the capitalistic bourgeoisie. The dictatorship of the proletariat, the politico-economic means of salvation demanded by our age, does not mean domination for its own sake and in perpetuity; but rather in the sense of a temporary abrogation, in the Sign of the Cross, of the contradiction between spirit and force; in the sense of overcoming the world by mastering it; in a transcendental, transitional sense, in the sense of the Kingdom. The proletariat has taken up the task of Gregory the Great, his religious zeal burns within it, and as little as he may it withhold its hand from the shedding of blood. Its task is to strike terror into the world for the healing of the world, that man may finally achieve salvation and deliverance, and win back at length to freedom from law and from distinction of classes, to his original status as child of God.'[117]

In this speech, which the narrator describes as 'trenchant', there is indeed a weird combination of Catholicism and Bolshevism. But where is the fascism? What fascist ever called on the name of the *world* proletariat? Since when has fascism had the political goal of establishing *the dictatorship of the proletariat* as the form of transition to *stateless* and classless society? In equating Naphta's strange and 'seductive' doctrine with fascism, Lukács does not even over-simplify matters, but rather

Preussentum', *Internationale Literatur*, 1943 (both translated here from Lukács, *Thomas Mann*, pp. 197, 205).
[117] Thomas Mann, *The Magic Mountain*, Harmondsworth, 1977, pp. 403–4.

offers an explanation which seems totally *inadequate* to its object. This is not to say that there is no 'rational kernel' in Lukács's interpretation; it is not altogether wrong to consider fascism as one possible development from 'Naphtaism' (if the reader will allow the neologism). However, an unprejudiced reading of the speeches by Mann's Jewish–Jesuit–Bolshevik character is quite enough to demonstrate the biased character of Lukács's argument. And in reality, his mistake cannot be understood in isolation from his general post-1934 attitude to the neo-romantic current – after, that is, the ideological trauma of the fascist victory in Germany. We shall return to this point later.

According to the other interpretation, Leo Naphta is a fictionalized depiction of Lukács himself, and more generally, a typical example of the communist doctrinaire. Let us now examine the latest variant of this hypothesis: that contained in Yvon Bourdet's very interesting and thought-provoking work, *Figures de Lukács* (Aspects of Lukács). Bourdet asserts that Naphta's declarations 'allow us to understand Lukács's whole life, right up to his last days', and that 'the basic principles of Lukács and Naphta are identical'![118] Thomas Mann, so the argument goes, traced in Naphta not only a life-portrait of Lukács, but 'a highly indicative portrait of the essential features of a Leninist militant'.[119] Naphta, then, has nothing of the Nazi *or the romantic*; while appearing to be a Jesuit, he is basically a *communist*, in the Third International sense of the term. 'With prophetic irony and the insight of a genius, Mann was able to detect in the Bolshevik militant a straightforward reincarnation of the churchman.' Now, as Bourdet himself explicitly points out, this thesis is not without political presuppositions: 'Our view of Naphta as a representative of Bolshevik Marxism suggests that Stalinism was a linear continuation of Leninism.'[120] How should we assess this interpretation, which is of course the symmetrical opposite of Lukács's own analysis?

In our view, there is no doubt that Mann partly used Lukács as his model in 'creating' Naphta: we need only mention the physical resembl-

---

[118] Yvon Bourdet, *Figures de Lukács*, Paris, 1972, pp. 139, 151.

[119] Ibid., p. 101. Bourdet mentions as 'other Marxists' who might have inspired Thomas Mann: Ernst Bloch and Walter Benjamin. This may well have been true in the case of Bloch. But, as Nicolae Tertulian has pointed out in his reply to Bourdet, Benjamin was far from being a Marxist before 1923. (Cf. N. Tertulian, 'Des contre-vérités historiques', *La Quinzaine Littéraire*, No. 170, 1–15 September 1973, p. 22.)

[120] Bourdet, pp. 116, 163, 128. See also p. 129: '[Naphta] is undoubtedly both a Leninist and a Stalinist', and p. 130: 'The character reveals both the essence and the consequences of Bolshevism.'

ance between the two; the name of Naphta's landlord, the ladies' tailor *Lukacek*, teasingly slipped into the text by Mann; the fact that Mann and Lukács first met in 1922, the year in which the new character was written into the next-to-last chapter of the novel (Chapter 6, section II: 'A Newcomer'); and the various statements and letters attributable to the author of *The Magic Mountain*. All these circumstances show that there is a link between the real-world Marxist and the fictional Jesuit.[121]

Still, we cannot disregard Mann's letter to Paul Sagave in which he states quite firmly: 'I beg you not to establish a relationship between Lukács and *The Magic Mountain* or the character of Naphta.... Character and reality are as different as could be; and quite apart from the differences in origin and life-history, there is nothing of Lukács in the mixture of communism and Jesuitism which I invented in this book and which, intellectually speaking, is perhaps not all that bad.'[122] Bourdet makes light of this letter, putting it down to the 'Jesuitical mind' of Thomas Mann. But we shall try in a moment to show that Mann's seemingly contradictory remarks about the Naphta-Lukács relationship are in reality 'complementary'; that although Lukács was, in part, the model for Naphta, the thought of the obscurantist Jesuit is not at all 'identical' with that of the people's commissar of the Hungarian Soviet Republic.

In arguing his 'identity thesis', Bourdet is forced arbitrarily to equate Naphta's mystical anti-nature cult and Lukács's critique of a dialectics of nature.[123] At another point, Bourdet cites Naphta's 'programmatic' speech (which we quoted earlier) as proof of the author's real preoccupations: 'Thomas Mann could not have done more to tell us that he cared very little about the Jesuits, and that the whole elaborate disguise refers to Marxist revolutionary militants.'[124] Is Naphta's Jesuitism, then, merely the 'disguise' of the 'Marxist revolutionary'? Thomas Mann himself explicitly states in his letter to Sagave that he created a *combination* and not a disguise. And far from 'caring very little about the Jesuits', he emphasizes the Catholic, obscurantist character of Naphta, most of whose

[121] Given the testimony of Bloch and Honigsheim concerning Lukács's 'Catholicism' during the 1912–14 period, it may seem that Naphta is a juxtaposition of two distinct stages in Lukács's ideological evolution. However, it is unlikely that Mann knew of his pre-war 'ecclesiastical' tendencies.

[122] Thomas Mann, 'Letters to Pierre-Paul Sagave (18 February, 1952)', *Cahiers du Sud*, no. 340, 1956, p. 384.

[123] Bourdet, pp. 153–3. Cf. Tertulian, p. 19.

[124] Bourdet, p. 145.

statements do not have much in common with even 'disguised' Bolshevism.[125]

Furthermore, it is obvious that Naphta's impassioned, mystical anti-capitalism, including his diatribes against 'the devilish domination of money and finance', are far removed from Marx and Lenin's critique of capitalism. Bourdet suggests that this discrepancy stems from Mann's 'inadequate knowledge of the analyses of *Capital*'. But is it really necessary to have studied all three volumes of *Capital* in order to know that Marx's economic propositions are distinct from those of the church fathers and have nothing to do with either nostalgia for the Middle Ages or a struggle against the Devil's temptations? Does Mann's ignorance of Marx's writings really explain the fact that Naphta's strictures against commerce 'are closer to a religious homily than to Marxist criticism'?[126] In our view, then, Naphta's Jesuitism, obscurantism, and clericalism are neither a 'disguise' nor a foible arising out of Mann's 'ignorance'; they form part of his specific ideology *by the same token* that the revolutionary-proletarian dimension is part of his ideology.[127]

Nicolae Tertulian of Bucharest University makes a rather more rigorous analysis of Mann's text in his polemical reply to Bourdet. Thus, basing himself on Lukács's own suggestion, he finds in Naphta's speeches 'the *leitmotiv* of a particular type of Germanic sociology and philosophy: a reactionary-conservative type which, from the Max Scheler of *Vom Umsturz der Werte* to Sombart, from *Von Ewigen im Menschen* and Othmar Spann to Hans Freyer, embraced themes and attitudes very precisely defined by Lukács's formula "romantic anti-capitalism".'[128] The neo-romantic thinkers mentioned by Tertulian are not the most relevant to the question at issue, for the authors who most influenced Mann at this time were Dostoevsky, Tolstoy, Novalis, Schopenhauer,

[125] Thus, Naphta praises Christian charity towards the sick, and even describes illness as a 'sanctified state'. He goes on to draw a highly provocative conclusion: 'The persistance of poverty and sickness had been in the interest of both parties, and the position could be sustained just so long as it was possible to hold to the purely religious point of view.' (*The Magic Mountain*, pp. 450–1.) With the best will in the world, it would be difficult to find much that is 'Bolshevik' in this kind of reasoning.

[126] Bourdet, p. 129.

[127] We shall not go into whether there is a continuity or a break between Leninism and Stalinism. The problem is too complex to be tackled in a discussion of Thomas Mann without even the briefest analysis of the political and historical questions involved. See Trotsky's essay *Bolshevism and Stalinism*, London, 1974.

[128] N. Turtulian, 'Le "Naphta" de *La montagne magique* n'est pas le jeune Lukács', *La Quinzaine Littéraire*, no. 170, September, 1973, p. 19.

Nietzsche, Bergson, and Sorel.[129] But his basic idea is correct. He is also on the right track when he analyses the 'Naphta enigma' in terms of those 'paradoxical amalgams' and 'unusual ideological alloys' of which Georges Sorel is one striking example. In the last analysis, however, Tertulian unfortunately returns to Lukács's 'classical' thesis, arguing that the themes of anti-capitalist romanticism lead inevitably to 'the demagogic literature of proto-fascist and fascist ideologies'. In equally peremptory fashion he declares: 'Ideas have a rigorous morphology and syntax which make it impossible to confuse "left-wing" thought with "right-wing" thought'[130]; whereas, in fact, the very existence of 'unusual ideological alloys' *à la* Sorel shows that things are not so straightforward.

We cannot at all agree with Tertulian when he asserts that Lukács's own thought is 'at the very antipodes of such ideological constellations', and that it was '*always* based on a eulogy of Aristotelianism, the Renaissance, the Enlightenment, and European democratic traditions'.[131] Indeed, in the 1967 preface to *History and Class Consciousness*, Lukács openly recognized that his thought was characterized for a whole period by 'an ethical idealism . . . with all its romantic anti-capitalist overtones'.[132] We shall return to this point.

Who then is Leo Naphta? Although completely opposed to each other, the answers given by Lukács and Bourdet are based on a similar premise: in either case, the author chooses *one aspect* of the character and tries to 'get rid of' the other. For Lukács, Naphta is a fascist and his communism is mere 'demagogy'; for Bourdet, he is a Leninist and his Catholicism is just a 'disguise'. Both arbitrarily seek to give coherence to a character whose very essence is contradiction and paradox. And so, they are both forced to turn Mann into a diviner, prophet, or visionary who, drawing upon miraculous powers of clairvoyance, foresaw fascism or Stalinism well in advance.

Now, as that eminent precursor of dialectics Blaise Pascal rightly pointed out: 'In order to understand an author's meaning, we must resolve all the contradictions in his work. Thus, if we are to understand the Scriptures, we must find a meaning which reconciles all the contradictory passages. It is not enough to have one meaning which fits a number of

[129] Cf. Georges Fourrier, *Thomas Mann, le message d'un artiste bourgeois (1896–1924)*, Besançon, 1960.
[130] Tertulian, pp. 19–20.
[131] Ibid., p. 19 (emphasis added).
[132] Lukács, *History and Class Consciousness*, London, 1971, p. x.

passages that already agree with one another; we must have one which reconciles even those that are contradictory. Every author either has a meaning which fits all the contradictory passages in his work, or he has no real meaning at all.'[133] Everything said in this chapter about the late-nineteenth- and early-twentieth-century German intelligentsia implies that all the contradictory passages of Naphta's strange, repulsive, and *ambiguous* discourse find a common meaning precisely in anti-bourgeois neo-romanticism – in that trend which already contained *in potentia* both communism *and* reaction, Bolshevism *and* fascism, Ernst Bloch and Paul Ernst, Georg Lukács and Stefan George. Thomas Mann's genius is manifest not only in his supposed powers of 'prophecy', but in his ironical and subtle description of a *contemporary* phenomenon and in the way he pushes it to its final, *contradictory* conclusion.

As we have already seen, Mann's 1918 *Reflections of an Unpolitical Man* was deeply impregnated with romantic anti-capitalism. In 1922–3, he partially distanced himself from this work – especially from its anti-democratic ideology – but he did not thereby embrace classical bourgeois liberalism: hence the way in which Hans Castorp wavers between Naphta and Settembrini. Far from waging an 'ideological struggle' against 'fascist demagogy', as Lukács would maintain, Mann shows in *The Magic Mountain* that he is at once attracted and disturbed by Naphta's discourse. As a matter of fact, the perspective of a synthesis of romantic conservatism and socialist revolution – which is Naphta's driving idea – *is not so far from Mann's own politico-cultural conceptions*. Thus, in *Culture and Socialism*, an essay written in the 1920s, Mann writes: 'What would be necessary, and indeed typically German, would be a union and pact between the conservative conception of culture and revolutionary social ideas – between Greece and Moscow, if I may be allowed this shorthand formula. This is the idea I have already once tried to promote. I declared that the situation in Germany would not be good, and that Germany would not rediscover itself, until Karl Marx had read Friedrich Hölderlin – a meeting, by the way, which is already about to take place. I forgot to add that any one-sided knowledge would necessarily remain sterile.'[134] Lukács quotes this passage, but tries to drain its content by arguing that

---

[133] Fragment 684 of Pascal's *Pensées*, quoted in L. Goldmann, *The Hidden God*, London, 1964, p. 13. Goldmann makes of this a methodological principle for his interpretative studies.

[134] Thomas Mann, 'Kultur und Sozialismus', in *Die Förderung des Tages*, Berlin, 1930, p. 196.

'Hölderlin was Germany's greatest *citizen*-poet' and was therefore 'not remotely connected with any kind of German "conservative conception of culture"'.[135]

What concerns us here is not so much the 'true' meaning of Hölderlin's work, but rather the meaning Mann attached to it. By associating Hölderlin with romantic cultural conservatism, Mann was merely following the tradition of German literary criticism. Indeed, Lukács admits as much when he complains, in his *Short History of German Literature*, that 'reactionary romanticism has appropriated that backward, solitary revolutionary, Hölderlin'.[136]

In what sense, then, does Naphta's ideology evince romantic anti-capitalism? He condemns without appeal 'the English [who] invented the economic theory of society', 'the empire of capital [which is] fuel for the fires of hell', 'the horrors of modern industrialism and speculation', the demonic power of money, 'the wolfish cruelty and baseness of the economic conflict within the bourgeois State', and so on.[137] He says these things in the name of the Catholic church and of a nostalgia for the Middle Ages and pre-capitalist society. His thought is thus 'a mixture of revolution and obscurantism', as Settembrini puts it. Hans Castorp, in a striking interjection, describes Naphta as a 'revolutionary in a conservative direction' – almost the same description as that used by Martin Buber about Gustav Landauer, the friend of Paul Ernst (in 1891) and Ernst Toller (in 1918–19)! And the narrator portrays him in the following terms: 'Naphta was both natural aristocrat and natural revolutionary; a socialist, yet possessed by the dream of shining in the proudest, finest, most exclusive and conventional sphere of life.'[138]

In one of his last homilies, Naphta himself reveals the source of all these contradictions and ambiguities: 'He spoke, among other matters, of the romantic movement, at the beginning of the nineteenth century, and its fantastic double meaning; pointing out how before it the conceptions of reaction and revolution went down, in so far as they were not incorporated in a new and higher one.'[139] Mann therefore crystallized in Naphta 'the fantastic double meaning' of romanticism, by developing *to the full* the two opposed meanings contained in the original matrix. Our thesis concerning

---

[135] Lukács, *Essays on Thomas Mann*, p. 44.
[136] Lukács, *Brève histoire de la littérature allemande*, p. 57.
[137] *The Magic Mountain*, pp. 377, 403, 405, 690.
[138] Ibid., pp. 522, 461, 443.
[139] Ibid., p. 694.

the hermaphroditism of romantic anti-capitalism is thus splendidly illustrated by the character of the communist Jesuit: in him we see, juxtaposed, combined, and sometimes simply mixed together, the extreme tendencies that may develop from the one root.

This interpretation allows us to understand Mann's contradictory statements about the Lukács-Naphta relationship. It also explains the merely *partial* truth of Lukács's and Boudet's positions, for they both fail to see that it is precisely the *contradictory unity* of neo-romanticism which is the ideological key to Leo Naphta's *princeps scholasticorum*. We can now understand why, in the course of his botched duel with Settembrini, Naphta commits that surprising act of suicide which imparts a *tragic* dimension to the shadowy Jesuit. For pre-1914 anti-capitalist romanticism was a current *with no way out*, tending towards despair and a tragic view of the world. Mann himself, in a letter written to a friend in 1917, spoke of his intention to set the liberal-republican Settembrini against the character of a 'despairingly witty reactionary' (*verzweifelt-zynischer Reaktionär*).[140] Naphta's despair should be seen in relation to the 'ideological climate' of Mann's major pre-war writings: the atmosphere of monumental decline in *Buddenbrooks*, and of morbid decomposition in *Death in Venice*. And in varying degrees and forms, a similar tendency appears in most neo-romantic writers: for example, Theodor Storm, Stefan George, and Paul Ernst. Not by chance does this tragic view of the world take on a more intense and dramatic form in the work of Paul Ernst, whose rejection of bourgeois-liberal society was the most forceful of all. (At first, in 1891, he went so far as to embrace the semi-anarchism of the 'Jünger' group in the SPD – only to become an arch-conservative in the twenties.) Nor is it an accident that Lukács, whose anti-capitalism was much more radical than that of most German intellectuals, would be attracted precisely by the work of Paul Ernst.

More generally, this 'tragic consciousness' appeared among the romantically anti-capitalist German intelligentsia as a whole, and especially among academic sociologists.[141] We have already pointed out the

---

[140] Thomas Mann, *Letters to Paul Amman*, London, 1961, p. 87. Tertulian quotes this letter as proof that Naphta really was conceived as a 'proto-fascist' rather than a 'Leninist'. ('Des contre-vérités historiques', p. 22.) It should not be forgotten, however, that the 'revolutionary' dimension was added to Naphta's character in the early twenties, at a time when an astonished Mann had witnessed the conversion to Bolshevism of Ernst Bloch, Georg Lukács, and other thinkers close to the neo-romantic current.

[141] Kurt Lenk, 'Das tragische Bewusstsein in der deutschen Soziologie', *Kölner Zeitschrift für Soziologie und Sozialpsychologie*, 1964, p. 258: 'Concentrated in this phenomenon, as in

66

tragic aspect of Tönnies's thought, and the deep pessimism about society which marked both Max Weber and Simmel's problematic of 'the tragedy of culture'. To these we could add Scheler's view of history as a continual decline of values, and the theme of cultural decadence taken up by such diverse authors as Alfred Weber, Werner Sombart, and Oswald Spengler. Max Weber once summed up, in the following remarkable terms, the attitude shared by a large section of the German intelligentsia including, to some extent, himself: 'They [intellectuals] look distrustfully upon the abolition of traditional conditions of the community and upon the annihilation of all the innumerable ethical and esthetic values which cling to these traditions. They doubt if the domination of capital would give better, more lasting guarantees to personal liberty and to the development of intellectual, esthetic, and social culture which they represent. . . . Thus, it happens nowadays in the civilized countries . . . that the representatives of the highest interests of culture turn their eyes back, and, with deep antipathy, [stand] opposed to the inevitable development of capitalism. . . .'[142]

The three main aspects of this tragic vision were:

1. A metaphysical variant of the problem of alienation, reification, and commodity fetishism. The most characteristic example, as we have already seen, was the work of Georg Simmel. It was he who transformed the socio-economic problematic of Marxism into an idealist vision – with neo-Kantian overtones – of the conflict or gulf between subject and object, 'life' and cultural 'forms', subjective culture and objective culture. The growing autonomy of social institutions from the concrete needs of individuals, the domination of men by their economic and cultural products – all this becomes a 'tragic destiny' (*tragische Verhängniss*) inevitable and irresistible in modern society.[143]

2. A neo-Kantian dualism whereby the sphere of values was divorced from reality, and the realm of the spirit from the realm of social and political life. While characteristic of the Heidelberg School of Rickert,

---

the beam of a mirror, are the *leitmotiv* of the social consciousness of certain German intellectuals from the wartime period to the end of Weimar.' However, as Lenk himself shows, this 'tragic consciousness' had emerged in Germany well before the First World War.

[142] *From Max Weber*, pp. 371–2.
[143] G. Simmel, *Philosophische Kultur*, Leipzig, 1911, p. 272. Cf. Lenk, pp. 261–4.

Lask, and others, this conception also emerged among the sociologists, especially Max Weber, albeit in more mediated forms.

3. The feeling of 'spiritual impotence' when faced with an uncultured, barbarian-civilized, and vulgarly materialist 'mass society'.[144]

To conclude, the tragic view of the world held by writers, sociologists, and other German intellectuals around the turn of the century was itself the product of two combined phenomena: a) the opposition, varying in intensity, between their ethico-cultural and socio-political values and the ruthless spurt of industrial monopoly capitalism in Germany; and b) despair of ever being able to contain or halt this process, which they saw as an irreversible 'fatality'. In any one writer, the intensity and radicalism of the tragic world-view depended upon the degree to which he was repelled by capitalism and reacted with resignation or indignation, or both, to its triumphant appearance. When we think of the suicidal frenzy with which some of their number left for the front in 1914 to fight against the Anglo-French Settembrinis, we are reminded somewhat of Leo Naphta's last, dramatic and despairing gesture.

4. The Revolutionary Intelligentsia in Hungary

Hungary was the only country that, through the establishment of the Soviet Republic in 1919, experienced an ephemeral yet real victory of the proletariat in the immediate wake of the Russian Revolution. What, we must ask ourselves, did Hungary have in common with Russia? And how did any similarity between the two affect the way intellectuals radicalized?

The conditions under which a revolutionary anti-capitalist current emerged among the late-nineteenth- and early-twentieth-century Hungarian intelligentsia were very different from those obtaining in Germany. Although the proportions were of course not the same, the problems of this mainly agrarian country, with its backward social and economic structure, were much closer to those of Russia. Lenin had observed that both Tsarist Russia and Austria-Hungary were marked by vestiges of the Middle Ages, survivals of absolutism and feudalism, privileges and property-holding by a landed nobility, and the oppression of national minorities.[145] We shall see that the analogy (but not, let us be

---

[144] Cf. K. Lenk, p. 282. See also Lenk, *Von der Ohnmacht des Geistes*, Tübingen, 1959.
[145] Lenin, *Collected Works*, vol. 18, Moscow, 1973, p. 368.

clear, identity) extended to other aspects of the social structure, above all if we make the comparison only between Russia and Hungary.

In analysing the pre-1917 Russian social formation, Trotsky formulated the concept of *uneven and combined development* to characterize the amalgam of the most archaic and the most modern forms: an agriculture still close to the level of the seventeenth century and a capitalist industry based on western imports and comparable to the level of the developed countries – in some respects even beyond it. Russian industry did indeed present two essential peculiarities: a) an exceptional degree of concentration, such that in 1914 the percentage of workers employed in enterprises with a labour-force of more than a thousand was already greater than in the United States (41.4 as against 17.8 per cent); and b) the hegemony of foreign, primarily West European, monopoly capital, which accounted for nearly 40 per cent of capital invested in Russia, and a much higher percentage in heavy industry (metallurgy, coal, petroleum), not to mention banking and the railways.

Trotsky drew out the political consequences of this situation: 'The proletariat immediately found itself concentrated in tremendous masses, while between these masses and the autocracy there stood a capitalist bourgeoisie, very small in numbers, isolated from the "people", half-foreign, without historical traditions, and inspired only by the greed for gain.' But not only was the proletariat concentrated in huge factories imported from Western Europe, it also rapidly absorbed the most advanced social thought of the European workers' movement: socialism, Marxism. Consequently, in the hearts of the Russian liberal bourgeoisie, 'the fear of the armed proletariat [was] greater than the fear of the soldiery of the autocracy'. The Russian bourgeoisie, then, could not and did not seek to play a genuinely revolutionary-democratic role: the democratic, anti-absolutist and anti-feudal revolution could be accomplished only by the proletariat, whose dictatorship (supported by the peasantry) would inevitably transform it into a socialist revolution.[146]

We cannot here undertake an analysis of the Russian intelligentsia. But it is evident that, under such conditions, major sections of the 'Jacobin', anti-Tsarist intellectual current were attracted to the camp of the workers' movement and socialism, seeing in it the only consistently oppositional

---

[146] Trotsky, 'Results and Prospects', in *The Permanent Revolution*, New York, 1978, pp. 51, 61; 'The Proletariat and the Russian Revolution', in *1905*, Harmondsworth, 1973, pp. 304–13; and *History of the Russian Revolution*, London, 1977, pp. 27–35.

and revolutionary force. Now, to a certain extent the articulation of the modes of production was similar in the case of the Hungarian social formation. About the turn of the century, a developing modern industry was grafted onto a semi-feudal and essentially agrarian socio-economic structure, more agrarian than not only German but even Italian or Danish society. This western, monopoly-based process was concentrated in coal, steel, and the other branches of heavy industry; and the advanced sectors of economic life were dominated by industrial or financial monopoly capital, foreign and above all Austrian in origin.[147] As in Russia, although on a smaller scale, industrial development produced a modern and highly concentrated proletariat: between 1880 and 1900 the number of workers in big factories (with a labour-force of more than a hundred) increased two-and-a-half times; and three-quarters of these workers were employed in factories with more than 500 employees. From 20 per cent of the class as a whole in 1880, the number of workers in big factories rose to 45 per cent in 1900; and by 1910, they made up 464,475 out of the total of 912,007.[148]

This partial similarity between the Hungarian and Russian social formations, with all that it implied for the political roles of the bourgeoisie and proletariat, helps us to understand why the revolutionary movements in Russia had such a great impact in Hungary. (In 1905, for example, there was a huge wave of workers' strikes and demonstrations, while the 1919 Hungarian Soviet Republic more or less took its inspiration from the Russian model of 1917.) In both countries, the uneven and combined development of capitalism laid the basis for a popular movement fusing the traditional tasks of bourgeois-democratic revolution with the tasks of the proletarian revolution.

In both cases, but to an even more striking degree in Hungary, the bourgeoisie's organic incapacity to impel and direct an anti-absolutist '1789' represented a key element in the political and social arena. It had deep social and economic roots in what Lukács termed 'the unequal

[147] Peter Hanak, 'L'Influence de la révolution russe de 1905 en Hongrie', *Acta Historica*, Budapest, 1955, vol. 4, sects. 1–3, p. 282. See also p. 287: 'With regard to its social structure and many violent antagonisms, early-twentieth-century Hungary *may be compared to Tsarist Russia*. . . . In the epoch of imperialism, both countries found themselves in a relation of dependence on foreign monopoly capital, even though their degree of dependence was not the same; this was one of the factors hindering capitalist development in both countries.'

[148] Hanak, p. 284. See also p. 287: 'Owing to certain peculiarities of capitalist development, the composition and situation of the proletariat in Hungary was in many ways similar to that in Russia.'

alliance between the feudal latifundia and developing capitalism for the joint exploitation of Hungarian workers and peasants'.[149]

The Hungarian big bourgeoisie, of which a large part was Jewish, may be traced back to its origins in the corn trade. Since it used to finance the land-holdings of the aristocracy and sometimes made direct investments in agriculture, it felt as threatened as the landed nobility itself by the agitation of rural labourers in the late nineteenth and early twentieth centuries.[150] Having thus become a partner of the rural aristocracy and the Austrian financial bourgeoisie, it shared in the ruling power bloc and formed one of the pillars of the semi-feudal monarchic regime. Not only did it show no inclination for a liberal, not to say democratic, opposition, but its most burning desire was to imitate the Hungarian aristocracy and to be received into its ranks. The Hungarian Social Democrat Diner-Denĕs, writing with a certain degree of irony, described as follows the assimilation of the bourgeoisie to the nobility and landed gentry: 'Just as in England one could be a gentleman without being of gentle birth, it was now possible to become an *ur* in Hungary without being a noble. The granting of this facility precipitated a literally epidemic passion for the title *ur* . . . this mania . . . scored most of its victims among the Jews. This social disease is designated by an almost untranslatable Hungarian term: *urhatnámság*. . . . To an outside observer, this onward march of a social disease appeared as a complete fusion of the old nobility with the new bourgeois class. . . . The whole process brought the gentry and the Jews together in a strange community. It is remarkable to see how the whole gentry rapidly became Jewish, and how the Jews even more quickly became gentrified.'[151] In 1911, Oscar Jaszi, the spokesman of the moderate democratic intelligentsia, began to denounce the 'servile' Hungarian bourgeoisie and its behaviour as a 'moral vassal' of the established conservative system;[152] while, in a text written in 1912, the left socialist and future Comintern economist Jenö Varga pointed out the big bourgeoisie's economic

[149] Lukács, 'Bela Bártok, On the 25th Anniversary of his Death', *The New Hungarian Quarterly*, No. 41, Spring 1971, p. 42.

[150] Tibór Süle, *Sozialdemokratie in Ungarn, Zur Rolle der Intelligenz in der Arbeiterbewegung 1899–1910*, Cologne, 1967, p. 7. Cf. Hanak, 'Skizzen über die ungarische Gesellschaft am Anfang des 20. Jahrhunderts', *Acta Historica*, vol. 10, 1964, p. 21: 'The Jewish bourgeoisie was for a long time linked to agricultural commodity production, to the system of big landed property.'

[151] Joseph Diner-Denĕs, *La Hongrie: olygarchie, nation, peuple*, Paris, 1927, pp. 113, 134, 137.

[152] Oscar Jaszi, *The Dissolution of the Habsburg Monarchy*, Chicago, 1961, p. 153.

collusion with the aristocracy, and its social adaptation to 'lordly' ways of thinking and forms of life.[153]

One of the most typical expressions of this *arriviste* enthusiasm for the semi-feudal establishment was the buying of titles through which Hungarian big bourgeois, of commoner or even Jewish origin, were 'ennobled'. To take but one example, József Löwinger, director of the Anglo-Austrian Budapest Bank and later of the General Credit Bank of Hungary, was ennobled in 1889 and became József 'von Lukács'. As is well known, this was the father of György.[154]

However, there was a factor still more important than this upward magnetism in making the new Hungarian bourgeoisie conservative: fear of 'those below', of the 'dangerous classes'. Even those sectors of the industrial and financial bourgeoisie not contaminated by the philo-aristocratic 'social disease' knew very well that any struggle for democratic rights against Count Tisza's conservative-clerical regime would have to involve an alliance with the urban and rural proletariat – with those menacing commoners being won in ever greater number to socialist ideas. It is not surprising, then, that the Hungarian working class, fighting with strikes, mass demonstrations, and mass agitation, was virtually alone in the great battles for democracy and universal suffrage, both in 1905 ('Red Friday', 15 September) and in 1912 and 1913. No significant section of the bourgeoisie saw fit to take part in the struggle.[155] For in the last analysis,

---

[153] Quoted in Süle, p. 7. Cf. Hanak, 'Skizzen', p. 23: 'With the sense of inferiority of the newly-accepted, and often therefore with an excess of zeal, the Magyar-oriented Jews did their best to adapt to given conditions, to the relations of domination of a not yet disintegrated feudal structure. They became assimilated to the "historic" ruling layers, embracing their Magyar-centric world view and their aristocratic way of life. . . . This upward-looking, assimilated bourgeoisie, which had neither origins, life-style, nor traditions of anti-feudal struggle in common with the people, sealed itself off from things below.'

[154] Cf. Hanak, 'Skizzen', p. 12: 'The financial bourgeoisie . . . would purchase a baron's title, a post as court advisor . . . land-holdings, castles, and family ties; it procured distinguished godfathers and added an aristocratic name to its (proudly kept) German-sounding name: "Csetei" would be added to Deutsch, "Hatvani" to Weiss. . . . But the result was still grotesque, and it was funny to see them wearing Hungarian gala costumes and honorary swords. . . .' One cannot help thinking of that well-known photograph (reprinted in Mészáros's *Lukács' Concept of Dialectic*, London, 1972) in which the distinguished Director of the Credit Bank József von Lukács is to be seen wearing his aristocratic costume and noble épée.

[155] Cf. Zoltán Horváth, *Die Jahrhundertwende in Ungarn: Geschichte der zweiten Reformgeneration 1896–1914*, Budapest, 1966, pp. 242–3: 'The bourgeoisie should have mobilized in support of extending democratic rights. But the socialists were also involved in that field. And the bourgeoisie – under the impact of the strikes of recent years – trembled at the thought of collaborating with the working class. . . . The capitalist bourgeoisie had

the policy of supporting the conservatives, the aristocracy, and the Tisza regime corresponded to the real class interests of the bourgeoisie, which wisely preferred the *status quo* to any revolutionary-democratic adventure, with all the attendant dangers for its own survival as a class.[156]

Thus, even less than in Russia was there a consistently liberal-democratic and anti-feudal bourgeoisie capable of attracting Jacobin intellectuals in revolt against the conservative and obscurantist *status quo*. Indeed, the big industrial and financial bourgeoisie could only be a *repellent force* for such rebellious intellectuals.

What, then, of the pre-1918 workers' movement? Did it appear as an alternative pole capable of assuming the historic role of the bourgeoisie and drawing the discontented intelligentsia in its wake? Here we find the most important difference between Hungary and Russia: the Hungarian Social Democratic Party was in no way comparable to the Bolshevik Party; it made even the Mensheviks look revolutionary. Profoundly reformist, sincerely parliamentarist, instinctively legalist, modelling itself on the German SPD, the *Magyarországi Szociáldemokrata Párt* (MSZP: Hungarian Social Democratic Party) embraced a strategy of fighting 'in the framework of existing laws . . . by a legal road and by legal means'.[157] In 1905, the MSZP leadership invoked Lassalle by name when duly endorsing an agreement with Kaiser Franz Josef arranged by His Majesty's Hungarian representative, Minister of the Interior József Kristóffy. The MSZP supported the pro-Habsburg party against the nationalist parliamentary coalition, in exchange for a vague promise of universal suffrage. The Social Democratic leader Sándor Garbai went so far as to declare at a mass rally: 'Let absolutism come so long as the bayonets also bring universal suffrage.'[158] After this manoeuvre had failed, the party leadership did everything possible, in 1905 and again in

---

understood very early on that no democratic change could be accomplished without the help of the peasants. But it saw the peasants as striking agricultural workers capable of being mobilized under the banner of socialism. . . . If that was the only way democratic advance could be achieved, then the bourgeoisie preferred to forget about it.'

[156] The historian William McCagg speaks with flattering sympathy about the way this 'bourgeois nobility' reasoned. See 'Jewish Nobles and Geniuses in Modern Hungary', in *East European Quarterly*, 1972, p. 224.

[157] *Népszava* (the MSZP daily), 3 June, 1899, quoted in Süle, p. 40.

[158] Quoted in Süle, p. 124. See also the speech delivered by the leader of the MSZP, Ernö Garami, on 10 September 1905, in which he referred to Lassalle as an example for the Hungarian workers. (Ibid., p. 118.)

1912–13, to curb, moderate, and keep within the established order the great mass workers' mobilizations for the right to vote.[159]

In the left wing of the MSZP, however, a number of intellectuals tried to wage a fight within the party. The most important of these attempts was led by Ervin Szabó. Together with a group of students, including Jenö László and Béla Vago, both of whom became founding members of the Hungarian Communist Party in November 1918, Szabó criticized the party's opportunism and parliamentarism from a standpoint close to revolutionary syndicalism.[160] In response, Gerami denounced the ideas of Szabó and his comrades as 'highly excitable playing at revolution', typical of 'semi-anarchist academics'. By 1907 the left current had been effectively isolated and neutralized by the party apparatus. Shortly afterwards, a more orthodox Marxist-revolutionary opposition sprang up under the leadership of the young journalist and future HCP and Comintern leader Gyula Alpari, who was in contact with the German *linksradikalen* – Karl Liebknecht, Rosa Luxemburg, and others. Alpari and his comrades, including the young office-worker Béla Szantó (also to become a founding member of the Communist Party), were denounced by the trade-union bureaucracy as 'intellectual vagabonds' and eventually expelled by the MSZP leadership in 1910.[161]

Thus, by virtue of its reformism, its distrust of intellectuals, and its hostile indifference to peasant struggles and the oppressed national minorities, the MSZP leadership disqualified the party from becoming the political vanguard of a powerful revolutionary-democratic mass movement with a socialist dynamic. Hungarian Social Democracy was never an adequate pole of attraction for the 'red' intelligentsia, and the small groups of revolutionary intellectuals who tried to become members were gradually marginalized and expelled between 1905 and 1910. In Hungary, the intelligentsia was 'left to its own devices'; the moderate wing was deprived of its natural allies by the liberal-democratic bourgeoisie, while the revolutionary wing was rejected by the Social Democratic labour movement.

The two currents therefore found themselves together in a number of politico-cultural centres of influences: the literary review *Nyugat* (West),

---

[159] Cf. Süle, pp. 116–24; and Hanak, 'L'Influence de la révolution de 1905', pp. 296–9.
[160] László was executed by the counter-revolution in 1919, Vage during the Stalinist purges in 1939.
[161] Süle, pp. 106–7, 207–9. Alpari appealed against his expulsion but was defended by only two international leaders – Luxemburg and Lenin.

the Social Science Society and its journal *Huszadik Század* (Twentieth Century), the 'Martinovics' masonic lodge (named after a Hungarian Jacobin), and the 'Galileo Circle' at the University. These various groups were linked by a network of friendship and affinity, and their audience was to a great extent the same. Hegemony undoubtedly rested with the ideology of the moderates, who served as the mediators of 'modern' European ideas in Hungary; theirs was an eclectic combination of positivism, French 'radical socialism', Bernstein-type revisionism, masonic anti-clericalism, Enlightenment evolutionism, and the cult of progress, science, and industry. The sociologist Oscar Jaszi, the most typical and best-known figure in this current, has recalled that his aim in founding *Huszadik Század* in 1900 was to create 'a front against feudalism . . . Magyar-centred chauvinism . . . and faithless clericalism'.[162]

Also participating in this 'anti-feudal front' were the 'red' intellectuals who wrote for *Nyugat* and *Huszadik Század* but who rejected, for aesthetic-literary, moral, and/or political reasons, the 'enlightened' bourgeois liberalism which then held sway. Legitimate offspring of Hungarian conditions, these intellectuals were radically opposed to the established economic, social, and political regime: they were at once *anti-feudal* and *anti-capitalist*. Disgusted with the 'servile bourgeoisie' and dissatisfied with the 'social-liberal' platitudes of intellectual circles, they placed their hopes in the Hungarian proletariat, despite the character of the Social Democratic Party. This anti-bourgeois intellectual current, a large part of which eventually went over to communism in 1918–19, was inspired primarily by Endre Ady and Ervin Szabó. These two, each in his own way, may be regarded as the 'spiritual fathers' of the generation that carried out the social revolution of 1919.

József Révai rightly speaks of the poet Ady as having 'two souls': that of the bourgeois-democratic revolutionary and that of the artist who detests the bourgeoisie and its regime. And indeed, Ady proudly depicts himself as a man with 'two convictions', explaining this in the following terms: 'We call for the most complete democracy: we proclaim with loud shouts, acting honestly and as martyrs, the principle of a universal, secret ballot – even though, without anyone knowing it, the results obtained by highly civilized societies many centuries ahead of us have already spoiled our

---

[162] Quoted in Süle, p. 22. In 1914 Jaszi founded an impotent Hungarian Radical Party that had little political influence.

appetite.'[163] These contradictory moments of Ady's poetry and thought develop according to a logic of their own and result in a *sui generis* ideological synthesis.

First of all, Ady was a Hungarian Jacobin, a resolute enemy of feudalism, church power, and landowners' privilege. Here he had much in common with the masonic, free-thinking anti-clericalism of radical Hungarian bourgeois – with the Galileo Circle, *Nyugat*, and Oscar Jaszi. Yet despite this common ground in the struggle against 'the masters of Hungary', Ady already displayed a significant difference: his democratism was Jacobin, plebeian, and genuinely revolutionary; he appealed to the heroic example of György Dózsa, the leader of the sixteenth-century Hungarian *jacquerie*, who was burned alive on a red-hot throne by the feudal lords:

> He was finer than eighty abbots
> More holy than any of our lords
> Enthroned there on his seat of fire
> Like God in Heaven.[164]

Ady's faith in revolution sharply differentiated him from the timid reformism of the liberal-modernist current; his links with the socialist peasant movement led by András Áchim expressed his hope in a peasant insurrection that would destroy the foundations of the old regime. But there is also Ady's 'second soul': his artist's hatred of the bourgeoisie and his revulsion from capitalism. He severely criticized bourgeois democracy in France and the United States, describing it as 'illusory', 'mediocre', and 'immoral'. In an article written in 1909 he gave free rein to his bitterness against the French Third Republic: 'It has replaced the emperor or king with money. . . . Europe can set its mind at rest, since money is king in France, and that king is more conservative than any Habsburg emperor.'[165] But it was above all in the name of art that Ady rebelled against the grey monotony and dreary staleness of capitalism; and it was the ideal of an authentic, beautiful, exalted, and heroic life which he invoked against the insignificant, hideous, and corrupt life of bourgeois society. In his 'second soul', then, Ady was sensitive to the influence of certain late-

---

[163] Cf. J. Révai, 'Endre Ady', in *Etudes historiques*, Budapest, 1955, vol. 10, pp. 64–5, 77.

[164] 'Dózsa György Lakomáján' (Dózsa's Banquet), in *Ady: Összes Versei*, Budapest, 1936, p. 191.

[165] Ady, 'Nem lesz forradalom' (There Won't Be a Revolution), *Pesti Naplo*, 28 April 1909. (Quoted in *Nouvelles Etudes hongroises*, vol. 7, 1972, p. 174.)

76

nineteenth-century currents: to aristocratic anti-democratism, romantic anti-capitalism, and aesthetic opposition to the bourgeoisie; to the Parnassus School, Nietzsche, Bergson, and Tolstoy.[166]

It should be added that, in Ady, these aesthetic-moral anti-bourgeois tendencies are combined with more political sentiments. In fact, disgust with the urban bourgeoisie's 'cowardice' and passive adaptation to the feudal-aristocratic establishment played a decisive role in the radicalization of the Hungarian intelligentsia. Unlike Western Europe, Ady argued, Hungary was then witnessing the development of 'a weak, scattered, and flabby bourgeoisie with lordly airs, one that lacks the strength or talent to open its mouth and swallow the choicest morsels' (1908).[167]

The tension between Ady's 'two souls' therefore led to a seemingly contradictory result: a bourgeois democrat contemptuous of the bourgeoisie, and an anti-feudal revolutionary who spurned West European society. The Jacobin element in this unstable ideological equilibrium was too powerful for the scales to tip towards reaction, as happened with many romantically anti-capitalist intellectuals in Germany and France. And so, in the end the balance swung towards socialism and the workers' movement.[168] In the absence of a revolutionary-democratic bourgeoisie, the Jacobin intellectual tended to be irresistibly drawn to the ideological camp of the proletariat.

This socio-historical background enables us to understand Ady's solution to the conflict between his 'two souls'. For his intense and burning hope in revolution also had a *dual nature*, both anti-feudal and anti-bourgeois; it reconciled the plebeian *élan* of the democratic revolution with the proletarian critique of bourgeois democracy. With the insight of true genius sometimes to be found among poets (Heine, for example), Ady *alone* in pre-war Hungary had a foreboding of the *combined, democratic and socialist* revolution with which uneven and combined development had impregnated the social formation. *What Marx in 1850 and Trotsky in 1906*

[166] Révai, pp. 64–71.
[167] Quoted in Révai, p. 55.
[168] Cf. ibid., p. 82: 'Hungary carried within it the seeds of the democratic revolution. . . . That is why in pre-war Hungary the disillusionment caused by capitalism, which had already gripped a considerable section of European bourgeois intellectuals, did not pass into counter-revolution and cultural-literary aristocratism. Since a new awareness of the decay of the bourgeoisie was grafted onto the problems of the democratic revolution, working-class socialism began to exert a deeper ideological attraction over the really sincere supporters of democratic change.'

called 'the permanent revolution' can be found in Endre Ady in the form of a lyrical vision. This prophetic insight first appeared in an article Ady wrote in 1903: 'We must tackle the problem head-on, starting with the first estate, then passing to the second, and finally to the third. We must *at one and the same time* put an end to orders of precedence, privileges, ancestral brutality, the aristocracy, the clergy and *exploitative capital.*'[169] This idea would be developed above all in the light of the 1905 Russian Revolution. In his remarkable article *Earthquake*, Ady wrote: 'Russia has undergone a massive tremor. . . . The Slavs are teaching the world a new kind of revolution. . . . *Russia is carrying out two revolutions at once*: the old one, which Europe has already experienced, and a new one. . . . Russian democracy is triumphantly shaking the throne by means of blood, rubble, and ashes. But it will also triumph over enemies stronger than the throne: over the egotistic lordly manor, the exploitative factory, the stupefying clergy, and the heartless barracks.'[170] With his astonishing lucidity, Ady was able to grasp not only the dialectical unity of the 'two revolutions' in Russia, but even the leading role of the proletariat in the popular movement: 'History will be proud of this formidable earthquake. . . . *Here we see the proletariat giving the people back to the people.* The people has risen up to shape the world.' The article ends by stressing the import for Hungary of the 1905 events in Russia: 'We should be edified by the Russian example. Rotten and impotent societies can be saved only by the people, the working people invincible and irresistible.'[171]

The 'people' that had to save rotten, impotent Hungary were the workers and peasants, the people 'of the cities and hamlets' of whom Ady

---

[169] Quoted in Révai, p. 60. Révai comments: 'At times, his awareness of the social character and driving forces of the Hungarian revolution brought him so close to the spirit of revolutionary Marxism that he would have had to take but one more step to draw out the final conclusions. . . . We do not know whether Ady was familiar . . . with Marx's views during and after the 1848 revolution concerning the course of the German revolution. But in any case, the idea to which he stuck in this short article was a brilliant approximation of the Marxist theory of uninterrupted revolution.'

[170] Quoted in Hanak, 'L'Influence de la révolution russe de 1905', p. 308, emphasis added. Hanak also takes note of the poet's extraordinary political intuition: 'This discovery of two successive revolutions in Russia was unique for Hungary at that time; we may even say that it was a stroke of genius. According to this view, the old, bourgeois revolution would not stop at bringing down the throne and destroying "the egotism of the manor", but would inevitably continue until it triumphed over "the exploitative factory", that is to say, the capitalist system itself. In short, Endre Ady's verse poetically expresses the transformation of the bourgeois-democratic revolution into a socialist revolution.'

[171] Quoted in Hanak, p. 309; emphasis added.

speaks in his famous poem *The Warriors' Path*, announcing the 'red revolution' to come:

> Today Hungary is a country on fire
> Its frozen body licked by flames
> A miracle has happened, come down on earth.
> The Milky Way is alive with people.
>
> The earth is shaking, and we greet the sun
> With the great joy of red flowers
> And every street we stream along
> Is a river of flame, a holy river of flame . . .
>
> There is a new army on the Milky Way
> A new legend, a new battle-hymn
> This is the future, the future at hand
> In the dawn of the Hungarian sky . . .
>
> News and song today echo around
> The city walls, in village and plain
> There is the people, the people has come
> With the strength of the storm on the Milky Way.[172]

Ady looks especially to the Hungarian proletariat, whose enormous revolutionary potential he celebrates in *Poem of a Proletarian Son*:

> My father, from morning to night
> He slaves away with sweat on his brow . . .
>
> My father is prisoner of the rich
> My poor one, they hurt and humiliate him . . .
>
> My father, if ever he wished it
> The rich would be no more . . .
>
> My father, if he said but one word
> Many would start to tremble . . .
>
> My father works and fights
> Probably no one is stronger than he.[173]

However, such rousing calls to revolt appear in Ady's lyrical verse

---

[172] 'A Hadak Útja', in *Ady: Összes Versei*, p. 195.
[173] 'Proletár Fiu Verse', ibid., p. 303.

alongside a tragic, despairing, and pessimistic mood:

> Since I expect what cannot be had
> Expect only what cannot be had,
> Oh, I suffer the most bloody of bloody tortures . . .
>
> My brain is dizzy, my throat is hoarse
> And borne down by the demented twilight
> Oh Blessed accursed impossibility
> I intone thy consuming song.[174]

This anguished despair was rooted in the poet's *isolated position* between a 'flabby', corrupted bourgeoisie, an opportunist and blinkered Social Democratic movement, and a timid, reformist urban intelligentsia. Society seemed to him frozen in a condition of stability destined to last forever – stability accentuated by the apparent social immutability of Hungarian and European capitalism. 'In the writings of disillusioned revolutionaries and thinkers,' he wrote, 'I read that existing society will remain in equilibrium for a long time to come. . . . But what shall we do then, those of us alive today who aspire to the morality of a society which, even if it is probable, will still be several thousand years late?'[175]

Nevertheless, despite this isolation – which manifested itself within *Nyugat*, the literary review he helped to found – Ady exercised a real fascination over certain radicalized sections of the intelligentsia. Lukács, himself a typical representative of this fringe, wrote the following impassioned words in 1909: 'Ady is conscience, and a fighting song, a trumpet and standard around which all can gather should there ever be a fight.'[176] Sixty years later, in an article polemicizing against those who had tried to present Ady as simply a Hungarian nationalist, Lukács stressed his influence on the revolutionary intellectual milieu: 'What demonstrates the poet's real place, and I consider it an interesting piece of literary evidence, is the fact that Ervin Sinkó's novel *Optimisták* (Optimists) contains a number of young characters who constantly refer to Ady. In the Sinkó-Révai revolutionary circle in which the scene of this novel is laid, Ady is a living influence in 1918–19. It was in all probability not the only group of

---

[174] 'Szent Lehetetlenség Zsoltárja' (Psalm of Blessed Impossibility), ibid., p. 512.
[175] Quoted in Revai, p. 79.
[176] Lukács, 'Endre Ady' (1909), quoted in Ferenc Tökei, 'Lukács and Hungarian Culture', *The New Hungarian Quarterly*, no. 47, autumn 1972, p. 119.

this kind. . . .'[177] We may add that the 'Sinkó-Révai Circle' was to a large extent also 'the Lukács Circle'. But we shall return later to Ady's role in Lukács's ideological evolution.

One of those 'red' intellectuals who fervently admired Ady's verse was Ervin Szabó, the spiritual guide of revolutionary socialism in Hungary.[178] Lukács also speaks about a 'Russian' current in Hungarian thought, including in it Petöfi, Ady, Attila József and Béla Bártok. But we could add, with greater justification, the name of Ervin Szabó. The young Szabó was initiated into socialist politics by a Russian populist refugee in Vienna, Samuel Klachko, through whom he became familiar with the works of Bakunin, Nechaev, and Lavrov, as well as with Tolstoy and Dostoevsky. His first political writings were a hymn to the glory of Russian students and intellectuals – 'who for a century have been waging a struggle of unparalleled courage and self-sacrifice against Tsarism'.[179] For a long time Szabó's thought would remain marked by Lavrov's subjectivist philosophy, which he regarded as 'complementary to Marxism'.[180] According to Ilona Duczynska, his close collaborator in 1917, 'Szabó's roots lie in the ethic of *narodnichestvo*, highly revolutionary and not at all opposed to violence – rather profoundly opposed to statism and bureaucracy'.[181]

These anarcho-populist roots help us to understand why the Marxist Szabó worked with the libertarian group initially formed around the gnostic anarchist philosopher and agrarian socialist Eugen Heinrich Schmidt. (This group, which later came under the leadership of the Tolstoyan count Ervin Batthyány, published a review called *Társadalmi Forradalom* – Social Revolution – which had considerable influence over the socialist peasant movement founded by the former Social Democrat István Varkonyi.[182]) Szabó, in fact, was one of the few pre-1918

[177] Lukács, 'The Importance and Influence of Ady', *The New Hungarian Quarterly*, no. 35, autumn 1969, p. 58.

[178] A socialist militant, librarian, and scholar, Szabó edited the first Hungarian collection of Marx's works. He also wrote an outstanding history of the social struggles in Hungary in 1848.

[179] Cf. McCagg, p. 73; and Sule, p. 53. Szabó seems to have kept in touch with the Russian Social Revolutionaries up to his death.

[180] See Szabó's contribution to a February 1903 debate organized by the Social Science Society (Süle, p. 97).

[181] Letter to the author, 3 April 1974.

[182] Cf. Süle, pp. 126, 146. Szabó and the 'red count' Batthyány had bonds of deep friendship and mutual admiration with Bakunin, Kropotkin, and Tolstoy. Cf. Oscar Jaszi, 'Erwin Szabó and sein Werk' *Archiv für die Geschichte des Sozialismus und der Arbeiterbewegung*, vol. x, 1922, p. 29.

Hungarian Marxists who took an interest in the peasantry; yet his sympathy for social-agrarian currents was deeply imbued with anti-capitalist romanticism. His personal friend and political opponent Oscar Jaszi gave the following richly detailed description of this aspect of his ideology: 'Unlike the majority of Marxists, Szabó was intimately attached to the peasants and the village. He was instinctively aware of the morbid and corrupt nature of the big city; and in his thought, or at least in his sub-conscious feelings, the countryside took on a much greater role than it did for most socialists of urban origin. His moral and aesthetic attitude to the peasantry was quite different from that of routinist communism. Even under the superficial "conservatism" or "backward mentality" of the peasantry, he could distinguish the warmer and richer atmosphere of that instinctive, universal-human life which marks off the sons of the earth from the rationalist and mechanical life of the towns.' Jaszi recounts a strange conversation with Szabó, in which this romantic anti-capitalism appears with quite striking clarity: 'I vividly recall Szabó's satisfaction when showing me an almanac from which it was apparent that a well-organized and multi-ramified movement of Catholic inspiration was then being constituted. Pointing to pictures of those who had helped to prepare the almanach, Szabó said: "Just look at those faces! Nothing but peasant blood! I know that right now the movement is being driven forward by Jesuits and that it is reactionary. But that doesn't matter: it is only a sign of the ferment beginning in the countryside, and of the destruction of the 'Jewish-capitalist' press monopoly".'[183] In Szabó's thought and teach-ings, this anti-capitalist tendency stands in unresolved contradiction with another, 'orthodox-Marxist' orientation – in the evolutionary-materialist sense of the Second International (Kautsky and Plekhanov). It was this that sometimes made him write that Hungary would not be ripe for a socialist revolution until it had passed through a bourgeois-democratic industrial stage.[184]

On the basis of his romantic-revolutionary anti-capitalism and his anarchistic sympathies, Szabó found common ground with French revolutionary syndicalism, utilizing its ideological arsenal in struggle

[183] Jaszi, pp. 31–2. In order to avoid any misunderstanding, we should make clear that Szabó – real name Schlesinger – was himself of Jewish extraction.

[184] This second orientation may also be due to the influence of the anti-feudal liberal-democratism of the Social Science Society, of which Szabó was an active member. Cf. Révai, 'Ervin Szabó et sa place dans le mouvement ouvrier hongrois', *Etudes Historiques*, Budapest, 1955, pp. 138–41.

against mediocre, routinist parliamentarism, against the compromises and
lack of moral grandeur characteristic of the Social Democratic bureaucracy. Thus, while he was staying in Paris in 1904, Szabó made the
acquaintance of the intellectuals of the *Mouvement Socialiste* review; he
fervently studied the writings of Sorel, Lagardelle, Arturo Labriola, and
Robert Michels, and became the Hungarian correspondent of the review.
However, he failed in his attempts to create a revolutionary-syndicalist
movement in Hungary around a wing of the Social Democratic Party and,
above all, based on the trade unions. Like Michels in Marburg, he could
find a responsive audience only among limited circles of intellectuals.[185]

Beyond a number of real doctrinal and political differences, what
attracted Szabó to Sorel was above all the problematic of revolutionary,
ascetic, noble, and heroic morality, radically opposed to capitalist
hedonism and the crude materialism of the bourgeoisie. This tendency to
moral rigorism, which in Szabó's case strengthened during the war,
brought him closer to the ethical idealism of the *Geisteswissenschaften*
group around Lukács. (He encouraged them, for example, to set up their
'Free School'.) It was a tendency that expressed itself politically in such
extreme and intransigent formulas as: 'The struggle for pure ends can be
waged only by pure means'; or even: 'It is better to tolerate evil than to
change it by evil means'. We shall see below the influence these slogans
had on the young Lukács in 1918.[186]

Szabó's influence bore mainly upon two circles of students and intellectuals, most of whose members later became communists, in 1918–19:

1.   The revolutionary-socialist group which, stemming in part from the
'Galileo Circle', had begun anti-militarist agitation in 1917 under the
impact of the Zimmerwald Conference. It was initially led by Ilona
Duczynska, who had brought the Zimmerwald material into the country;
but when she was arrested in January 1918, it continued its activities under
the impetus provided by Ottó Korvin (future leader of the Hungarian
Communist Party and head of the Soviet Republic's Red Security force –

---

[185] Cf. Süle, pp. 92–3, 176–90; O. Jaszi, p. 33; and J. Jemnitz, 'La correspondence d'Ervin
Szabó avec les socialistes et les syndicalistes de France (1904–1912)', *Le Mouvement Social*,
no. 52, July–September 1965, pp. 111–19.

[186] Cf. Jaszi, pp. 32, 35; and E. Szabó, 'Müveltség es Kultura' (Learning and Culture),
Szabad-Gondolat, June 1918. This latter source was pointed out to us by M.G. Litvan of the
Budapest Institute of History. According to Jaszi, Szabó at first enthusiastically greeted the
October Revolution, but then expressed to close friends his moral reservations about the
practice of the Bolsheviks.

murdered in 1919 by the counter-revolution), Sallai (future deputy-head of the Red Security), the writer József Lengyel (who would join the party in 1918), and the future communist philosopher and leader József Révai. Both the first leaders and this so-called 'second group' (*masodik garnitura*) were in close touch with Ervin Szabó, who directly or indirectly inspired most of the anti-militarist leaflets distributed by the revolutionary socialists.

Ideologically, this current displayed a mixture, then fairly common, of revolutionary syndicalism, anti-militarist Zimmerwald internationalism, and passionate support for the October Revolution.[187] Révai, who at the time had also been attracted by the dash of Szabó's ideas, gave the following explanation forty years later of their impact on rebellious intellectuals: 'This doctrine . . . was not at all tarnished with the treachery of war: quite the contrary, anti-militarist work had endowed it with exceptional prestige, and its merciless critique of Social Democracy made it especially attractive. Thus it suddenly took on inordinate importance – above all among socialist intellectuals who, groping in the confusion of the years 1917–18 and already hearing the rumble of collapse and social revolution, were looking for a compass, a guiding force, a doctrine. Only in the light of these facts can we understand how Ervin Szabó, although completely lacking a mass base, acquired disproportionate ideological ascendancy over a whole social layer.'[188]

2.   The *Geisteswissenschaften* circle, in which the influence of Szabó, combined with that of Ady's aesthetico-political universe, was above all mediated by Lukács himself. The somewhat esoteric ideology and world view of this group had their intellectual roots not merely in Hungary (Ady and Szabó) but above all in German sociology and philosophy. The *szellemkék*,[189] as they were then called in Budapest with affectionate irony,

[187] József Lengyel, *Visegrader Strasse* (1929), Berlin, 1959, pp. 36–40, and Ilona Duczynska's letters to the author of 31 January and 1 August 1974. Duczynska states that she obtained Ervin Szabó's agreement to the eventual execution of Count Tisza. Révai also refers to Szabó's close ties with the group: 'Ervin Szabó remained very active . . . behind the scenes: he animated, directed, developed, and educated the anti-militarist movement which, under his spiritual patronage and guidance, had come out in opposition to the war through the co-operation and fusion of a group of Hungarian syndicalist workers (Mosolygo) and a group of left-wing socialist students (Duczynska, Sugar, et al.). This movement played a considerable role in preparing the great mass strikes of 1918.'
[188] Révai, pp. 135–6.
[189] Roughly translatable as 'the small minds': from the Hungarian word for 'mind' or 'spirit', *szellem*.

were poles apart from the positivist-tinged rationalist liberalism of the Social Science Society; rather they inclined towards a passionately romantic anti-capitalism, not at a political but at an ethico-cultural level.[190]

In its struggle against the evolutionary scientism of Jaszi and his colleagues, this group drew on the refined and subtle 'German ideology' brought by Lukács from the Max Weber Circle in Heidelberg, and by Mannheim from the Simmel Circle in Berlin. As for the conservative Hungarian anti-capitalism of broad layers of the traditional petty bourgeoisie, the gentry, and the Catholic peasantry (represented by the so-called '1848' opposition party), this was of such an obscurantist, vulgar, chauvinist, and anti-Semitic nature that it could not serve as a reference-pole for the *szellemkék*. Moreover, German romantic anti-capitalism acquired specific features in this intellectual hothouse, the dimension of nostalgia for a 'community' past being more or less discarded in favour of a genuinely *cultural* critique of capitalism. The Hungarian *szellemkék*, unlike the German sociological and literary circles discussed earlier, did not form part of a privileged university establishment, nor were they socially linked to a declining rural or urban petty bourgeoisie. In their eyes, the pre-capitalist and semi-feudal world was less a nostalgically remembered past than the oppressive and stifling present reality of Tisza's Hungary. It is in the light of the general character of the Hungarian social formation, its state of relative backwardness, that we can understand why the anti-feudal Jacobin dimension and a *sui generis* romantically anti-capitalist tendency could appear *complementary* rather than contradictory for certain sections of the Hungarian intelligentsia. This peculiar combination, which we have already mentioned in discussing Ady, was a potentially explosive mixture. Not by chance did many members of this current, unlike both liberal-democratic intellectuals and anti-bourgeois conservatives, become communists in the year 1919. Furthermore, unless the *ambivalence* of the neo-romantic 'spiritualist' intellectuals is taken into

[190] Cf. David Kettler, 'Culture and Revolution: Lukács in the Hungarian Revolutions of 1918/19', *Telos*, no. 10, winter 1971, pp. 56–7: 'Much the most important factor in this trend against the Social Scientists appears as an intellectual rather than political or purely literary development. Speaking generally, the new departure can be described as reception of the neo-romantic, "vitalist", or even "irrationalist" tendencies which had been spreading in France as well as Germany during the first decade of the new century. This was a reaction against what came to be perceived as the philistinism of the apostles of "progress", an expression of fear that the interests of high culture were being sacrificed in the ruthless pursuit of material prosperity.'

account, it is impossible to grasp their relative co-existence with the liberal-progressive trend – witness their involvement in the Social Science Society (of which Szabó and Mannheim, for example, were members), the *Huszadik Szádad*, *Nyugat*, and so on – that is, in the 'front against feudalism, chauvinism, and clericalism' to which Jaszi refered.[191]

The public expression of the *szellemkék* was the Free School of *Geisteswissenschaften*, which embraced a number of seminars and lectures intended for a highly selective intellectual elite. The group was generally rather isolated in Hungarian society, having much less contact or affinity with the petty bourgeoisie and middle layers than had German intellectuals at the turn of the century. Whether consciously or not, Mannheim probably used the *szellemkék* as a model when he later formulated his well-known analysis of the *freischwebende Intelligenz*.[192]

In a letter to David Kettler written in 1962, Lukács made an important statement about this 'spiritualist' seminar: 'Insofar as I can recall the School for Studies of the Human Spirit (*Geisteswissenschaften*), the basic tone in it was by no means generally conservative. That which essentially bound the lecturers together was opposition to capitalism in the name of idealist philosophy. The unifying factor was this rejection of Positivism.' This remark was in fact a polemical reply to his friend Horváth's view that the Free School was 'on the right rather than the left of' of the Social Science Society. We should note how Lukács, when referring to the perspective held in the years between 1915 and 1918, asserts a relation of identity between capitalism and positivism. Yet in the same letter, he warns Kettler not to exaggerate the revolutionary role of the School: 'It would be good in general if you would tone down your notion of the influence of the Free School for Studies of the Human Spirit in preparing the way for Communist ideology. The fact that several of its prominent members became prominent Communist ideologists simply belongs to the character of the time.' Kettler rightly points out, however, that although certain reservations are necessary and over-simplification should be avoided, we cannot overlook the fact that many more members of the Free School than of the Social Science Society later followed 'the character of the time' and became communists.[193]

---

[191] It should not be forgotten that one of the prominent *szellemkék*, the poet Anna Lesznai, was married to Oscar Jaszi. On the 'fluidity' of these opposed tendencies, see Kettler, p. 55.

[192] Cf. J. Gabel, 'Mannheim et le marxisme hongrois', *L'Homme et la Société*, no. 11, January-February-March 1969, p. 139.

[193] Kettler, pp. 60, 69, 70.

The communist writer József Lengyel, who had little sympathy for the group, describes it in the following terms: 'The "Human Spirit Boys" had opened a special school with courses of study during the war, a Budapest branch office of German idealist philosophy, where the old mystics and Husserl, Bolzano, and Fichte were studied; they were anti-militarist and occupied themselves with social science in the spirit of Max Weber, which was the fashion at the time.'[194]

Together with Lukács, Karl Mannheim was undoubtedly the *spiritus rector* of the School. Having studied for a year with Simmel in Berlin, Mannheim returned in 1913 a fervent supporter of German sociology and the neo-Kantian *Geisteswissenschaften* school (Dilthey, Rickert, et al.). In a programmatic talk given to the Free School in 1917, he well summarized a number of concerns common to the *szellemkék*. Under the title *Soul and Culture*, Mannheim developed Simmel's problematic of the tragedy of culture, the contradiction between subjective soul and objective culture. The soul creates culture, he argued, but culture becomes 'a Golem . . . leading an independent existence and a life of its own', an alienated life foreign to the soul. At the beginning of the lecture, Mannheim drew up a highly illuminating list of what he called 'the precursors of our road': 'Dostoevsky's world view and sense of life, Kierkegaard's ethics, the German review *Logos* and the Hungarian review *Szellem*, Lask, Zalai. I could also mention among our guides the aesthetic conceptions of Paul Ernst and Riegl, new French poetry . . . the Hungarians Bártok and Ady . . . and lastly the *Thalia* theatre movement.'[195] The other authors mentioned in the talk make up a no less significant list: Meister Eckhardt, Rousseau, Kant, Schlegel, Schiller, Marx, Simmel and— Lukács. But Mannheim adds that these names do not evoke the real essence of the school: 'an ethical and aesthetic normativism' located within 'a metaphysical-idealist' view of the world.[196]

---

[194] Lengyel, *Visegrader Strasse*, p. 140. A general announcement of the lecture series – responsibility for which rested with Mannheim, Lukács, Fogarasi, Béla Balázs, Arnold Hauser, Ervin Szabó, Bela Bártok and others – set out the approach of the Free School: 'The culture of Europe is turning, after the Positivism of the Nineteenth Century, once again towards metaphysical idealism.' The aim of the lectures was 'to express the point of view which speaks of the importance of the problem of transcendence, as against the materialism which is already receding into the past, of the unconditional validity of principles, as against relativistic impressionism.' (Quoted in Kettler, p. 61.)

[195] Originally written in Hungarian, this text appears in a full German translation in Mannheim, 'Seele und Kultur' (1917), *Wissenssoziologie*, pp. 67, 74.

[196] Ibid., p. 68.

We shall see below the similarity between such a *Weltanschauung* and Lukács's own problematic. As a matter of fact, in 1920 Mannheim published an enthusiastic review of *The Theory of the Novel*, emphasizing the close relationship between Lukács's methods of interpretation and medieval thought: 'The Middle Ages always tended to take the path leading from the uppermost to the lowermost point; it was Descartes who first introduced the fatal principle of deducing the whole from the parts, the top from the bottom.' Of course, Lukács takes the right path, basing his interpretation of works of literature on a 'spirit capable of description only in metaphysical terms'.[197]

Here we come to the problem of the ideological relations between Mannheim's thought, as typical of the *szellemkék*, and that German romanticism whose *intellectual* (but not social) nostalgia for the Middle Ages he seemed partly to share. This affinity emerges clearly in his essay on conservative thought, regarded by many as his finest production. A detailed analysis of this work is beyond the bounds of our study of the turn-of-the-century Hungarian intelligentsia. Suffice it to say that it involves a subtle and finely-shaded 'rehabilitation' of romantic thought, in its opposition to the abstract, calculating rationalism peculiar to the capitalist system.[198] The 'rehabilitation' refers above all to German writers such as Adam Müller, Justus Moser, and Novalis, but it extends to English romantics like Burke, 'whose merit was to have stressed the positive value of the Middle Ages at a time when they were a direct synonym of obscurantism'.[199] One of the most original and provocative aspects of Mannheim's essay is the parallel he draws more than once between romantic and socialist opposition to the abstract, individualist, and contemplative character of bourgeois-liberal thought. The example of Marxist thought he most often invokes is precisely *History and Class Consciousness*.[200]

The Free School of *Geisteswissenschaften* was the outward manifestation of a more or less esoteric group of friends meeting weekly around Lukács.

[197] Mannheim, 'Besprechung von Georg Lukács' *Die Theorie des Romans*', *Wissenssoziologie*, pp. 88–9.
[198] In a highly illuminating footnote, Mannheim mentions as examples of writers who analyse the structure and specificity of modern rationalism: Max Weber, Sombart, Simmel (*The Philosophy of Money*), and Lukács (the chapter on reification in *History and Class Consciousness*). See Mannheim, 'Conservative Thought', p. 147.
[199] Mannheim, 'Das konservative Denken: soziologische Beiträge zum Werden des politisch-historischen Denkens in Deutschland', *Wissenssoziologie*, p. 471.
[200] Ibid., pp. 425, 429, 504.

The atmosphere in this renowned 'Sunday Circle' has been outstandingly reconstructed by Anna Lesznai and Tibór Gergely: 'These Sunday discussions were, in general, organized and dominated by Lukács: some topic would be thrown out for discussion by him and pursued in detail by the group. Typically, the subject would be a moral and/or literary problem, with much attention paid to Dostoevsky and to German mystics like Eckhardt. In a vague sense, one could say that the group was "left" in its political sympathies; but it is more accurate to emphasize how unpolitical we all were. In fact, the group had more in common with a religious meeting than with a political club: there was a ceremonial, quasi-religious tone to the meeting.'[201]

A strikingly high proportion of communists and supporters of the 1919 Soviet Republic's 'cultural revolution' would eventually emerge from this coterie of 'aristocrats of the spirit' – a fact that cannot be understood unless we take account of the potentially explosive character of the *szellemkék* ideology. As we have seen, an anti-feudal, Jacobin dimension was there

---

[201] Kettler, p. 59. Kettler quotes another very interesting testimony given by the famous art historian Arnold Hauser: 'Lukács was tied to Lask, Weber and Jaspers, and was interested in philosophy and religion, having come back from Heidelberg a kind of mystic. . . . The Sunday circle met weekly at the home of Béla Balázs from about 1915 to 1918. . . . We never talked about politics, but about literature, philosophy and religion. . . . The guardian saints of the group in those early times were Kierkegaard and Dostoevsky.'

A list of the main participants in the Sunday Circle between 1915 and 1919 would include the following names: Frigyes Antal, a Marxist art historian, during the Commune of 1919 deputy head of the Directorium for Art; Béla Balázs, poet, writer, and communist militant from 1919 onwards, during the Commune head of the Literature and Art Section of the People's Commissariat for Education; Béla Fogarasi, philosopher, translator of Bergson into Hungarian before 1914 (gave a highly acclaimed talk in 1917 to the Free School on *Conservative and Progressive Idealism*; disciple of Lukács, Communist Party member and director of higher education during the 1919 Commune); Lajos Fülep, philosopher and art historian, close friend of Lukács, co-founder with him of the *Szellem* journal in 1911; Tibór Gergely, painter, Anna Lesznai's second husband; Arnold Hauser, sociologist and art historian close to Marxism; Anna Lesznai, poet and novelist, one of Lukács's closest friends, at this time married to Oscar Jaszi; Karl Mannheim, sociologist; Emma Ritoók, at the time a close friend of Bloch and Lukács (later supported the Horthyite counter-revolution and denounced her former friends in a book entitled *Adventures of the Spirit* published – in Hungarian – in 1922); Ervin Sinkó, novelist, at the time a Tolstoyan socialist, during the 1919 Commune officer in charge of the House of the Soviet (the residence of people's commissars); Wilhelm Szilasi, philosopher, disciple of Husserl and Heidegger; Charles de Tólnay, art historian; Eugene Varga, economist, former left-socialist, founding member of the Hungarian Communist Party in 1918, people's commissar for finance under the Soviet Republic; John Wilde, art historian (worked in 1919 with the Art Department of the Commissariat of Education).

(*Sources*: I. Mészarós, *Lukács' Concept of Dialectic*, London, 1972, pp. 124–5; Lukács, 'La politique culturelle de la Commune de Budapest', *Action Poétique*, no. 49, 1972, pp. 23–31.)

simply juxtaposed to an anti-capitalist, romantic dimension; they were like two inflammable substances that explode when an external shock brings them into contact with each other. In the case of our 'spiritual scientists', that shock was the 1918–19 revolutionary movement in Hungary.

These brief observations on the radicalized intelligentsia in Hungary may be summed up as follows. The Hungarian social formation – a specific articulation of capitalism with semi-feudal structures resulting from a process of uneven and combined development – displayed many similarities with the Russian. In both cases, the lack of a revolutionary-democratic bourgeoisie and the specific weight of the proletariat tended to impel the rebellious intelligentsia into the camp of the workers' move-ment; but in Hungary, because of its deeply reformist character, that movement was unable to serve as a pole of attraction. The 'red' wing of the intelligentsia, represented by Ady, Szabó, and the current under their influence, was simultaneously Jacobin-democratic and anti-capitalist (close to European neo-romantic tendencies). In a confused manner it aspired to a total change of Hungarian society; yet the lack of a revolutionary social force, whether bourgeois or proletarian, made it an isolated and 'free-floating' layer. Until 1917, the more these thinkers, writers, or philosophers became radically opposed to the feudal-bourgeois *status quo*, the more their isolation and impotence before the existing system led them into a sense of despair and a tragic view of the world.[202] However, in comparison with the tragic view current in Germany at the turn of the century, this phenomenon distinguished itself by greater radicalism, lack of resignation, and a genuinely revolutionary potential sharpened by the incipient radicalization of intellectuals. As an example of this developing process, we may quote the following anguished appeal to the Emperor issued by a group of Hungarian conservatives in 1918: 'Revolutionary tension is further heightened by the circumstance that the majority of the intellectually-working middle class sank to a proletarian standard of living – yes, even abandoned its special position and went over into the camp of the Social Democracy.'[203]

[202] As Lukács points out in an article on Béla Bártok (1970): 'Honest and sincere political thinkers . . . perceived the great deformation of human beings through the alliance between the remnants of feudalism and the beginning of capitalist production. Feeling and thought protested against it, but they believed *a priori* that, even theoretically, any possibility of radical opposition leading to or encouraging action was hopeless.' ('Béla Bártok, On the 25th Anniversary of his Death', p. 44.)

[203] Quoted in Kettler, pp. 46–7.

The twofold, anti-feudal and anti-bourgeois, aspirations of the Hungarian revolutionary intelligentsia would find a historical answer and concrete synthesis only with the 1918–19 Hungarian revolution; only then would the proletariat, led by its communist vanguard, appear on the social and political arena as the subject of a twofold, democratic and socialist revolution. Thus, in its programme of 'uninterrupted' or 'permanent' revolution, the Communist Party fused together those Jacobin and anti-capitalist aspects which had remained at the level of intuition (Ady) or unresolved contradiction (Szabó) for the 'red' intelligentsia. The ideological crisis of intellectuals influenced by Ady and Szabó would find a logical and coherent solution when large numbers of them passed over to the Communist Party and the Soviet Republic. For with the appearance of the Communist Party and the revolutionary proletariat as a massive social force, their bitter, anguished despair was transformed, through a brilliant explosion, into immense, passionate and messianic hope.

II
How an Intellectual Becomes a Revolutionary

> For socialism is not only the labour question, or the question of the so-called fourth estate, but . . . the question of the Tower of Babel which is deliberately being created without God, not for the sake of reaching heaven from earth, but for the sake of bringing heaven down to earth.
>
> DOSTOEVSKY, *The Brothers Karamazov*

1. Lukács's Anti-Capitalism and Tragic View of the World

Lukács's evolution occurred within the general ideological crisis of the Central European intelligentsia, in whose life he directly participated through various German and Hungarian intellectual groups. Early in his development, he met two figures who made a profound impact on him: Endre Ady, the most revolutionary representative of Hungarian Jacobin democracy, and Ernst Bloch, the most radical representative of German cultural anti-capitalism.

The starting point for Lukács's political thought, as he himself points out in a 1969 autobiographical text, was 'a passionate rejection of the order then existing in Hungary'.[1] Nevertheless, he did not identify with the 'liberal-democratic' opposition of moderate intellectual circles, being like a 'tolerated guest' in the Social Science Society, *Nyugat*, and *Huszadik Század*.[2] Not by chance was his book on the evolution of modern drama described by a Hungarian critic (Géza Feleky) as 'embarrassing' for both progressives and conservatives. Nor was it an accident that Endre Ady was the only, or almost the only, Hungarian thinker with whom he shared this

---

[1] Lukács, 'Elöszó' (Preface) to *Magyar Irodalom, Magyar Kultura*, Budapest, 1970, p. 6. Lukács also speaks of his 'feelings of violent hostility towards the whole of official Hungary'.

[2] Ibid., p. 11.

radical and global rejection of established society. Lukács situates Ady's poetry – his own encounter with which he describes as 'a veritable shock' – within an extremely broad philosophico-historical context: 'German philosophy . . . remained . . . conservative as far as the evolution of society and history was concerned: reconciliation with reality (*Versöhnung mit der Wirklichkeit*) was one of the cornerstones of Hegelian philosophy. Ady had such a determining influence precisely because he never for a single moment reconciled himself to Hungarian reality or, on that basis, to the overall reality of the epoch. . . . When I first met Ady, this irreconcilable spirit followed me in all my thoughts like an inescapable shadow. . . . In his poem *The Hun, A New Legend*, he describes this attitude to life, history, what was yesterday, what is today, and what will be tomorrow: "I am . . ./the faith that protests and the mission to veto/Only the dog has a master/Ugocsa non coronat".'[3]

Ugocsa is a small county in East Hungary which refused to support the monarch during the election of the first Habsburg king. And so *Ugocsa non coronat* is a historical, though doomed, symbol of the rebellious Hungarian spirit and, more generally, of courageous and indomitable protest.[4] This is a crucial point for understanding Lukács's political evolution: his itinerary began with a complete rejection of Hegelian *Versöhnung* with reality[5]; and he ceased to be a consistent revolutionary in 1926, at the very moment when he embraced the Hegelian realism of 'reconciliation'.

What attracted the young Lukács to Ady's lyricism was the fact that, unlike the *Nyugat* and *Huszadik Század* 'modernists', he rejected not only the old feudal Hungary, but also western bourgeois 'progress': 'At bottom, this entire phase of my development was inspired . . . by discontent and revolt against the Hungarian capitalism that had sprung to life in the "gentry". These same feelings lay behind my unconditional admiration for Ady; yet not for a moment did they give me the idea – generally accepted by the Hungarian intellectual left – that a way out had first to be prepared by the introduction of western capitalist civilization into

[3] Ibid., p. 8. Cf. Lukács's October 1969 interview with András Kovács: 'It was Ady who, in the name of "Ugocsa will not crown", aroused our rejection of the capitalist-aristocratic Hungary of the time. . . .' (Lukács, *L'Uomo e la rivoluzione*, Rome, 1973, pp. 67–8.)

[4] Cf. Ferenc Fehér, *Das Bündnis von Georg Lukács und Béla Balász bis zur ungarischen Revolution 1918*, typescript p. 17, published in Hungarian in *Irodalomtörténeti Tammanyok*, 2/3, Budapest 1969.

[5] In a series of notes written about 1915–16, Lukács returned to this question and criticized Hegel for his tendency to 'deify what exists'. Quoted by F. Fehér in *Am Scheideweg des romantischen Antikapitalismus*, unpublished manuscript, 1975, p. 123.

Hungary. . . . Even though my ideas were confused from a theoretical point of view, I saw the revolutionary destruction of society as the one and only solution to the cultural contradictions of the epoch.'[6]

For both Lukács and Ady, a tragic view of the world logically followed from this ethical revolt against the feudal-bourgeois order, combined as it was with the lack of a really revolutionary force in the political and social arena. In one of his first articles on Ady, dating from 1909, Lukács clearly sketched out this problematic; Ady is seen as the poet 'of Hungarian revolutionaries without a revolution'. 'Ady's public is absurdly touching. It consists of men who feel that there is no way out except revolution . . . who see that everything in existence is bad, cannot be corrected, and must be destroyed to make room for new possibilities. The need for a revolution does exist, but it is impossible to hope that one could be attempted even in the distant future.'[7] Obviously Lukács himself was part of this 'public' condemned to absolute, despairing negativity.

It was at this time (1910) that Lukács's first meeting with Bloch 'gave a crucial impetus to my philosophical development'.[8] Right up to 1914, the two thinkers would experience a veritable 'ideological symbiosis', united in a single ethico-messianic utopianism.[9] Circulating in Heidelberg was a very amusing epigram coined by Emil Lask which admirably captured the *Weltanschauung* common to the two young philosophers: 'What are the names of the four evangelists? Matthew, Mark, Lukács, and Bloch.'[10] It was because of this mystical idealism that the anti-capitalist Lukács refused to identify with working-class socialism: 'The only possible hope would be the proletariat and socialism . . . [but] socialism does not appear to have the religious power capable of filling the entire soul – a power that used to characterize early Christianity.'[11] Not only Christianity but also

[6] Lukács, 'Mon chemin vers Marx' (1969), *Nouvelles Etudes hongroises*, Budapest, 1973, vol. 8, pp. 78–9.

[7] Lukács, 'Ady Endre' (1909), in *Magyar Irodalom*, vol. 1, p. 45. Our study of Lukács's political thought begins with this 1909 article, probably his first statement of a revolutionary position.

[8] Lukács, 'Elöszó' (1969), p. 12.

[9] In the interview he granted me on 24 March 1974, Bloch said: 'We were like communicating vessels.' (See the appendix to the French edition of this work.)

[10] Karl Jaspers, 'Heidelberger Erinnerungen', *Heidelberger Jahrbücher*, 1961, p. 5. See also Leandre Konder's unpublished thesis, *Revolution und Gemeinschaft, Einige Grundzüge, Leistungen und Entwicklungsprobleme des politischen Denkens von Georg Lukács*, typescript, II, p. 9.

[11] Lukács, 'Esztétikai Kultura', *Renaissance*, Budapest, 1910, in *Müvészet es társadalom* (Art and Society), Budapest, 1969, p. 77.

94

Hindu and Jewish mysticism had an attraction for Lukács, in the latter case through the mediation of the utopian socialist theologian Martin Buber. The 1911–21 correspondence between Lukács and Buber, recently discovered in Heidelberg and Jerusalem, reveals the surprising degree of friendship and understanding that united the two thinkers. Thus, in his 1911 letters Lukács wrote that his reading of Buber's book on Baal-Shem had been an 'unforgettable' experience, and that the texts of Hasidic mysticism should be published in as complete a form as possible.[12] And three years later, the Hungarian poet Béla Balázs wrote this in his diary about his friend Lukács: 'Gyuri's great new philosophy. Messianism. A homogeneous world as the goal of redemption. . . . Gyuri has discovered the Jew in himself. The Hasidic sect. Baal-Shem.'[13]

Bloch had a very profound influence on Lukács at this time. Paul Honigsheim, who met them in Heidelberg in 1912, later described them as 'Ernst Bloch, the Catholic-leaning Jewish apocalyptic, together with his follower Lukács'.[14] It was also Bloch who persuaded Lukács to accompany him to Heidelberg, where he would find in the Max Weber Circle 'exceptional understanding of my uncommon ideas'.[15] Lukács's recently discovered pre-1917 correspondence shows the extent of his contacts with the Heidelberg Circle and the broader current of German romantic anti-capitalism. Lukács was then corresponding with, among

[12] Lukács Archivum, Budapest. Lukács's notes from 1911 contain numerous extracts from Buber's works, *Die Legende des Baalschems* and *Geschichten des Rabi Nachmann*. After one passage, Lukács remarks on the Jewish mystics' 'sharp rejection of the world'. (*Notizbuch C*, Lukács Archivum, p. 29.) During the same year, Lukács published a study of Jewish mysticism, in the form of a review of Buber's works on Hasidism. He saw this as the greatest and most authentic movement since German Reformation mysticism, pointing out the deep affinity between the Baalshem, the Vedes, Eckhardt, and Böhme. ('Zsidó miszticizmus', *Szellem* (Spirit), no. 2, 1911, pp. 256–7.)

[13] Béla Balázs, 'Notes from a Diary (1911–1921)', *The New Hungarian Quarterly*, no. 47, 1972, p. 173.

[14] P. Honigsheim, 'Der Max-Weber-Kreis in Heidelberg', *Kölner Vierteljahrschrift für Soziologie*, vol. 5/3, 1926, p. 284. When I asked him about this, Bloch gave the modest reply: 'It was mutual. I was as much a follower of Lukács as he was of me. There was no difference between us.' Another contemporary witness, Karl Jaspers, described the following scene in Heidelberg before 1914: 'After one of Lukács's talks, Bloch solemnly declared: the world-spirit has just passed through this room.' (Jaspers, p. 5.) It should be added that *The Theory of the Novel* was written at almost the same time as *Geist der Utopie*, and that Bloch would refer to his friend's early work in his polemics with the 'orthodox' Lukács of the thirties. In 1962, Lukács himself recognized the affinity between *The Theory of the Novel* and Bloch's early works (*Geist der Utopie* and *Thomas Münzer*), describing their common structure as a fusion of 'left' ethics and 'right' epistemology. (Lukács, *The Theory of the Novel*, London, 1971, p. 21.)

[15] Lukács, 'Elöszó' (1969), p. 13.

others: Margarete Bendemann, Richard Beer-Hoffmann, Ernst Bloch, Martin Buber, Max Dessoir, Hans von Eckhart, Paul Ernst, Friedrich Gundolf, Karl Jaspers, Emil Lask, Emil Lederer, Karl Mannheim, Rudolf Meyer, Gustav Radbruch, Heinrich Rickert, Georg Simmel, Hans Staudinger, Ernst Troeltsch, Alfred Weber, Max Weber, and Leopold Ziegler.[16] What, then, were the 'uncommon ideas' that Lukács put forward in Heidelberg? According to the testimony of Paul Honigsheim, himself a member of the Max Weber Circle, Lukács 'was very much opposed to the bourgeoisie, liberalism, the constitutional state, parliamentarianism, revisionistic socialism, the Enlightenment, relativism and individualism'.[17] Lukács's contempt for German Social Democracy was limitless. Thus, Honigsheim describes a scene after a meeting they attended at which the SPD revisionist Ludwig Franck had spoken: 'As we left the meeting hall, Lukács shook his head excitedly and said in a rage, "A socialist who wants to defend the constitution!"'[18] Max Weber's wife, writing in her *Memoirs*, says that Lukács was 'moved by eschatological hopes of a new emissary of the transcendent God', seeing 'the basis of salvation in a socialist social order created by brotherhood'.[19] However, Lukács's messianism did not draw him closer to the other Heidelberg intellectual coterie: the mystical-esoteric group of Stefan George's friends. In a letter about German literature sent to Félix Bertaux in March 1913 (and recently discovered in the 'Heidelberg suitcase'), Lukács dismissed the prophetic pretensions of the great lyrical poet and his ardent admirers: 'When the person in question is not really a prophet, not a true emissary and messenger, he cannot amass all the contradictions in himself, bearing all suffering on the path through clarity toward redemption.'[20] The striking feature of this letter from Heidelberg, more striking than its sceptical attitude to George, is its profoundly religious problematic and its

[16] Lukács Archivum, Budapest.

[17] P. Honigsheim, *On Max Weber*, New York, 1968, p. 24. In 1910, Lukács began to take an interest in French revolutionary syndicalism, especially its critique of bourgeois parliamentary democracy. In a 1910 notebook, we find under the heading 'Democracy' a highly revealing list of books: Bougle, 'Syndicalisme et bergsonisme', *Revue du Mons*, 10 April 1909; Sorel, 'Le socialisme est-il réligieux', *Mouvement Socialiste*, December 1906; Sorel, 'Bürgerlichkeit und Demokratie', *Mouvement Socialiste*, December 1906; Paul Louis, 'La crise du parlementarisme', *Mercure de France*, 1 February 1910; and other works by Sorel, Berth, Lagardelle, and the revolutionary syndicalist Emile Pouget. (*Notizbuch 1*, 1910, Lukács Archivum.)

[18] Honigsheim, p. 26.

[19] Marianne Weber, *Max Weber: A Biography*, New York, 1975, p. 466.

[20] Letter from Lukács to Félix Bertaux, March 1913, p. 4, Lukács Archivum.

implicit belief in the coming of a 'true' prophet. This problematic also appears in Lukács assessment of socialism: 'The last culturally active force in Germany, naturalist-materialist socialism, owes its efficacy to hidden religious elements.'[21]

This remark should be compared with a surprising analysis of Marxist socialism which he developed a few years later in *The History of Modern Drama* (1911): 'The system of socialism and its view of the world, Marxism, form a synthetic unity – perhaps the most unrelenting and rigorous synthesis since medieval Catholicism. When the time comes to give it an artistic expression, this will necessarily take a form as severe and rigorous as the genuine art of the Middle Ages (Giotto, Dante), and not that of the purely individual art, pushing individualism to the extreme, which is produced by our own times.'[22] This passage is typical of the romantically anti-capitalist problematic to be found in several texts written by Lukács during this period. Interestingly enough, Max Weber showed a certain understanding, if not sympathy, for these positions of Lukács. According to Honigsheim, Weber said that 'one thing became evident to Lukács when he looked at the paintings of Cimabue . . . and this was that culture can exist only in conjunction with collectivist values'.[23]

Despite the favourable echo his *Weltanschauung* found within the Max Weber Circle, Lukács's ethical-revolutionary orientation left him rather marginalized in the group.[24] It is indeed true that Lukács rejected capitalism much more violently than the majority of German intellectuals in Heidelberg; moreover, he criticized their lack of a consistently tragic vision and, particularly in the cases of Dilthey and Simmel, their tendency to moral and human 'reconciliation' (*Versöhnung*) with society.[25]

---

[21] Ibid., p. 5. The letter also talks of hope in a philosophical rebirth in Germany, in a philosophical system that will 'be the articulated expression of the silent religiosity of our age'. In our view, this is a reference to Ernst Bloch.

[22] *A Modern dráma története*, vol. 2, Budapest, 1911, pp. 156–7. Quoted in Fehér's unpublished manuscripts, *Die Geschichtsphilosophie des Dramas, die Metaphysik der Tragödie und die Utopie des untragischen Dramas* and *Scheidewege der Dramen-theorie des jungen Lukács*, pp. 416–42. It is unlikely that Thomas Mann knew of Lukács's Hungarian text when he created the character of the Jesuit-communist Naphta.

[23] Honigsheim, *On Max Weber*, p. 27.

[24] 'A certain world view, which I then considered to be revolutionary, brought me into conflict with the *Nyugat* review, isolated me within *Huszadik Szäzad*, and made me an outsider among my future German friends.' (Lukács, 'Elöszó' (1969), p. 9.)

[25] See the interesting work by Lukács's Hungarian disciple and friend György Márkus, *Lukács' 'erste' Ästhetik, Zur Entwicklungsgeschichte der Philosophie des jungen Lukács*, typescript, pp. 11–12. In a private letter of 3 August 1974, Markus drew my attention to another significant difference between Lukács and Simmel: 'Even during the pre-1918

We have already noted that elements of a tragic world view appear in the writings of Simmel, Tönnies, and the whole current of *Lebensphilosophie*. But whereas Tönnies, for example, was a reformist linked to the right wing of Social Democracy, for Lukács the routinist and parliamentarist character of German or Hungarian Social Democracy ruled it out as a genuine alternative to the bourgeois status quo; and Lukács, who was much more radical in his idealist rejection of the world, also exhibited a much deeper tragic vision. Lukács's 'politico-moral' thought in the period from 1910 to 1916 was that of a *sui generis* romantic anti-capitalist[26]: he embraced the problematic of both the German intelligentsia (irreversible development of capitalism) and the Hungarian intellectuals (stability of an ultra-conservative, feudal-bourgeois society), combining the two in an extremely radical 'ideological amalgam' that tended towards a consistently tragic world view. Directly or indirectly, this deep ethico-cultural opposition to capitalism and this tendency towards the tragic are reflected in most of Lukács's aesthetic writings of the time.

In 1909 he wrote *A History of the Development of Modern Drama* – a book which, published in Budapest in 1911, already contained some Marxist elements, albeit of a Marx seen 'through spectacles tinted by Simmel and Max Weber'.[27] There is no doubt that this work shares the romantically anti-capitalist problematic of German intellectuals, speaking as it does in terms of the 'reification (*Versachlichung*) of life' and 'the tendency to depersonalization and reduction of quality to quantity' in bourgeois society. Lukács also criticizes rationalization, 'that desire to reduce

period, he was never entirely happy with the tragic world view at which he had arrived; he was never marked by the self-satisfaction of a Simmel; he was always testing – in vain – new ways in which he might *leave* this tragic dualism.... To a degree that increased every year, he found it impossible to accept as definitive the verdict of *non possumus*.' This aspect of the young Lukács's ideology helps us understand why he went beyond the tragic world view with his political *engagement* of 1918.

[26] In his 1967 preface, Lukács himself characterizes his ideology at this time as 'ethical idealism...[with] all its romantic anti-capitalist overtones'. (*History and Class Consciousness*, p. x.) He also recognizes that it 'made a number of real contributions' to his evolution towards Marxism. It should be added that about 1907–8 Lukács had written the plan for a work on *Die Romantik des XIX. Jahrhunderts*, (Romanticism of the Nineteenth Century) and that he had closely studied the main German romantic thinkers (compiling notebooks on Schelling, Schlegel, Novalis, Schleiermacher, and others). See G. Márkus, pp. 5–6.

[27] Lukács, 'Preface' to *History and Class Consciousness*, London, 1971, p. ix. Lukács's work on modern drama has not yet been translated from Hungarian, except for one chapter, 'Zur Soziologie des modernen Dramas', *Archiv für Sozialwissenschaft*, vol. 38, 1914.

everything to figures and formulae', which eliminates from cultural life 'the sense-element of the visible and the audible, the palpable and the indefinable'; he vigorously denounces intellectualism on the grounds that it 'tends to break up every community, isolating men from one another'. He further points out that modern culture has become a bourgeois culture in which 'the economic forms of one class dominate the whole of life'; even agricultural production, the traditional base of feudalism, is assuming an increasingly capitalist character.[28]

The analysis of capitalism that Lukács unfolds is borrowed from both *Capital* and Simmel's *The Philosophy of Money*. Particular stress is laid on the phenomenon of alienation: 'Capitalism's main economic tendency ... is objectification (*Objektivierung*) of production, through which it is separated from the personality of the producer. In capitalist economy, the objective abstraction of capital itself effectively becomes the producer, no longer having any organic link with its chance owners; it is not even necessary that the owner should be an individual (joint-stock companies). ... Work takes on an objective life of its own opposed to the individuality of any single man.' This capitalist tendency to depersonalization appears in every field, whether the organization of the state (bureaucracy, a modern army) or the forms of economic life (the universal sway of money, the stock exchange, etc.).[29] Society is therefore the arena of a tragic conflict between the desire for personal fulfilment and reified objective reality. This conflict is, in turn, the socio-cultural basis of modern dramatic literature: 'Even pure being as such is becoming tragic. With the growing power of external conditions, the least movement or unadapted capacity is enough to

[28] Lukács, 'Zur Soziologie des modernen Dramas', in *Schriften zur Literatursoziologie*, Neuwied, 1961, pp. 271, 285, 287, 288. The concept of *reification*, which was to play a central role in *History and Class Consciousness*, appears here for the first time in Lukács's work.
[29] Lukács, (Zur Soziologie', pp. 287, 288. In 1909 Lukács sent Simmel a German translation of one chapter of an early draft of this work. He was then invited to Berlin to present his views at the seminar run by Simmel. Simmel took the opportunity to ask his student Ernst Bloch for an assessment of this unknown Hungarian writer. (See my interview with Bloch mentioned in note 9.) Simmel's own opinion of his disciple emerges from Lukács's 1900–17 correspondence, recently discovered in a suitcase he left in Heidelberg on returning to Hungary. In a letter to Lukács dated 22 July 1909, the Berlin sociologist writes: 'I have no wish to hide from you that, *methodologically speaking*, I was very attracted by the first pages I read. I found fruitful and interesting the attempt to derive what is most inward and sublime from the most external and commonplace conditions' (Lukács Archivum). Andrew Arato, who has read both Hungarian volumes of the work, argues that Lukács had a more historicist approach than Simmel and that the book contains elements of a Marxist analysis of social classes. (Arato, 'Lukács's Path to Marxism (1910–1923)', *Telos*, no. 7, spring 1971, p. 134.)

provoke insoluble discord.'[30]

Lukács's first work in which this tragic world view is consistently and systematically developed is *Soul and Form* (1910). Lucien Goldmann has rescued this book from undeserved oblivion, not only analysing its structure of meaning with incomparable rigour, but also drawing out its relationship to Kant, Pascal, and Racine on the one hand, and to twentieth-century existentialist thought (particularly Heidegger's *Being and Time*) on the other. Thus, in *The Hidden God* (1955) Goldmann uses *Soul and Form* to unravel Pascal's *Pensées* and, conversely, Pascal's paradoxes to explain the antinomies of the early Lukács – all through a process of reciprocal illumination in which the tragic world view emerges in all its richness and consistency.[31]

Soul and Form is a work whose deep philosophical and moral significance is not immediately apparent: most of the essays seem purely aesthetic in content, partly referring to minor contemporary authors now virtually unknown. The meaning of the work becomes clear only on the basis of a remark in the first chapter defining the irony employed by essayists: 'The irony I mean consists in the critic's always speaking about the ultimate problems of life, but in a tone which implies that he is only discussing pictures and books, only the inessential and pretty ornaments of real life – and even then not their innermost substance but only their beautiful and useless surface.'[32] In other words, the essays contained in *Soul and Form* should be read as relating to *the ultimate problems of life*; as in much of Lukács's other literary criticism, aesthetics is here intimately bound up with an *ethical* problematic, with a moral point of view on contemporary life and capitalist society. It is thus no accident that many of the writers discussed in *Soul and Form* belong, directly or indirectly, to the current of romantic anti-capitalism: Novalis, Kierkegaard, Theodor

---

[30] Lukács, 'Zur Soziologie', p. 289. In the autobiography written just before his death, Lukács makes the following evaluation of his work on modern drama: 'Synthesis of the problematic of my childhood and youth: a meaningful life impossible under capitalism; the fight for such a life; tragedy and tragi-comedy. . . .' (*Gelebtes Denken*, 1971, unpublished manuscript, p. 15.) A series of uncompleted notes, this autobiographical sketch and true balance-sheet of a life is a treasure-trove of information about Lukács's intellectual and political development.

[31] L. Goldmann, 'Georges Lukács l'essayiste', *Revue d'Esthétique*, no. 1, January-March 1950; *The Hidden God*, London 1964; 'The Aesthetics of the Young Lukács', *The New Hungarian Quarterly*, no. 47, autumn 1972; 'The Early Writings of Georg Lukács', *Tri-Quarterly*, no. 9, spring 1967; *Kierkegaard vivant*, Paris, 1966, pp. 125–64; 'Lukács, György', *Enciclopaedia Universalis*, vol. 10, 1971; *Lukács and Heidegger*, London, 1977.

[32] Lukács, *Soul and Form*, London, 1971, p. 9.

Storm, Stefan George, Paul Ernst, and so on. Nor is it by chance that Thomas Mann drew on *Soul and Form* when writing his short story *Death in Venice*,[33] and that he enthusiastically acclaimed Lukács's work in the most 'conservatively anti-capitalist' of his own writings, *Reflections of an Unpolitical Man.*

What then is the *structure of meaning* of *Soul and Form*? In the essay on tragedy, Lukács describes the plays of Paul Ernst as 'built into the clear architecture of a rigid, transitionless dichotomy'.[34] Now, this may also be said of Lukács's own work; for its axis is precisely a 'rigid dichotomy' between two types of life: absolute and relative life, life in which 'mutually exclusive opposites . . . are separated from one another sharply and definitively' and the life of 'the melting chaos of nuances'; life in which problems appear in the Kierkegaardian form of 'either-or' (*entweder-oder*) and life ruled by the 'not only – but also' (*sowohl-als auch*). On the one side is 'real life', 'always unreal, always impossible in the midst of empirical life'; and on the other is that empirical life itself, 'an anarchy of light and dark' in which nothing is carried through to the end. Here, 'everything flows, everything merges into another thing, and the mixture is un-controlled and impure . . . nothing ever flowers into real life (*zum wirklichen Leben*)'.[35]

Tragedy stems from this contradiction between the demand for absolute values and the empirical, corrupt and corrupting world; it stems, that is, from nostalgia for an authentic life incapable of realization in the concrete life of society. The tragic vision, understood as radical and consistent rejection of the world, is more fully analysed in the last essay, 'The Metaphysics of Tragedy', which is devoted to the writings of Paul Ernst. By contrast, most of the preceding essays explore forms of rejection that Lukács considers, in the last analysis, to be inauthentic and insufficiently radical.[36]

This judgement applies especially to those attempts to reconcile authentic life and empirical life most clearly expressed in the 'art of living' (*Lebenskunst*) of Kierkegaard and the romantics. In criticizing such efforts, Lukács employs two fine, almost identical images: Kierkegaard, he argues,

[33] Cf. Judith Tarr, 'Georg Lukács, Thomas Mann und *Der Tod in Venedig*', *Die Weltwoche*, 2 July 1971.
[34] Lukács, *Soul and Form*, p. 166.
[35] Ibid., pp. 4, 31, 152–3.
[36] L. Goldmann, 'The Aesthetics of the Young Lukács', p. 131. The only exception, in Goldmann's view, is the first chapter, 'On the Nature and Form of the Essay', which sounds a dissonant chord in the Kantian rigour of the work.

sought 'to build a crystal palace out of air', while the romantics tried 'to erect a spiritual Tower of Babel . . . with nothing but air for its infrastructure'.[37] This metaphor spotlights the contradiction between the ('crystal') clarity and rigour of the universe of forms, pointing towards the absolute ("Tower of Babel'), and the amorphous unsubstantiality of the raw material employed: empirical life.

In the essay on Kierkegaard, Lukács criticizes the possibility of performing a noble and authentic *gesture* in one's actual life. (He refers to the Danish poet's break with his fiancée, Regine Olsen, who was thereby sacrificed to an exclusive love of God.) Here Lukács adopts a standpoint more Kierkegaardian than Kierkegaard, expressing astonishment at the latter's inconsistency with his own rigorous positions: 'How could he do it – he of all men, who saw more clearly than any other the thousand aspects, the thousand-fold variability of every motive – he who so clearly saw how everything passes gradually into its opposite?' For Lukács, the will to reconcile the absolute with life by means of a gesture is nothing other than 'self-delusion, however splendidly heroic'. Kierkegaard wished to perform an absolutely honest (*ehrlich*) action; but 'can one be honest in face of life, and yet stylize life's events in literary form (*ins Dichterische*)'? The answer is clear: 'In life, nothing is unambiguous . . . and not every note that has once been struck must necessarily be silenced in the end.' In short, 'poetry and life' must be kept 'tragically, definitively distinct'.[38]

In Lukács view, the failure to make such a 'definitive distinction' is the cardinal weakness of romantic *Lebenskunst*. Novalis and the romantics wished to turn life into poetry: 'They transformed the deepest and most inward laws of poetic art into imperatives for life.' Not understanding the unbridgeable gulf between the clear, unequivocal universe of poetic form and the ambiguous universe of empirical reality, 'they created a homogeneous, organic world unified within itself and identified it with the real world'.[39]

In the essay on Paul Ernst, 'The Metaphysics of Tragedy', Lukács rejects any illusory reconciliation, compromise, or fusion of the two universes; and in this sense, he consciously identifies with the tragic *Weltanschauung* as a total rejection of the empirical world in favour of 'a different life opposed to and exclusive of ordinary life', one that would be

[37] Lukács, *Soul and Form*, pp. 28, 42.
[38] Ibid., pp. 28, 29, 32, 40. See also p. 40: 'Kierkegaard's heroism was that he wanted to create forms from life. . . . His tragedy was that he wanted to live what cannot be lived.'
[39] Ibid., pp. 49–50.

governed by the quest for the absolute and expectation of the miracle.[40] For Lukács, the miracle 'is a gleam, a lightning that illumines the banal paths of empirical life: something disturbing and seductive, dangerous and surprising . . .'; it is 'clear and unambiguous', admitting of 'no relativity, no transition, no nuance'. The miracle-enlightened soul judges the world and judges itself: 'The judgement is a cruelly harsh one, without mercy or reprieve; sentence is passed ruthlessly upon even the smallest fault, the faintest suggestion of a betrayal of the essence.'[41]

In the tragic world view of *Soul and Form*, the only authentic attitude is, as Goldmann puts it, 'one which, governed by the category "all-or-nothing", spurns the more and the less, rejects all degrees and transitions. For the man who is aware of his condition, there are only the extremes of the authentic and the inauthentic, the true and the false, the just and the unjust, value and non-value; there is no point in-between. However, such a man faces a world in which absolute value is never encountered; everything there is relative and, as such, non-existent and totally devoid of value.'[42]

Is this the world *in general* or is it the *historically determined* world of modern capitalist society? At one point in 'The Metaphysics of Tragedy', Lukács allows the real scope of the problematic to break through: 'And because nature and fate have never been so terrifyingly soulless as they are today . . . we may again hope for the coming of tragedy.'[43] Still, the thrust of the essay is rather ahistorical, rooted in the abstract categories of 'life', 'essence', and so on. Lukács moves beyond all concrete social reality in the realm of ethical tension between the absolute and the relative, the 'miracle' and the empirical reality. How then should we understand this 'miracle' which inaugurates the authentic life?

Part of the answer can be found in a 1912 essay that is also typical of his world view: *Von der Armut am Geiste* (On Poverty of Spirit). Very rich and beautiful, this is perhaps the most 'literary' work ever published by Lukács. It appeared in the *Neue Blätter* review together with poems and essays by Theodor Däubler, Rudolf Kassner, Martin Buber, Francis Jammes, and Rainer Maria Rilke – the list is a whole programme in itself. Lukács employs the form of a letter and a dialogue to situate a tragic

[40] Ibid., p. 158. Cf. L. Goldmann, 'Lukács l'essayiste', in *Recherches dialectiques*, Paris, 1959, pp. 147–52; and *Kierkegaard vivant*, p. 131.

[41] Ibid., pp. 153, 157–8.

[42] L. Goldmann, *Kierkegaard vivant*, pp. 130–1.

[43] Lukács, *Soul and Form*, p. 154.

incident: a man has been unable to foresee or prevent the suicide of the woman he loved; eventually, metaphysical and mystical despair brings him to commit suicide as well. The story is evidently related to the writer's own life: for Irma Seidler, who had a relationship with him in 1908, had just killed herself in 1911 after an unhappy marriage.[44] Rather than this real-life incident, however, it is Lukács's overall ideological development that enables us to understand *Von der Armut am Geiste*. Its structure of meaning recalls 'The Metaphysics of Tragedy'; as in that work, there is a rigorous and inflexible, clear and trenchant dualism of two forms of life – 'living' (*lebendige*) or 'true' (*wahre*) life, and 'unliving', 'impure', or 'ordinary' life. These two worlds should be 'kept rigorously distinct' (*streng voneinander zu scheiden*), and the main character of the dialogue proclaims his deep aversion to the lower world: 'I can no longer bear the unclarity and dishonesty of the everyday life.'[45]

What is the content of the true life – which, Lukács implies, is extraordinary and pure, honest and clear? The expression he uses, 'the

---

[44] Basing herself on Lukács's recently discovered diary, Agnes Heller, Lukács's friend and disciple, brings out the deep ethical and personal significance of this episode in her unpublished philosophical parable, *Das Zerschellen des Lebens an der Form: Georg Lukács und Irma Seidler*.

[45] Lukács, 'On Poverty of Spirit: A Conversation and a Letter', *The Philosophical Forum*, vol. 3, nos. 3–4, spring-summer 1972, pp. 374, 375, 380. Also discussed is 'the grubby flux' of everyday life (p. 375). By stressing the essential opposition of 'two lives', we have neglected an important aspect of *Von der Armut am Geiste* and other of Lukács's early writings: the mediating role of *the work* and its complex relationship to life. György Márkus has drawn my attention to the lack of analysis of this question: 'I agree with you completely about the importance in Lukács's early philosophy of the dualism of "ordinary" life and "living" life (or other such terms). But I think that he introduced a third, problematic element into this conceptual framework – namely, *die Werke*. Both ordinary life and authentic life are *life*, existence, *Sein* – but beyond, or in a sense 'between' the two, there are cultural objectifications, that is, objectified and corporealized values which, *qua* values, do not exist but *gelten* [hold good]. He calls these *Formen* [forms] in *Soul and Form*, *die Werke* [works] in the Heidelberg manuscripts, and *Gestaltungen des absoluten Geistes* [figures of the absolute spirit] in the analysis of Croce – but the general concept is the same in each case. They spring empirically from everyday life, and only in relation to them can the very notion of authentic life be formulated; in other words, the problem of *Vermittlung* [mediation] was posed from the beginning for the young Lukács. However, this only highlights the tragic character of his vision, for in most if not all his early writings, the values are still transcendent and unrealizable in real-individual life. The problem of these *geschichtlich* [historical] and *zeitlos* [timeless] objectifications, considered as possible *Vermittlungen* between authenticity and inauthenticity, lends a specifically dialectical character to his dualism . . . and also leaves it open to other solutions.' (Letter to the author dated 3 August 1974). Although Márkus's observation is of great interest, it would appear that this dialectical moment remained subordinate to a fundamentally dualist and 'metaphysical' (pre-dialectical) general framework and world view.

descent of the heavenly realm to earth', was in 1912 still charged with individualist mysticism, but it would soon acquire an ethico-social and political significance for him. The descent of heaven takes place through the *miracle* of 'Goodness' (*Güte*), to be conceived not as a quality but as a *gift of grace*: 'Goodness is the miracle, the grace, and the redemption.' The Protestant, Kierkegaardian influence is quite apparent here. But one cannot help comparing his dualism of 'Goodness' (grace) and 'ordinary life' with Max Weber's counter-position of 'charisma' (a Greek word meaning precisely 'gift of grace') and 'routine'.[46]

As in 'The Metaphysics of Tragedy', a tragic rejection of the world ('ordinary life') leads to a life of waiting for the miracle; man's principal task is to prepare himself to receive grace. For Lukács, such *possession* (*Besessenheit*) by 'Goodness' requires as its precondition *poverty of spirit* (*Armut am Geiste*) – a profoundly mystical concept that holds a key place in the work of Meister Eckhardt (see his sermon *Beati pauperes spiritu*). In Lukács's eyes, poverty of spirit involves 'preparing oneself for virtue': it is 'the prerequisite – the negative principle – the way out of the bad infinite of life'; or again, it is 'liberating myself from my psychological limitations, in order to deliver myself up to my own deeper metaphysical and metapsychical necessity'.[47] This problematic refers not only to Christian mysticism, but also to those eastern, particularly Hindu, religious doctrines in which Lukács was then interested, probably as a result of Max Weber's influence. Most important of these was the Brahmanic doctrine that grace (*bhakti*) can be obtained only by the *sacrificium intellectus* or surrendering oneself to passive receptivity, to consciousness emptied of all content.[48]

Lukács also displayed his Kantian dualism in a total, metaphysical opposition between the subjective universe of intention and the objective

---

[46] Lukács, 'On Poverty of Spirit', p. 375. A. Mitzman has argued that this dialogue probably reveals the kind of discussions held in the Weber Circle about this time. (See A. Mitzman, *The Iron Cage: An Historical Interpretation of Max Weber*, New York, 1971, p. 273.)

[47] Lukács, 'On Poverty of Spirit', pp. 381, 383 (modified). Cf. Jeanne Ancelet-Hustache, *Maître Eckhart et la mystique rhénane*, Paris, 1956, p. 60: 'What he preaches is therefore poverty of spirit, exactly as recommended by the Gospel. . . . One is always on the path of *Gelassenheit*, of complete abandonment. . . . To this self-renouncing soul God will give his grace.' Lukács's 1911 Heidelberg notebooks contain extracts from and comments on S. Frank, Eckhardt, Anselm, and various Jewish mystics; in part, these were used in the writing of the dialogue. CF. G. Márkus, *Lukács' 'erste' Ästhetik*.

[48] On the pertinent writings of Max Weber, see Reinhard Bendix, *Max Weber: An Intellectual Portrait*, New York, 1962, pp. 167, 175, 176.

universe of the external consequences of one's action. 'Goodness' is given an exclusively subjective definition (in the spiritual-ethical, rather than psychological sense): 'Why should Goodness concern itself with the consequences? "Our duty is to do the Work, not to try to win its fruits", say the Indians. Goodness is useless, just as it has no foundation (*grundlos*). Because consequences lie in the outer-world of mechanical forces – forces that are unconcerned with us.' As an example of this mystical Goodness, proudly indifferent to the results of one's action, Lukács refers us to Dostoevsky's 'saintly figures': 'Do you remember Sonya, Prince Myshkin, Alexei Karamazov, in Dostoevsky? You have asked me if there are any good humans: here they are. And you see, even their Goodness is fruitless, confusing and without result. . . . Whom did Prince Myshkin help? Didn't he actually bring tragedy wherever he went? . . . Goodness is no guarantee of being able to help; it is, however, the safeguard of the absolute and perceptive *desire* to help.'[49] Implicitly, Lukács here enters Weber's problematic of the antinomy between an ethic of conviction (*Gesinnungsethik*) and an ethic of responsibility (*Verantwortungsethik*). It is no accident, therefore, that Weber read Lukács's 'On Poverty of Spirit' with the most lively interest and, in conversation with a friend, placed it on the same level as *The Brothers Karamazov*. He saw it as a striking confirmation of his own thesis that moral behaviour should be judged not by its results but by its intrinsic value.[50]

Corresponding in *Armut am Geiste* to the 'two lives' concept is a duality of men: on the one hand, those 'possessed' or capable of being possessed by 'Goodness'; on the other, those condemned to the gloomy purgatory of ordinary life. Here the aristocratic tendencies already apparent in *Soul and Form*[51] re-emerge in a strange doctrine of 'castes'. Martha, holding a dialogue with the tragic hero, asks him: 'If I understand you correctly, you want to establish new foundations for the castes. In your eyes, there is only one sin: the mixing of castes.' The answer is affirmative: 'You have

---

[49] Lukács, 'On Poverty of Spirit', pp. 374–6. In a commentary on Dostoevsky written in 1943, Lukács again mentioned this aspect of *The Idiot*, although now rather in a negative context: 'It may be said in passing that the limitless compassion of Myshkin causes at least as much tragic suffering as the darkly individualistic pathos of Raskolnikov.' ('Dostoevsky', in *Marxism and Human Liberation*, New York, 1978, p. 196.)

[50] Cf. Marianne Weber, *Max Weber: A Biography*, p. 490.

[51] In 'The Metaphysics of Tragedy', Lukács declares: 'In vain has our democratic age claimed an equal right for all to be tragic. . . . And those democrats who are consistent about their demand for equal rights for all men have always disputed tragedy's right to existence.' (*Soul and Form*, p. 173.)

understood me marvellously well. . . . There are only personal duties; it is according to these that we humans are sorted into the several castes. . . . Goodness is the duty and the virtue of a caste that is higher than mine.'[52]

In a passage from *Geist der Utopie*, Ernst Bloch refers to Lukács as 'the absolute genius of morality' who sought 'to re-form the castes on a metaphysical basis'.[53] When I raised this problem with him in my interview, Bloch stressed the aristocratic-Catholic dimension of Lukács's 'metaphysical castes': they revolved around virtues specific to each social estate, running in an 'inverted' hierarchy in which difficulties, ascesis, and self-sacrifice mounted with the rung of the ladder – witness the monastic institution.[54] In point of fact, Martha says as much in accusation against her interlocutor in *Armut am Geiste*: 'You want to become a monk. . . . Doesn't your asceticism just make things easier for you?' But Lukács did not choose the word *caste* lightly; again it refers us to Hindu mysticism, which, while attributing specific duties and rules to each caste, sharply distinguishes between those capable of receiving grace through the path of ascesis, and 'all the others'. It also names caste-mixing and rule-breaking as the cardinal sin, poor execution of one's own caste duties being considered preferable to the most fervent performance of those of another caste.[55] Hence the despair of the tragic figure in *Armut am Geiste*: 'If I wanted to live, it would be over-stepping the bounds of my caste. That I loved her and wanted to help her was already a violation of those bounds. Goodness is the duty and virtue of a caste that is higher than mine.'[56]

In this tendency to mystical elitism, Lukács was also influenced by his best friend of the time, Béla Balázs, who carried it to absurd lengths. In 1919, for example, Balázs wrote an entry in his diary about a meeting he had had with Lukács shortly after Irma Seidler's death: 'I talked a lot about God with Gyuri. . . . There are very few men in the religious sense. . . . There is a greater difference between metaphysical man and animal man than between man and dog. . . . Here perhaps my thoughts (most of them generally fertilized by Gyuri) link up with his "metaphysical castes". . . . Religion can only be aristocratic.'[57]

---

[52] 'On Poverty of Spirit', pp. 385–6.
[53] E. Bloch, *Geist der Utopie* (1918), Frankfurt, 1971, p. 347. The reference to Lukács does not appear in the 1923 edition.
[54] 'On Poverty of Spirit', pp. 380–1.
[55] See Max Weber's studies in Bendix, *Max Weber*, pp. 172, 183.
[56] 'On Poverty of Spirit', p. 385 (modified). The text concludes at once: 'Two days later, he had shot himself.'
[57] Béla Balázs, 'Notes from a Diary (1911–1921)', p. 124. In her penetrating essay on *Von*

Nothing better sums up the ideological climate of *Armut am Geiste* – circumscribed as it is by the tragic view of the world – than the very last scene of the dialogue. After the central figure has committed suicide, his friend Martha finds a half-open Bible lying on his desk, with the following sentence from the Apocalypse underlined: 'I know your Works, that you are neither cold nor warm; oh, if only you were cold or warm. Because you are lukewarm, however, and are neither cold nor warm, I will spit you out of my mouth.'[58] The 'lukewarm' for Lukács was that impure and cross-blended ordinary life, with its daily 'grubby flux' – in short, the real social world of his age. His tragic rejection of the world could give rise to but two forms of action: either mystical expectation of grace and the miracle, or, for those not believing themselves among the elect, suicide. Either-or, *entweder-oder*: the 'fire' of redemption or the 'cold' of death; the 'drabness' of inauthentic life is passionately discarded.

Lukács's recently discovered journal shows clearly that he *personally* experienced this dilemma about 1911. On 17 November 1911, he composed some notes on 'Redemption' (*Erlösung*), arguing that it is not granted according to 'merit' but depends solely on God. He wonders whether a miracle will happen to him, whether he will go through a *Damaskus* (road to Damascus) in which his soul will be metamorphosed. Above all, he looks to suicide as a consistent rejection of vulgarity and compromise. On 30 November, he wrote this crucial sentence: 'I cannot bear an inessential life.' In the end Lukács mastered his dizzy inclination to suicide, but he regarded his survival as a moral defeat: '15 December. The crisis seems to be over. . . . But I look on my "life", my "capacity to go on living" as a kind of Decadence; if I had committed suicide, I would be alive, at the height of my essence, consistent. Now everything is just pale compromise and degradation.'[59] Far from being a mere literary interlude, then, *Armut am Geiste* expressed with rare power the very ethical-

---

der Armut am Geiste, Agnes Heller gives an exact definition of Lukács's ideology as 'a peculiar mixture of proud aristocratism and submissive humility'. According to Heller, 'these "castes" are not social; they are the castes of life as such': one is the caste of the 'everyday life', the second of the forms that bring about the 'works', and the third is the caste of the 'living life' that breaks through all forms, having received the grace of goodness. (A. Heller, '*Von der Armut am Geiste*: A Dialogue by the Young Lukács', *The Philosophical Forum*, vol. III, nos. 3–4, spring-summer 1972, pp. 363–4.)

[58] Lukács, '*On Poverty of Spirit*', p. 385. It should be noted that this sentence appears above Rosa Luxemburg's trenchant 1915 article against the lukewarm Kautsky.

[59] *Tagebuch*, p. 53, Lukács Archivum.

existential problematic the young Lukács experienced at a certain stage of his life.

In 1969 Lukács wrote an autobiographical text to introduce a selection of his writings on Marxism. This highly interesting document contains a passage on *Armut am Geiste* which throws remarkable light on the connection between this dialogue and the romantically anti-capitalist problematic then underpinning Lukács's *Weltanschauung*: 'Even during my Hegelian period, my intellectual attitude to any social activity was dominated . . . by Ady's "mission to veto", above all, of course, in the field of ethics. . . . For this reason, I was constantly searching in the present and the past for ethical tendencies that could satisfy the demands of the romantic anti-capitalist I still was. This is how I came to replace Ibsen, the idol of my youthful criticism, with Tolstoy and, even more, Dostoevsky . . . This search, which I pursued even in Kierkegaard, lay behind my inclination towards medieval Christian thinkers – actually heretics like Meister Eckhardt – and certain aspects of eastern philosophy and morality. The dialogue entitled "On Poverty of Spirit" is nothing other than an attempt to lend such efforts a theoretical and practical foundation. . . .'[60]

In other words, *Lukács's mystical flight, suicidal despair, ascetic spiritual aristocratism, and tragic world view can be understood only in relation to his deep, radical, absolute, and intransigent rejection of the impurity and lack of authenticity of the bourgeois world.* In his outstanding thesis on Lukács and Korsch, Paul Breines has this to say about this dialogue: 'Although expressed in mystical-messianic terms, the concept of "Goodness" in *Von der Armut am Geiste* is an image for an earthly social utopia. . . . Naturally . . . Lukács standpoint carries these implicitly social-revolutionary intentions towards a cosmic realm far beyond all concrete historical and social problems and possibilities. But it should be clear that, without being inevitable, the "leap" from this singular cosmic realm to the camp of communist revolution may well be short and rational.'[61] In our view, however, it is rather the *negative*, critical side of this dialogue that makes it an important stage in Lukács's 'long march' to social revolution and communism. But it is also true that the moral ideal embodied in various Dostoevskian characters (here termed 'Goodness') lies at the heart of his

[60] Lukács, 'Mon chemin vers Marx', pp. 80–81.

[61] Paul Breines, 'Lukács and Korsch 1910–1932: A study of the Genesis and Impact of "Geschichte und Klassenbewusstsein" and "Marxismus und Philosophie"', unpublished thesis, University of Wisconsin, 1972, p. 53.

post-1914 political radicalization.

Why, then, was Lukács gripped by this tragic *Weltanschauung* between 1910 and 1912 – just at the height of the *belle époque*, with its relative social and political stability? According to Goldmann, Lukács was one of the first to expose the crisis of western society, to perceive the hidden cracks in an apparently still solid façade. In short, Lukács had foreseen the looming catastrophe.[62] In our view, *precisely the opposite was the case*: what drove Lukács to despair was the very stability and immutability of the capitalist society he hated[63] – a society in which it was impossible to realize the absolute, idealist aesthetic-philosophical values to which he was so deeply attached. The conflict between authentic values and the inauthentic (capitalist) world was tragically insoluble, for Lukács could see no social force capable of changing the world and making those values a reality.[64] The conflict therefore assumed the eternal, ahistorical, unchangeable character of *metaphysics* – hence the title of Lukács's essay 'The Metaphysics of Tragedy'.

The Theory of the Novel, published in 1916, to some extent prolongs the tragic vision of 1910–12; but it also bears a new and surprising element of hope. In his preface to the 1962 edition, Lukács describes the climate in which this book was written as one of 'permanent despair over the state of the world'. Its ideology is characterized as 'ethically-tinged pessimism' reflected in a definition of the present as 'the age of absolute sinfulness' and in 'opposition to the barbarity of capitalism'.[65]

The work falls into three parts. First, a study of Greek art in which the epic (Homer) is seen as expressing a closed and harmonious totality. This

---

[62] L. Goldmann, 'The Early Writings of Georg Lukács', p. 170.

[63] This frame of mind prevailed even in some revolutionary circles of the time. Thus, in his *Memoirs* Victor Serge described his attitude and that of his anarchist friends around 1913 as 'desperate' and 'enraged', because 'the world was an integrated structure, so stable in appearance that no possibility of substantial change was visible within it'. (V. Serge, *Memoirs of a Revolutionary*, London, 1963).

[64] Here lies the social basis of Lukács's acute *idealism*. In a 1911 letter to Paul Ernst, he writes: 'Go back inside yourselves! The outside cannot be changed – create a new world starting from what is possible! . . . You can act *only* on the Spirit.' ('Letter to Paul Ernst', September 1911, in *Paul Ernst und Georg Lukács, Dokumente einer Freundschaft*, Emsdetten, 1974, pp. 23–4.)

[65] Lukács, 'Preface' (1962) to *The Theory of the Novel*, pp. 12, 18. Rejection of the epoch as a *Zeitalter der vollendeten Sündhaftigkeit* (Fichte's expression) is, in reality, another form of Ady's 'mission to veto', and is thus opposed to Hegel's *Versöhnung* with the present. *The Theory of the Novel*, despite the influence of Hegel's aesthetics, is *politically* a Fichtean work.

epic form corresponded to an absolute equivalence of individual and community, man and universe. It belonged to an epoch marked by 'adequacy of the deeds to the soul's inner demand for greatness, for unfolding, for wholeness. . . . Being and destiny, adventure and accomplishment, life and essence are then identical concepts'.[66] Now, clearly such a picture has little in common with the reality of pre-classical Greece. At bottom, it is rather an ideal model, an imaginary 'golden age' into which Lukács (like many German thinkers before him) projects his own aspirations and dreams of the Absolute, of wholeness and ethical-aesthetic harmony. Second, and more centrally, an analysis of the world of the novel in terms of a fissure (*Zerissenheit*) between individual and community, an insurmountable schism between the hero and the world. For Lukács, the novel expresses the 'historico-philosophical realities' of modern society. Similarly, Lucien Goldmann, in his study of the novel, discovers a structural homology between the novel form and the functioning of market-dominated capitalist society.[67]

Finally, a chapter on Tolstoy and Dostoevsky containing a strange and complex glimmer of hope (almost prophetic, given that the Russian Revolution was still two years away). In Lukács's estimation, Tolstoy's work was to some extent a return to the epic; for his art 'aspires to a life based on a community of feeling among simple human beings closely bound to nature . . . which excludes all structures which are not natural, which are petty and disruptive, causing disintegration and stagnation'.[68] It is difficult to account for the emergence of such art in capitalist society – since 'art can never be the agent of such a transformation: the great epic is a form bound to the historical moment.' Moreover, present-day capitalist society is the exact opposite of the harmonious Greek world, and its literary expression is precisely the novel: 'The novel is the form of absolute sinfulness, as Fichte said, and it must remain the dominant form so long as the world is ruled by the same stars.'[69] This being so, Tolstoy and Dostoevsky can be explained only as *precursors of the future*: 'In Tolstoy, intimations of a breakthrough into a new epoch are visible; but they remain polemical, nostalgic and abstract. It is in the works of Dostoevsky that this new world . . . is drawn for the first time simply as a seen society. . . . He belongs to the new world. Only formal analysis of his works can show

---

[66] *The Theory of the Novel*, p. 30.
[67] L. Goldmann, *Towards a Sociology of the Novel*, London, 1975, p. 11.
[68] Lukács, *The Theory of the Novel*, pp. 145–6.
[69] Ibid., p. 152.

whether he is already the Homer or the Dante of that world. . . . It will then be the task of historico-philosophical interpretation to decide whether we are really about to leave the age of absolute sinfulness or whether the new has no other herald but our hopes.'[70]

We now find ourselves *at the very frontier between literature and politics*, aesthetics and revolution: the transition from the one to the other would be effected by what Lukács, in his 1962 preface, terms 'left ethics'. Undoubtedly, it was the great crisis of 1914, the war with its procession of crimes and misery, that sparked off Lukács's 'politicization'. His 1915 letters to Paul Ernst, recently published in Hungary, testify to his growing interest in political questions: the war problem ('madness and absurdity'), military conscription ('the vilest form of slavery that ever existed'), struggle against the state (which he seeks to arouse by 'ethical means'), Russian terrorism (whose 'mystical morality' he admires, with some reservations), and so on.[71] Also, the war began to distance him politically from the Heidelberg Circle, whose main leaders, such as Max Weber, supported German imperialism. Georg Simmel, for example, in a letter to Marianne Weber dated 14 August 1914, complains about Lukács's anti-militarism, putting it down to his 'lack of experience'.[72]

This anti-militarism was but the logical consequence of Lukács's anti-capitalism. Indeed, he saw the Great War as a typical expression of the capitalist reification and mechanization of social life. In an imaginary conversation written about 1917, Paul Ernst puts the following words into

---

[70] Ibid., pp. 152–3.

[71] *Paul Ernst und Georg Lukács*, pp. 66, 74, 117. In *Gelebtes Denken* (pp. 24–7), Lukács describes his state of mind between 1914 and 1915: 'All the social forces I had hated since my youth, and which I aimed in spirit to annihilate, now came together to unleash the first global war; at the same time, they were globally without any ideas, the very enemies of ideas. Right from the beginning, I was among the negative forces (*Verneiner*).' Lukács adds that his opposition to the war gradually 'shifted the centre of my interests from aesthetics to ethics'.

[72] In *Buch des Dankes an Georg Simmel*, p. 77. Bloch speaks of a small group of people in Heidelberg who opposed the war: Lukács, Jaspers, Bloch, Lederer, Radbruch. (See the interview mentioned in note 9.) Radbruch, a well-known Social Democratic jurist, published an article in 1917 entitled 'On the Philosophy of the Present War', in fact a lucid critique of various German war-apologists (Scheler, Gomperz, et al.). He compared the war to 'a clay figure which, thanks to a cabalistic parchment in its mouth, has mysteriously succeeded in acquiring a soul of its own, and which subsequently unfurls a life that is blind, stupid, and terrifying, yet quite omnipotent'. (G. Radbruch, 'Zur Philosophie dieses Krieges', *Archiv für Sozialwissenschaft*, vol. 44, 1917–18, p. 148.) The reference to the Golem requires no comment. In a letter to Radbruch, Lukács discussed this article and added: 'I agree completely with your analysis. . . . I even find it hard to discover any point of difference.' (Lukács to G. Radbruch, 11 March 1917, Lukács Archivum.)

Lukács's mouth: 'Just as existing economy has replaced the independent worker with the machine and workers who serve it, thereby causing the personal value of work to disappear, so does the present war pit against one another no longer men but machines and servants of machines.'[73] And writing in 1915 about German intellectuals and the war, Lukács contrasted the terrorist hero of the Russian revolution, whose actions are guided by an ideal goal, with the soldier of 1914–15 enrolled in a 'thing-like', technical, and impersonal process.[74]

Lukács's attitude to the powers at war was at once that of a (Hungarian) anti-absolutist democrat and a (German) romantic anti-capitalist. The 1962 preface to *The Theory of the Novel* offers a retrospective account of his position: 'When I tried at this time to put my emotional attitude into conscious terms, I arrived at more or less the following formulations: the Central Powers would probably defeat Russia; this might lead to the downfall of Tsarism; I had no objection to that. There was also some probability that the West would defeat Germany; if this led to the downfall of the Hohenzollerns and the Habsburgs, I was once again in favour. But then the question arose: who was to save us from western civilization?'[75] In Lukács's ethico-social anti-capitalism, the collapse of two anachronistic empires was little consolation for the crushing victory of bourgeois-industrial *Zivilisation*.

Lukács's political views during the 1914–16 period were obviously still very abstract and, above all, profoundly utopian.[76] Their idealist character was rooted in the lack of a concrete social perspective, in the inability to find a real force that might open the road to the new world:

[73] *Paul Ernst und Georg Lukács*, p. 86.
[74] Lukács, 'Die deutschen Intellektuellen und der Krieg' (1915), in *Text und Kritik*, nos. 39–40, 1973, pp. 67–8.
[75] Lukács, 'Preface' (1962) to *The Theory of the Novel*, p. 11. There is a telling error in the French edition of this text: the translator (or proof-reader) has inadvertently replaced 'qui *nous* sauvera *de* la civilization occidentale' with 'qui sauvera la civilisation occidentale'! (*La Théorie du roman*, Paris 1963, p. 5.) Cf. the German original: 'Wer rettet uns von der westlichen Zivilisation?' (*Die Theorie des Romans*, Neuwied, 1963, p. 5.) This 'slight' difference marks off two distinct views of the world: the difference between Naphta and Settembrini, or between Georg Lukács and Georges Clemenceau. In the 1969 preface to his writings on Hungary, Lukács returns to this idea, expressing it in even more violent terms: 'The question is: who will free us from the yoke of western civilization?' (Lukács, 'Elöszó', pp. 13–14.)
[76] In the 1962 preface, Lukács describes his thought at this time as 'a highly naive and totally unfounded utopianism – the hope that a natural life worthy of man can spring from the disintegration of capitalism and the destruction, seen as identical with that disintegration, of the lifeless and life-denying social and economic categories'. (*The Theory of the Novel*, p. 20.)

'Clearly my rejection of the war and, together with it, of the bourgeois society of that time was purely utopian; nothing, even at the level of the most abstract intellection, helped to mediate between my subjective attitude and objective reality.'[77]

Why did this 'left ethics' take Tolstoy and above all Dostoevsky as its starting point? In his 1969 preface to a collection of writings on Hungary, Lukács gives the following answer: 'In this way [i.e., under Ady's influence] the great Russian writers, especially Dostoevsky and Tolstoy, were integrated into my world as decisive revolutionary factors. And slowly, but ever more resolutely, this world shifted towards the belief . . . that ethics is methodologically superior to the philosophy of history.'[78] This may seem strange, given that the work of Dostoevsky and Tolstoy is far from clearly revolutionary.[79] But an article written in 1916 provides the initial elements of an explanation by pointing to these writers' opposition to the bourgeois civilization of Western Europe. In Lukács's view, 'the writers of world-historical importance in Russia are seeking to go beyond "European" individualism (with its resulting anarchy, despair, and godlessness): to overcome it in the depths of one's being and, on the ground thereby captured, to instal a new man and a new world.'[80]

[77] Ibid., p. 12. Lukács's sympathy for the working class, as well as his scepticism that it might become a socio-cultural alternative to capitalism, are apparent in a little known article written in 1915: his review of the work of a socialist writer, M. Staudinger. According to Lukács, 'Staudinger's hope (which, as a hope, I myself share) that the synthetic and organic character of the world of labour will lead to a cultural synthesis in which the universal will prevail over the individual, and union (*Bindung*) over freedom – this is merely an object of hope rather than knowledge, since no positive content can be found and presented in this universality.' (Lukács, 'Zum Wesen und zur Methode der Kultursoziologie', *Archiv für Sozialwissenschaft*, vol. 39, 1915, p. 220.)

[78] Lukács, 'Elöszó' (1969), pp. 8–9.

[79] However, as Rosa Luxemburg has argued: 'Patterns such as "revolutionary" or "progressive" in themselves mean very little in art. Dostoevsky, especially in his later writings, is an outspoken reactionary, a religious mystic and hater of socialists. . . . Tolstoy's mystic doctrines reflect reactionary tendencies, if not more. But the writings of both have, nevertheless, an inspiring, arousing, and liberating effect upon us. And this is because their starting points are not reactionary; their thoughts and emotions are not governed by the desire to hold on to the status quo . . . or by caste egotism. On the contrary, theirs is the warmest love for mankind and the deepest response to social injustice.' ('The Spirit of Russian Literature: Life of Korolenko', in *Rosa Luxemburg Speaks*, New York, 1970, p. 345.) Cf. the penetrating remarks of Nikolai Berdyaev, written from a quite different point of view: 'Tolstoy and Dostoevsky were possible only in a society which was moving towards revolution, in which explosive materials were accumulating. . . . Tolstoy and Dostoevsky were the mouthpieces of a universal revolution of the spirit.' (*The Origin of Russian Communism*, London, 1937, pp. 101–2.)

[80] Lukács, 'Solovieff', *Archiv für Sozialwissenschaft*, vol. 42, 1916–17, p. 978. Paul

It is easy to understand Tolstoy's role in shaping Lukács's revolutionary ethics, if we consider the fact that, especially through his social and philosophical writings, he directly inspired a number of anarchist, populist, and socialist currents. More subtle and complicated, but also more important, is the influence of Dostoevsky. In order to illustrate his 'elective affinity' with the mystical and messianic ideology of Lukács, let us take a passage from the work which, to a degree, served as Lukács's ethico-literary gospel, *The Brothers Karamazov*: 'The moment he thought seriously about it, he was overcome by the conviction of the existence and immortality of God, and he quite naturally said to himself: "I want to live for immortality, and I won't accept any compromise." Similarly, if he had decided that there was no immortality and no God, he would at once have become an atheist and a Socialist (for Socialism is not only the labour question, or the question of the so-called fourth estate, but above all an atheistic question, the question of the modern integration of atheism, the question of the Tower of Babel which is deliberately being created without God, not for the sake of reaching heaven from earth, but for the sake of bringing heaven down to earth).'[81]

In Alyosha Karamazov, then, Dostoevsky's 'positive' character *par excellence*, we discover both Lukács's ethical radicalism (living for the absolute, rejecting all compromise) and an almost metaphysical moral conception of socialism as the earthly fulfilment of supreme principles. The formula 'make heaven come down to earth' cannot fail to recall the Bolshevik Lukács of 1919: 'The Marxist theory of class struggle . . .

Honigsheim, who was a member of the Max Weber Circle in Heidelberg, recalls that Bloch and Lukács were fascinated by Russian literature and religion, and that they identified the collectivist kingdom of justice with a life led in the spirit of Dostoevsky. (Honigsheim, *On Max Weber*, p. 91.)

[81] Dostoevsky, *The Brothers Karamazov*, pp. 26–7. This trajectory had actually been foreseen by Dostoevsky himself. Suvorin refers to a conversation he had with the Russian writer: 'His hero (Alyosha) had at the right moment to commit a political crime and be executed; a character thirsty for truth, who quite naturally became a revolutionary by following his chosen course.' This is confirmed by Dostoevsky's *Notebooks*, in which the novelist depicts Alyosha's long and painful spiritual path to revolutionary action. Moreover, it would seem that the model for Alyosha – who, apart from one letter, gave him his surname – was none other than the famous terrorist Karakazov, the initiator of an attempt on the life of Tsar Alexander II. (Cf. G. Philippenko, 'Commentaires', in Dostoevsky, *Les Frères Karamazov*, Paris, 1972, pp. 488–9.) It should be noted that the revolutionary significance of Alyosha was already clear to intellectuals of the anti-capitalist current. Thus, Paul Ernst wrote in 1918: 'The Bolsheviks are today seeking to accomplish what Dostoevsky envisaged through Alyosha.' (P. Ernst, *Gedanken zur Weltliteratur*, Gutersloh, 1959.)

changes the transcendent objective into an immanent one.'[82] And does not the young Alyosha's potential itinerary from moral-mystical rigorism to atheist, yet ethical, socialism prefigure the early Lukács's spiritual journey between 1909 and 1919? As a matter of fact, in an article written in 1916, Lukács actually refers to Alyosha Karamazov as the prototype of 'the new man' who goes beyond the old, corrupt world of individualism.[83]

Writing about Dostoevsky a quarter of a century later, Lukács cast a revealing light on the (revolutionary) political significance the great Russian writer had for his development up to 1919. In this essay by 'the older Lukács', Dostoevsky's greatness appears in 'his powerful protest against everything false and distorting in modern bourgeois society. It is no chance that the memory of a picture by Claude Lorrain, *Acis and Galatea*, recurs several times in his novels. It is always called "The Golden Age" by his heroes and is described as the most powerful symbol of their deepest yearning.'[84] Lorrain's paintings present an idealized vision of ancient Greece as a realm of absolute harmony between man and nature, man and man. *Acis and Galatea*, which typifies this glowingly nostalgic elegy of the Greek world, hangs in the museum of Dresden – a town in which Dostoevsky lived for a considerable time. The painting appears three times in his work as a plastic representation of paradise lost, each time in the telling of a dream. The most striking case is the dream of Stavrogin – that fascinating, shadowy character in *The Devils*, that socialist and enemy of God, a fallen angel, 'an absolute atheist [standing] on the last rung but one before most absolute faith'.[85] Let us quote the main parts of this epic account, in which a whole world view is concentrated: 'I had quite an extraordinary dream. I had never had one like it before. In the Dresden gallery there is a picture by Claude Lorrain, called, I think, "Acis and Galatea" in the catalogue. . . . It was that picture that I saw in my dream, not as a painting, but as a fact. A corner of the Greek archipelago; blue, caressing waves, islands and rocks, a foreshore covered in lush vegetation, a magic vista in the distance, a spell-binding

[82] Lukács, 'Tactics and Ethics', in *Political Writings, 1919–1929*, London, NLB, 1972, p. 5.

[83] Lukács, 'Solovieff', p. 978. The continuity between Lukács's revolutionary Bolshevism and his Dostoevskian problematic is very well described by Bloch: 'Lukács will follow to the end the road charted by Tolstoy and Dostoevsky; linked as ever to Russia, he will carry the philosophy of Ivan and Alyosha Karamazov to its final conclusion.' (E. Bloch, 'Zur Rettung von Georg Lukács', *Die weissen Blätter*, 1919, p. 529–30.)

[84] Lukács, 'Dostoevsky', p. 196.

[85] Dostoevsky, *The Devils*, Harmondsworth, 1978, p. 679.

116

sunset – it is impossible to describe it in words. Here was the cradle of
European civilization, here were the first scenes from mythology, man's
paradise on earth. Here a beautiful race of men had lived. They rose and
went to sleep happy and innocent; the woods were filled with their joyous
songs. . . . The sun shed its rays on these islands and that sea, rejoicing in
its beautiful children. A wonderful dream, a sublime illusion! The most
incredible dream that has ever been dreamed, but to which all mankind
has devoted all its powers during the whole of its existence, for which it has
sacrificed everything, for which it has died on the cross and for which its
prophets have been killed, without which nations will not live and cannot
even die.'[86]

Lukács's 1943 commentary highlights the revolutionary implications of
this problematic, enabling us to grasp with precision the structural
homology between Dostoevsky's ideological universe and Lukács's own
utopian messianism of 1915–18: 'The golden age: genuine and harmonious relations between genuine and harmonious men. Dostoevsky's
characters know that this is a dream, but they cannot and will not abandon
the dream. . . . This dream is the truly genuine core, the real gold of
Dostoevsky's utopias; a state of the world in which men may know and
love each other, in which culture and civilization will not be an obstacle to
the development of men. The spontaneous, wild and blind revolt of
Dostoevsky's characters occurs in the name of the golden age, whatever
the contents of the mental experiment may be. This revolt is poetically
great and historically progressive in Dostoevsky: here really shines a light
in the darkness of Petersburg misery, a light that illuminates the road to
the future of mankind.'[87]

What really matters in this text is not the truth or falsity of Lukács's
interpretation of Dostoevsky, but his actual pre-1919 *reading* of the
Russian writer, with its probable echoes, however distant, in this article of
1943. For the young Lukács, who also dreamed of a 'golden age' of
harmonious and authentic men, saw Dostoevsky as a prophetic light in the
'dark misery' of the First World War.

Now, we know that *The Theory of the Novel* was conceived merely as the
introduction to a large work on Dostoevsky, going beyond the aesthetic
and literary domain towards an *ethico-political* problematic.[88] After

[86] Ibid., p. 695.
[87] Lukács, 'Dostoevsky', pp. 196–7.
[88] Cf. Lukács, 'Methodischer Zweifel', *Der Monat*, April 1966, p. 95: 'During the first
year of the World War I wrote *The Theory of the Novel*. This was conceived as the

Lukács's death, his disciples György Markus and Ferenc Feher discovered the original plan of the work; and this enables us to reconstitute its
general approach and to gain a rough idea of the questions he intended to
explore. The outline is divided into three broad chapter-headings.

I—'Interiority and adventure': a study of the epic and the novel,
particularly the 'terrestrial epic' of Dante and Dostoevsky. Apparently,
The Theory of the Novel was to have been just one part of this first chapter.

II—'The godless world': this contains the following cryptic notes charged
with a strange 'political religiosity':
'Russian and European atheism – the new morality.
'(Suicide) (Changing the world).
'Jehovah.
'Christianity.
'The State.
'Socialism.

'Solitude.

'Everything is permitted: problem of terrorism (Judith: transgression).
'Natural man: impossibility of loving one's neighbour.
'Abstract idealism: the line from Schiller to Dostoevsky.'[89]

We cannot make a thorough analysis of these laconic and rather
mysterious remarks here. But let us note the alternative 'suicide or
changing of the world', conceived as forms of radical rejection of reality.
After being momentarily tempted by suicide in 1911, Lukács moved
during the years up to 1918 closer and closer to the other pole:
Veränderung der Welt.[90] The *Judith* in question is the tragedy by Hebbel,

---

introduction to a historico-philosophical analysis of Dostoevsky's poetic work. But since I
was called up in 1915, I had to interrupt this work. It was never re-started.' See also Lukács's
1915 letter to Paul Ernst: 'At last I have begun a new book on Dostoevsky (leaving the
aesthetics aside for the moment). The book will cover much more than Dostoevsky: it will
contain most of my metaphysical ethics and philosophy of history, and so on.' (*Paul Ernst und
Georg Lukács*, p. 64.)
    [89] Lukács Archivum.
    [90] Lukács deals with this question in a little-known 1922 article on Stavrogin's confession.
On the one hand, he discusses Dostoevsky's 'utopian sensitivity', his dream of 'a world in
which all the inhuman mechanics and all the soulless reification (*Verdinglichte*) of capitalist
society will simply not exist'. On the other hand, he judges Stavrogin's 'demonic' character as
a typical example of those Russian intellectuals who, 'insofar as they were sincerely looking

in which the key problem is the justification of murder (of the tyrant Holophernes) from an ethico-religious point of view; hence the link with terrorism. The expression 'everything is permitted' refers to *Crime and Punishment*, in which Dostoevsky questions whether the act of killing a man can be given a moral foundation (as against Raskolnikov, who maintains that 'everything is permitted' for a just end). Lukács long hesitated between these contradictory answers to a single problem. But, as we shall see, between November and December 1918 he went over from Dostoevsky's to Hebbel's position, thereby laying the ethical basis for his decision to join the Hungarian Communist Party. As for 'Jehovah', Lukács sees this as a symbol for false, authoritarian religion and for any institutional power whatever: the church, the state, the judicial system, etc. Unlike Jesus Christ or Francis of Assisi, ecclesiastical Christianity makes its peace with the 'Jehovistic' (*das Jehovaische*), the state, property, and so on. This problematic recurs in Lukács's further notes for the Dostoevsky book (notes that develop the main themes of the outline plan), and its similarity with the parable of the Grand Inquisitor is quite apparent. Finally, in Lukács's view of things, the Russian terrorist is the one who, by his very nature, expresses rebellion against everything 'Jehovistic'.[91]

Then follows III—'The light to come (The breaking dawn). Poverty of spirit. Goodness (*Güte*). . . .' Here are some of the points he makes on this chapter:

'Dostoevsky's misunderstanding: attitude to Christianity and revolution.
'"All men": Metaphysics of socialism.
'Ethical democracy: Metaphysics of the State. (Related to II.)
'Russian mysticism. Community (*Gemeinde*).
'Russia and Europe. (Theme: England, France and Germany.)'

The title itself speaks volumes about Lukács's grandiose moral-utopian outlook: it reveals that the problematic of *Von der Armut am Geiste* still preoccupied him in 1915, and that the new world ('the light to come') was

---

for an aim to their lives, had no way out other than suicide, decadence, or revolution (Stavrogin chose the first of these)'. Thus, Dostoevsky's 'political curse on revolution . . . is imperceptibly transformed into poetic glorification of its absolute spiritual necessity'. (Lukács, 'Stavrogins Beichte', *Die Rote Fahne*, 16 July 1922.)

[91] See F. Fehér, *Am Scheideweg des romantischen Antikapitalismus*, pp. 111–14, 136, 161. Lukács's notes were found in the famous 'Heidelberg suitcase'.

seen as the reign of 'Goodness' embodied in the Dostoevskian 'saints': Prince Myshkin, Aloysha Karamozov. However, Lukács no longer refers to the 'Goodness' of a caste, as he did in 1911, but to that of a genuinely human community of *Gemeinde* explicitly located within the *Russian* social, cultural, and religious context. This explains the note on the relationship between community and mysticism, which should be read together with the observation in his 1915 notes on Dostoevsky dealing with the oneness of community and 'Goodness' in the Russian world.[92]

Of course, this mysticism has nothing in common with established religion; indeed, it may even take the form of *atheism*. In his 1915 notes, Lukács rigorously distinguishes between genuine and deeply 'religious' Russian atheism and the 'perverted (egotistic) and mechanical (Neils Lyhne)' atheism of Western Europe. The most interesting point here is that the highest expression of such mystical atheism is seen in the *Russian terrorist*: 'We would have to portray ... the new, silent God in need of our help, and those like Kaliayev who believe in him while considering themselves atheists. Are there not, in fact, three levels of atheism: 1) Niels Lyhne; 2) Ivan Karamazov; 3) Kaliayev?'[93] Ivan Kaliayev was the poet and terrorist fighter who killed the Grand Duke Sergei, Governor General of Moscow, in February 1905. Savinkov, the leader and ideologue of Russian terrorism (whose books Lukács discovered about 1915), describes Kaliayev as follows: 'For those who know him closely, his love of revolution and his love of art blaze with one and the same fire – with a religious feeling that is timid and unconscious, yet sturdy and deep-rooted. He found his way to terrorist activity along a fresh path all his own. And he saw in such activity not only the best form of political struggle, but also a moral or perhaps even a religious sacrifice.'[94] The Russian terrorist, then, appeared alongside the Dostoevskian heroes as a paradigmatic figure of the Russian universe from which Lukács expected 'the dawn' to come. This was a very important factor in his subsequent development, since the ethico-social problematic of Russian terrorism would lie at the heart of the moral crisis that led him to join the Communist Party in 1918.

[92] Here we are following the interpretation of Ferenc Fehér (pp. 156–7), who has recently deciphered Lukács's notes on Dostoevsky and made an exceptionally penetrating analysis of them.

[93] Quoted in Fehér, pp. 143, 148.

[94] Savinkov, *Souvenirs d'un terroriste*, Paris, 1931, p. 60. Savinkov adds that Kaliayev was an implacable enemy of established religion, and that he refused the services of a priest at the moment of his execution.

Let us now examine the other points contained in Lukács's outline of Chapter III: 'Dostoevsky's misunderstanding: attitude to Christianity and revolution.' Lukács did not share Dostoevsky's mystical anti-revolutionism, with its absolute contradiction between genuine Christianity and atheistic socialist revolution. If he spoke of a mis-understanding, it was because he considered that a certain kind of religiosity was itself intrinsic to real socialism.

'"All men": Metaphysics of socialism.' Once again, it is impossible to understand this laconic formulation except by referring to Dostoevsky. In the chapter of *The Brothers Karamazov* devoted to the Grand Inquisitor, the Russian writer drew a contrast between the figure of Christ, preaching to the virtuous chosen few who are capable of choosing freedom and the bread of heaven, and the Grand Inquisitor who, intending to give earthly bread to all, says to Jesus: 'You pride yourself upon your chosen ones, but you have only the chosen ones, while we will bring peace to all. . . . With us . . . *all* will be happy and will no longer rise in rebellion nor exterminate one another, as they do everywhere under your freedom.'[95] Dostoevsky was here attacking, in the person the Grand Inquisitor, not only the Church of Rome but also what he saw as the closely related phenomenon of atheist socialism. But did Lukács, whose elitist tendencies emerged in *Von der Armut am Geiste*, feel that socialist redemption was necessary for 'all men'? The cryptic note gives no answer, but it does allow us to identify the problematic.

'Ethical democracy: Metaphysics of the State.' A letter to Paul Ernst of 14 April 1915 throws considerable light on this remark, which has its roots in Lukács's morally anti-statist and (politically) anti-Hegelian idealism: 'It is a mortal sin for the spirit to enclose all power in a metaphysical aura. Such was the prevailing concept of German thought before Hegel. The state is a real power – but should it be recognized as existing in the utopian philosophical sense of a true ethic active at the level of essence? I do not think so. And I hope, in the non-aesthetic part of my book on Dostoevsky, to make a vigorous protest against that view.'[96] These directly political aspects are missing from *The Theory of the Novel*. However, if we read the book 'philosophically', relating it to Lukács's outline of the projected broader work, then we rediscover Dostoevsky's dream of the golden age in the form of nostalgia for pre-classical Greece[97] – that blissful time when

[95] Dostoevsky, *The Brothers Karamazov*, p. 303; emphasis added.
[96] *Paul Ernst und Georg Lukács*, pp. 66–7.
[97] For Lukács, as for Dostoevsky, the earthly Greek paradise was not the prosperous and

men could read in 'the starry sky . . . the map of all possible paths'. For 'the fire that burns in the soul is of the same essential nature as the stars'; this is a 'closed and perfect' universe, harmonious and homogeneous, in which 'knowledge is virtue and virtue is happiness', and 'beauty is the meaning of the world made visible'.[98] Lukács, of course, regards Dostoevsky's 'golden age' as the absolute negation of the cursed, venal, corrupt and loathsome world of capitalism (*Zustand der vollendeten Sündhaftigkeit*)[99]; it is not only the dream of a mythological past, but above all *the premonition of a messianic future*; and Dostoevsky himself is the herald of 'a new era' destined to blossom forth in Russia.[100] In this way, the tragic view of the world is partly transcended in *The Theory of the Novel*.[101]

Our last question is also the most difficult: how could Lukács, writing about Tolstoy and Dostoevsky at the height of the First World War (1915), when the anti-militarist opposition was only just beginning to organize, and when even the most steadfast revolutionaries were not exempt from feelings of anxiety and even despair – how could Lukács then have voiced a *presentiment*, although not, of course, a prediction, *of the*

---

refined Athens celebrated by the bourgeoisie of the Renaissance and the French Revolution. Against this classical bourgeois ideal, they opposed the archetype of a mythical and mythological Greece, the imaginary realm of absolute harmony between men and the world. It is no accident, therefore, that Dostoevsky placed the scene of Stavrogin's dream 'three thousand years in the past' (i.e., in pre-classical Greece), and that Lukács refers to the Greek world of Homer's epic.

[98] Lukács, *The Theory of the Novel*, pp. 29, 33, 34.

[99] On Dostoevsky's romantic anti-capitalism, see Lukács, *The Meaning of Contemporary Realism*, London, 1972, p. 62: 'His hero's sufferings derive from the inhumanity of early capitalism, and particularly from its destructive influence on personal relationships. . . . His protest against the inhumanity of capitalism is transformed into a sophistical, anti-capitalist romanticism, into a critique of socialism and democracy.'

[100] See, in the French edition of the present work, Bloch's remarks on Lukács's 'passionate' relationship with Dostoevsky. He places this within the framework of the 'Russophilia' of western anti-bourgeois intellectuals.

[101] In an essay published in 1916, Lukács explicitly presented Dostoevsky's Russian heroes as pointing beyond the tragic vision: 'And what if the darkness of our lack of aim were but the night-darkness between the twilight of one god and the dawn of another? . . . And it is certain that we have discovered the final meaning, here in the tragic world deserted by every god? Is there not in our abandonment rather a cry of suffering and longing for the god to come? In any case, is the still weak and distant light not more essential than the hero's illusory shout? . . . From this duality spring Dostoevsky's heroes: Prince Myshkin beside Nikolai Stavrogin, Alyosha Karamazov beside his brother Ivan.' (Lukács, 'Ariadne auf Naxos', in *Paul Ernst und Georg Lukács*, p. 56.) This text casts a superb light on the contemporary *Theory of the Novel* as a stage in Lukács's evolution from a metaphysics of tragedy towards a historico-social utopia.

approaching revolution?[102] More research is required before this question can be answered. We know of only one other comparable case: speaking at the Genet Theatre in 1966, two years before May 1968, Lukács's disciple Lucien Goldmann detected 'the symptoms of a historical turning-point', 'the first swallow announcing the arrival of spring'.[103]

A few words should now be said about Lukács's attitude to Marxism between 1909 and 1916. In the 1967 preface to *History and Class Consciousness*, Lukács explains that he read *Capital* about 1908 in order to find a sociological basis for his work on modern drama;[104] he adds, however, that he approached Marx as if he were a 'sociologist' similar in kind to Simmel and Weber. Also very revealing is a brief reference to Marx the philosopher, contained in the first chapter of the monograph on drama. 'In the last analysis,' Lukács wrote, 'the whole philosophy of both Marx and Stirner has its origins in Fichte.'[105] Now, there is no need to insist that this assertion is highly dubious from the point of view of the history of philosophy, and that it is more a symptom of Lukács's own Fichteanism, then influenced by, among other things, Marianne Weber's *Fichtes Sozialismus und Sein Verhältnis zur Marxschen Doktrine*. In an article written the following year, Lukács recognized the 'epoch-making' importance of historical maerialism as a 'sociological method' – provided, 'of course', that it is 'drained of its metaphysical conceptualizations',[106] largely through the mediation of a neo-Kantian epistemology for which any form of materialism could only be 'metaphysical'.[107]

[102] However, a similar insight does seem to have appeared among certain far-left currents at the beginning of the war – for example, the anarchists. In his *Memoirs*, Victor Serge writes that for him the war 'heralded another, purifying tempest: the Russian Revolution. Revolutionaries knew quite well that the autocratic Empire . . . could never survive the war. A gleam of light was at last visible: this would be the beginning of everything, the prodigious first day of Creation. An end to deadlock! This huge gateway would be open towards the future'. (*Memoirs of a Revolutionary*, p. 47.)

[103] L. Goldmann, *Structures mentales et création culturelle*, Paris, 1970, p. 339.

[104] Lukács's notebooks for the years 1908–1910 contain a number of extracts from *Capital* which indicate that he read the whole work thoroughly. They also contain extracts from Engels's *Anti-Dühring* and Kautsky's *Vorläufer des Sozialismus*, jumbled up with passages on capitalism taken from Werner Sombart. (*Notizbuch Z*, pp. 88–103, Lukács Archivum.)

[105] This first chapter was published in German: 'Zur Soziologie des modernen Dramas', *Archiv für Sozialwissenschaft*, vol. 38, 1914, p. 669.

[106] Lukács, 'Croce, Zur Theorie und Geschichte der Historiographie', *Archiv für Sozialwissenschaft*, vol. 39, 1915, p. 884.

[107] About 1910, in his answer to a questionaire sent to various writers by a Hungarian editor, Lukács stressed the 'everlasting value' of Marx for his intellectual development. However, alongside Marx he mentions a list of other writers who influenced him: Hebbel, Novalis, Schlegel, Kierkegaard, Simmel, Schopenhauer, Nietzsche, Kant, Goethe, Hegel,

During the First World War, however, Lukács would take a greater interest in Marxism and examine it in a fresh light: 'As the imperialist nature of the war became clear, and as I deepened my study of Hegel and Feuerbach . . . so did I begin for the second time to concern myself profoundly with Marx. . . . This time, however, it was a Marx seen through Hegelian rather than Simmelian spectacles. I no longer regarded Marx as "an outstanding man of science", an economist or a sociologist, but began to see in him the universal thinker and great dialectician.'[108]

How, then, did Lukács greet the outbreak of the Russian Revolution? Our only direct testimony comes from Paul Ernst's account of his Heidelberg meeting with Lukács in the autumn of 1917. In a dialogue-novel written late that year, Ernst attributes the following views to his Hungarian friend: 'Herr von Lukács drew attention to the Russian Revolution and the great ideas becoming a reality through it. The Russian Revolution is an event of whose European significance we do not yet have so much as an inkling; it is just taking its first steps to lead humanity beyond the bourgeois social order of mechanization and bureaucratization, militarism and imperialism, towards a free world in which the Spirit will once again rule and the Soul will at least be able to live.'[109] Although this account is impossible to verify, it does have a strong ring of truth when it describes the idealist and romantically anti-capitalist grid through which Lukács perceived the Russian October.

Still, in 1917 the mystical dream of a Russian *Gemeinde* began to mutate by stages into political fascination with the Bolshevik Revolution. During this year and the next, Lukács became more and more deeply political, under the impact of the Russian experience and the revolutionary-syndicalist ideas of Ervin Szabó. He read (or re-read) Sorel and the anarcho-syndicalists, the Dutch far left (Pannekoek and Henriette Roland-Holst), and Luxemburg. Yet his old reservations about socialism

---

Dilthey, Meister Eckhardt, Dostoevsky, Tolstoy, and others. (See Béla Köhalmi, *Könyvek könyve*, Budapest, 1918, pp. 166–8.)

[108] Lukács, 'Mein Weg zu Marx' (1933), in *G. Lukács, Zum 70. Geburtstag*, Berlin, 1955, p. 326.

[109] P. Ernst, 'Weiteres Gespräch mit Georg (von) Lukács' (1917), in *Paul Ernst und Georg Lukács*, p. 128. Answering along the same lines, Paul Ernst shows that the various currents of the German intelligentsia (seemingly) concurred in a kind of abstract commitment to the Russian Revolution: 'What the Russians and you want is a linear development from our classical ideals: in other words, a politics of Humanity.' (Ibid., p. 132.)

are repeated in a Hungarian article published in 1917: 'The ideology of the proletariat, its understanding of solidarity, is still so abstract that – whatever importance we attach to the military arm of the class struggle – the proletariat is incapable of providing a real ethic embracing all aspects of life.'[110] Once he became a communist, Lukács would do his best to explain that Marxism involves precisely an ethic of this type. In the 1969 preface to his writings on Hungary, he has this to say about this epoch: 'At that point in my development, French anarcho-syndicalism exerted considerable influence over me. I could never accommodate myself to the Social Democratic ideology of that time, and above all to Kautsky. My knowledge of the works of Georges Sorel, to which I had been introduced by Ervin Szabó, helped me to combine the influences of Hegel, Ady and Dostoevsky in a certain organic vision of the world that I then considered to be revolutionary.'[111] It is difficult to precisely assess Sorel's role in shaping this 'revolutionary . . . vision of the world': what Lukács drew from Sorel's work was less the cult of violence than its moral rigorism, its contempt for parliamentarism and reformist Social Democracy, its romantically anti-capitalist hatred for the pleasure-seeking individualism of the 'liberal' bourgeoisie, and its peculiarly apocalyptic vision of the future.[112]

One text that sheds considerable light on Lukács's growing interest in politics and on his radically idealist, 'classical' (German) method of approach, is his contribution to the debate on *Conservative and Progressive Idealism* held at the Social Science Society early in 1918. Lukács's speech, following an intervention by his friend Béla Fogarasi, was perhaps *his first systematic attempt* to broach the key problem of the relation between politics and ethics – a problem which, as we shall see, lies at the heart of his theoretical and practical activity between 1918 and 1921. Hence the exceptional importance of this text, virtually unknown in the West and

---

[110] 'Halálos fiatalság' (*Mortal Youth*), in *Magyar Irodalom, Magyar Kultura*, p. 116. In this article (whose title refers to a work by Béla Balázs), Lukács contrasts the ideology of the proletariat with Dostoevsky's work, which 'is addressed not to a socially defined group of men, but – independently of all social links – to every soul that has discovered the concrete reality of the soul'.

[111] 'Elöszó' (1969), pp. 8–9.

[112] Given this view of the world, it is not at all surprising that Lukács had nothing but contempt for the MSZP. We have very little information about Lukács's attitude to this party. In an interview with an American revolutionary journalist in 1919, Lukács said that before the Hungarian revolution he had been 'a socialist', but had been 'inactive because . . . disgusted with the compromise parliamentary policy of the party'. ('In Communist Hungary', *The Liberator*, August 1919, p. 6.)

never before translated from Hungarian.

Let us first note in passing that Lukács here sharply and explicitly criticizes the Hindu caste philosophy that had inspired him in *Von der Armut am Geiste*. He now regards it as fundamentally conservative and inimical to progress: 'The stagnation of Indian culture is closely bound up with the ethic and rules of behaviour current in India – with the doctrine ... that scrupulous observance of caste regulations is the highest virtue and rejection of one's caste the greatest crime.' In Lukács's view, this ethic was responsible for the fact that Hindu culture 'rules out any social advancement'.[113] Of course, this has nothing in common with a Marxist analysis of the Asiatic mode of production. But it does indicate the ideological ground Lukács covered between 1912 and 1918, and above all his final break with the 'caste metaphysics' Bloch was still attributing to him in *Geist der Utopie* (1918).

Lukács opens his contribution quite abstractly. Operating within a neo-Kantian and Fichtean theoretical framework that is idealist in the extreme, he draws a rigorous distinction between the field of 'authenticity' and the field of 'metaphysics.' Authenticity, whether aesthetic or ethical, is defined as *total independence* of everything that exists; a morally authentic action is thus completely independent of the consequences it may entail in the real world. Lukács here weaves together German idealism and the *Gesinnungsethik* of Tolstoy and Dostoevsky – that 'cosmo-ethical rationalism' which Max Weber criticized in his famous 1919 talk 'Politics as a Vocation'. An authentic action, therefore, has an 'ought-structure' (*Sollen*), and the *Sollen* 'is by nature transcendent (totally independent of the existence to which its content attaches it).'[114]

For Lukács, this Kantian dualism of the Is and the Ought did not involve an attitude of indifference to empirical reality. It led rather to a categorical imperative: 'Make the kingdom of God come down to earth at once', as it had for those models of progressive idealism, the Anabaptist movements of the sixteenth century.[115] It would seem that we are still a long way from politics; and yet it is precisely towards political action that

---

[113] Lukács, 'A konservativ es progressziv idealizmus vitája: Hozzászólas' (The debate on conservative and progressive idealism: an intervention), *Huszadik Század*, no. 1, 1918, in *Utam Marxhoz, Válogatott Filozofiai Tanulmányok*, vol. 1, Budapest, 1971, pp. 179–80. For a French translation, see the original edition of this work.

[114] Ibid., pp. 178–9.

[115] Ibid., pp. 180. Cf. Dostoevsky, *The Brothers Karamazov*, pp. 26–7: 'Socialism ... [is] the question of the Tower of Babel which is being erected ... for the sake of bringing heaven down to earth.'

this moral messianism guides Lukács's thought. He distinguishes between two types of action stemming from ethical idealism: 1) ethical *action directe* (he uses the French term), which 'pays no heed to the detour of politics' and immediately sets out 'to change men's souls'; and 2) political action, conceived as an ethical instrument whose only aim is 'to create institutions corresponding as far as possible to ethical ideals, and to bring about the disappearance of those which hinder the realization of such ideals'.[116]

Thus, complete subordination of politics to ethics is the ideological axis around which Lukács's approach revolves: 'From the standpoint of ethical idealism, every institution (from property to the nation and the state) has value not in itself but only insofar as it serves the [moral] transformation' of men. In this regard, Lukács explicitly counterposes Fichte's ethics to what he calls Hegel's 'metaphysics of the state'.

There now follows a quite remarkable passage which, in spite of its ethical-idealist elation, demonstrates a surprisingly high degree of *political lucidity*: 'Whereas institutions have value for ethical idealism only as means to an end . . . any doctrine which tends to make of politics an autonomous domain is found to ascribe an intrinsic value to institutions. However, the structural necessity of the situation then gives rise to a conservative politics in which the goal of political activity is to defend the institution that embodies its own value: one no longer inquires whether an institution still corresponds to its original purpose, but merely seeks to promote further advance on the ground of that institution, and to extend its sphere of influence. Every institution, once it becomes an end in itself, has a conservative character – which explains not only the reactionary politics of the church . . . but also the fact that movements that are initially very progressive stagnate as soon as the institutions they created as a means become independent of the end. (The history of German socialism, even before the war but especially since it began, provides an all-too-instructive example of this process.)'[117] As we read these lines today, it is difficult not to be reminded of other cases that would involve, ten or twenty years later, the 'stagnation of initially very progressive movements'. Unfortunately, Lukács had by then exchanged his ethical idealism for a Hegelian-type 'political realism'.[118]

[116] Lukács, 'A konservativ es progressziv idealizmus', pp. 181–2.
[117] Ibid., p. 184.
[118] In his 1969 preface to *Utam Marxhoz*, Lukács commented about this essay: '. . . the idealist tendencies still within me, and even dominating me, then reached their apogée. . . . Perhaps the most striking outward expression of this internal state was my contribution to the

In 1918, however, Lukács suggested a way to prevent the process whereby institutions become frozen in a conservative autonomy. His solution to this problem of overcoming political stagnation is, once again, rather astonishing: 'Ethical idealism is a permanent revolution against what exists, simply because what exists does not measure up to its ethical ideal. And being permanent revolution, absolute revolution, it is capable of defining and correcting the course of true progress that never finds a point of equilibrium.'[119] Now, it is unlikely that the Lukács of 1918 had found the concept of 'permanent revolution' (*permanens forradolom*) in the writings of Trotsky or Marx; he 'invented' it himself, so to speak, lending it a peculiar meaning at once close to and distant from the Marxist concept.

The passages we have just discussed reveal the young Lukács's dazzling and moving *revolutionary radicalism*, which burst forth in his first strictly political text. But, of course, he held that politics was only the servant of ethics; the speech therefore ends by returning to Kant and Fichte's demand for human dignity (*Würdigkeit*). The general principle 'embracing all progressive demands in a homogeneous system' is the principle of classical German idealism: on no account must man ever become a mere instrument.[120]

In broaching the problem of whether revolutionary violence can be harmonized with such Kantian ethics, Lukács at first tended to answer in the negative. The *avant-garde* writer Lajos Kassák has described Lukács's ideology in 1918 as a form of 'Tolstoyan ethical socialism'.[121] And since

---

debate on conservative and progressive idealist tendencies organized by the Social Science Society and introduced by Béla Fogarasi.' Lukács insists that this text deserves attention only as a symptom of the intellectual crisis he was then going through – and even then, only 'for readers with a scientific interest in the various stages of my later development'. (Lukács, 'Mon chemin vers Marx', in *Nouvelles Etudes Hongroises*, Budapest, 1973, p. 83.) Why all these precautions and reservations? Is it just a question of modesty, or did Lukács realize that his 1918 speech was still explosive fifty years later? In our view, Lukács must have been aware that an unalerted reader could fall into the temptation of applying the criteria expounded in this text to the Hungary of 1969 – for example, by investigating whether certain present-day institutions correspond to their initial objective.

[119] Lukács, 'A konservativ es progressziv idealizmus', p. 185.

[120] Ibid., pp. 185–6.

[121] Quoted in Rudolf Tökes, *Bela Kun and the Hungarian Soviet Republic*, New York, 1967, p. 96. In an autobiography written in 1941, Lukács writes of his wartime 'bourgeois pacifism', describing his evolution between 1914 and 1918 as follows: 'The imperialist war threw my world-view into a deep crisis that initially took the form of bourgeois-pacifist rejection of the war and a pessimistic critique of bourgeois culture; only in the second half of the war, under the impact of the Russian Revolution and the writings of Rosa Luxemburg, did this crisis take on a political character. My opposition to the prevailing system became

the term 'Tolstoyan socialism' then referred above all to a *pacifist*, anti-militarist and 'non-violent' ideology, it is highly likely that violence was the supreme evil for Lukács's Tolstoyan ethics – or, at least, the prime moral problem. It is no accident that this problem would play a central role in his passage from 'Dostoevskian Tolstoyism' to Bolshevism.[122]

2. The Passage to Communism

> My decision to take an active part in the communist movement was influenced profoundly by ethical considerations.[123]

In October 1918, when the old regime collapsed in Hungary, a reformist coalition of Social Democrats and bourgeois radicals took power. Lukács was still a long way from communism in November of that year: he signed a liberal-democratic manifesto ('An Appeal by Hungarian Intellectuals for a Free Confederation of Nations') and wrote a rather lukewarm article on Bolshevism. Only late in the month, or early in December, did Lukács meet Béla Kún for the first time – Kún having founded the Hungarian Communist Party on 20 November shortly after his arrival from Soviet Russia. According to his friend Anna Lesznai, Lukács's 'conversion took place in the interval between two Sundays: from Saul came Paul'.[124] This lightning change was a surprise to all Lukács's friends. And indeed, its suddenness and irreversibility are reminiscent of religious conversion – rather in keeping with his mystical-ethical character at the time.

Nevertheless, despite the apparent break in continuity, the whole of Lukács's previous development had paved the way for this turn. Since his

---

ever more acute, and I made contact with a number of far-left circles (*linksradikale*).' Lukács, *Autobiographie*, German typescript, n.d., p. 1. This unpublished document can be found in the Lukács Archivum, Budapest.

[122] In an article written during the war, Lukács defended Tolstoy's consistent pacifism against the 'hate-filled polemic' of the Russian writer Solovyev, who had argued that killing in wartime is not murder, since intention is absent: the enemy at whom one shoots is not visible! Lukács contemptuously rejected this position as 'an evasive compromise'. (Lukács, 'Solovieff', p. 980.)

[123] Lukács, 'Preface' (1967) to *History and Class Consciousness*, London, 1971, p. XXXI.

[124] Our source is the letters sent by Lukács and Anna Lesznai to David Kettler and quoted in his remarkable study: 'Culture and Revolution: Lukács in the Hungarian Revolution of 1918/19', *Telos*, no. 10, 1971, pp. 68–9.

tragic world view had been rooted in the apparent lack of any social force capable of waging the revolutionary struggle against capitalism, the October Revolution (and to some extent the Hungarian events of 1918) made a deep impact on him, demonstrating that such a force did indeed exist: the proletariat and its Bolshevik vanguard.[125] On the other hand, Lukács clearly read into the Soviet revolution his own messianic hope that the new world would dawn *in Russia*.

The period between October 1917 and the December 1918 'conversion' was essentially one of transition during which Lukács remained at the level of 'Tolstoyan ethical socialism'. Before making the leap from tragic moralism to Marxist Bolshevism, he had to pass through a crucial mediation: *the Faustian dialectic of means and ends.*

As we have already pointed out, Lukács, hovering on the brink in November 1918, made one last attempt to shake off the temptation of 'the Bolshevik demon'. This was his article 'A bolsevizmus mint erkölsci probléma (Bolshevism as a Moral Problem), published in the 15 December issue of *Szabad-Gondolat*, the review of the Galileo Circle. In his 1967 preface, Lukács very sharply describes this article as 'a brief transitional phase: my last hesitations before making my final, irrevocable choice were marked by a misguided attempt at an apologia fortified with abstract and philistine arguments.'[126] In fact, this rather mysterious article, sometimes discussed[127] but never before translated in the West, needs to be analysed in detail as a turning point in Lukács's politico-philosophical development.

Those 'abstract and philistine arguments' which Lukács employed in his 'last hesitations' certainly did not involve Menshevik-type allegations about 'the unripeness of objective conditions'. For Lukács explicitly rejected 'the argument most often used in discussing Bolshevism, namely the problem of whether the economic situation is sufficiently mature for it to be immediately achieved'.[128] He dismissed this objection on the grounds that 'there can never be a situation about which *we are completely*

---

[125] In an interview given much later, Lukács pointed out: 'I would not venture to say – I could not – that the purely negative impact of the First World War would have been enough to make a socialist out of me.' ('The Twin Crises', *New Left Review*, no. 60, March/April 1970, p. 36.) See also 'Lukács on His Life and Work', *New Left Review*, no. 68, July/August 1971, p. 53: 'October gave the answer. The Russian Revolution was the world-historical solution to my dilemma.'

[126] Lukács, 'Preface' (1967), p. xi.

[127] Peter Ludz, Andrew Arato, Paul Breines, and David Kettler all mention it.

[128] Lukács, 'A bolsevizmus mint erkölcsi probléma', pp. 228–32.

certain beforehand: the *will* to carry something through at any cost is at least as integral to the "ripeness" of the situation as are the objective conditions.' Evidently, Lukács's neo-Fichtean voluntarism had nothing in common with Plekhanov's or Kautsky's eighteenth-century materialism. Similarly, Lukács had no hesitation in rejecting the argument of numerous conservative intellectuals that Bolshevism spelt the destruction of civilization and culture: 'Such a worldwide overturning of values cannot take place without the annihilation of the old values' and the creation of new ones by the revolutionaries.

The problem for Lukács, then, was not economic or cultural but *ethical*: it was here that he still had reservations about Bolshevism. His ideological starting point, *which lends its structure to the entire article*, is once again a neo-Kantian opposition between 'arid empirical reality' and 'the ethical, utopian human will'. This explains his demand that Marx's sociology, which takes note of such key realities as the class struggle, should be *separated* from 'the utopian postulate of Marx's philosophy of history: namely, his *ethical programme* for the new world to come'. Conceived as a purely sociological necessity, the proletarian class struggle leads only to a situation whereby those who used to be oppressed are transformed into oppressors: 'The victory of the proletariat is, of course, an indispensable precondition if the era of true freedom, with neither oppressor nor oppressed, is at last to become a reality. . . . But it cannot be more than a precondition, a negative fact. For the era of freedom to be attained, it is necessary to go beyond those mere sociological statements of fact and those laws from which it can never be derived: it is necessary to *will* the new, democratic world.' In this universe of dualist thought, social facts and the human will are seen as totally distinct and independent levels; the will to a new world lies in a sphere *beyond* the real course of the class struggle.

Now, Marx's dialectic negates/surpasses (*aufhebt*) such a rigid, metaphysical separation, pointing towards a unity of facts and values, 'sociological statements' and 'ethical programme'. Lukács criticizes as 'Marx's Hegelianism' precisely this dialectical unity, 'which has too great a tendency to place the different elements of the real on a single plane' and has consequently 'played a role in blurring these differences'. He further complains that Marx was 'constructing the historico-philosophical process after the manner of Hegel (*List der Idee*)' when he declared that 'the proletariat will free the world from all despotism by struggling for its own interests'. In opposition to Marx's 'Hegelianism' – or dialectical method – the neo-Kantian Lukács followed Ervin Szabó in describing the final goal of socialism as 'a new, democratic world' *beyond the limits* of the proletariat's class struggle for its concrete material interests. The will to this new world, Lukács argued, 'is not derived from any sociological statement of fact'.

Through the mediation of this abstract ethical will, Lukács discovers in the proletariat 'the bearer of the social redemption of humanity' and even 'the messiah-class of world history'. Driven by such messianic excitement, he also (like Engels) sees the proletariat as the legatee of German classical philosophy – 'of the ethical idealism of Kant and Fichte which, suppressing all earthly links, was supposed to tear the old world, metaphysically, from its hinges'. In Schelling's aesthetics and Hegel's philosophy of the state, German idealist thought 'strayed from the path of progress . . . and eventually became reactionary'; however, it will now find direct fulfilment through the redeeming role of the proletariat.

This grandiose philosophico-moral perspective, messianic and apoc-alyptic in character, illuminates the first steps through which Lukács committed himself to the workers' movement. But we are still talking of an abstract, idealist, and metaphysical commitment. His attitude to the proletariat continued to be marked by a profound dualism: he did not grasp the nexus between the gigantic historico-philosophical role of the proletariat and its 'petty' struggle to defend its material interests. Still wary of proletarian socialism, he asked whether it was really 'the subject yet self-willing bearer of world redemption' or rather 'a mere ideological envelope for real class interests, distinct from other interests not by their quality or moral force, but only by their content'. Yet again, Lukács's neo-Kantianism blinded him to the dialectical link between the *real content* and the *ethical quality* of the interests of the proletariat.

This dualism, which expressed the ethical rigorism of the tragic world view, also appears in the central theme of the article: a rigid, absolute separation between 'good' and 'evil', freedom and oppression, the Messiah and Satan. Bolshevism, in Lukács's view, wishes to abolish capitalist terror by means of proletarian terror, bourgeois oppression by means of working-class oppression; in short, it wishes 'to expel Satan by means of Beëlzebub'.[129] This raises a dilemma: 'Can good be achieved through evil

[129] If we accepted the Bolshevik ethic, he argues, 'we would be forced to take up the position of dictatorship, terror, and oppression; the position according to which we must replace the rule of previous classes with the class rule of the proletariat, believing all the while that – Beëlzebub having driven out Satan – this last, and by its very nature most cruel and overt class domination will abolish itself together with all class domination.'

means? Can freedom be reached along the path of oppression? Can a new world be born, when the means used to attain it differ only technically from those employed by the old order, rightly the object of hatred and contempt?' Lukács's reply is unambiguous: 'I repeat, Bolshevism rests on the metaphysical hypothesis that good can come out of evil, that it is possible, as Razumikhin puts it in *Crime and Punishment*, to attain the truth with a lie. The author of these lines cannot share this belief, and that is why he sees an insoluble moral dilemma in the very roots of the Bolshevik mentality.'[130]

The reference to *Crime and Punishment* at the climax of Lukács's argument is quite characteristic of the intellectual universe he inhabited during this crucial period. Dostoevsky's ethical rigorism, harmoniously combining with Lukács's neo-Kantian dualism, served as his main reference-point between 1918 and 1920: indeed, he would still be mentally arguing with the Grand Inquisitor even when he assumed his tasks as a people's commissar of the Hungarian Soviet Republic in 1919. It is precisely the problematic of *Crime and Punishment* that underlies the 1918 article we have been discussing. For everything suggests that Lukács saw the Bolsheviks as the inheritors of the dreaded Raskolnikov. They are supposed to have believed, like the hero of Dostoevsky's novel, that 'all . . . lawgivers and arbiters of mankind, beginning from ancient times and continuing with the Lycurguses, Solons, Mahomets, Napoleons, and so on, were without exception criminals because of the very fact that they had transgressed the ancient laws handed down by their ancestors. . . . Nor, of course, did they stop short of bloodshed, if bloodshed – sometimes of innocent people fighting gallantly in defence of the ancient law – were of any assistance to them. It is indeed a remarkable fact that the majority of these benefactors and arbiters of mankind all shed rivers of blood.'[131]

---

[130] Cf. Dostoevsky, *Crime and Punishment*, Harmondsworth, 1977, p. 219: '"What do you think?" cried Razumikhin, raising his voice louder and louder. . . . "I like people to talk rot. It's man's only privilege over the rest of creation. By talking rot, you eventually get to the truth. I'm a man because I talk rot. Not a single truth has ever been discovered without people first talking utter rot a hundred times or perhaps a hundred thousand times."'

[131] Dostoevsky, pp. 276–7. Cf. the famous words of the student who incites Raskolnikov to kill the miserly old woman: 'Hundreds, perhaps thousands of lives could be saved, dozens of families could be rescued from a life of poverty, from decay and ruin, from vice and hospitals for venereal diseases – and all with her money. Kill her, take her money, and with its help devote yourself to the service of humanity and the good of all. . . . For one life you will save thousands of lives from corruption and decay . . . why, it's a simple sum in arithmetic! And, when you come to think of it, what does the life of a sickly, wicked old hag amount to when weighed in the scales of the general good of mankind? It amounts to no more than the life of a

It is true that Lukács here poses a genuine political problem about the Bolsheviks' practice in power, which involved them in a number of serious curbs on democracy: 'Is democracy merely part of the tactics of socialism – a combat weapon for the period when it is in a minority and struggling against the legalized and illegal terror of the oppressor classes? Or is it rather an integral part of socialism?' But Lukács raises the question in an abstract, moralistic framework, thereby turning it into an insoluble ethical dilemma: socialism or democracy. It is interesting to compare Lukács's article with Rosa Luxemburg's notes on the Russian Revolution, written in prison in 1918. Although the Polish Marxist also criticized certain aspects of Bolshevik policy, she tackled the problem in a much more concrete and flexible manner, placing it in a thoroughly *realist* perspective: 'It would be demanding something superhuman from Lenin and his comrades if we should expect of them that under such circumstances they should conjure forth the finest democracy. . . . By their determined revolutionary stand . . . they have contributed whatever could possibly be contributed under such devilishly hard conditions. The danger begins only when they make a virtue of necessity and want to freeze into a complete theoretical system all the tactics forced upon them by these fatal circumstances.'[132]

In drawing out the political conclusions of his philosophico-moral critique of Bolshevism, Lukács appears to lean in the direction of the classical Social Democratic solution: the path of 'slow struggle, seemingly less heroic yet laden with responsibility – the long, pedagogic struggle shaping the soul of those who fully commit themselves to democracy'. But he admits that this path, just as much as Bolshevism, 'contains the possibility of hideous crimes and colossal mistakes'. In particular, it entails 'the necessity . . . of collaborating with classes and parties that agree with Social Democracy only on certain immediate goals, while remaining hostile to the final goal of Social Democracy'. Lukács points out that such compromises almost inevitably mar the purity of programme and the passion of the will – and so, this solution is clearly in blatant contradiction with Lukács's ethical rigorism, grounded precisely on the rejection of compromise. The Social Democratic road cannot be sustained within his

---

louse or a black beetle, if that, for the old hag is really harmful. For one thing, she is ruining the life of another human being.' (pp. 84–5) It is quite possible that, for Lukács in November 1918, this speech appeared as the quintessence of Bolshevik morality – provided only that 'the old hag' be replaced by the 'wicked', 'harmful' bourgeoisie 'ruining' the lives of other people.

[132] 'The Russian Revolution', in *Rosa Luxemburg Speaks*, New York, 1970, p. 394.

system of thought: it will not 'stand up'. As it happened, Lukács quickly reached the conclusion – illustrated by the social patriotism of the First World War – that the compromises of Social Democracy not only 'have a harmful effect on the purity of programme' but may also involve far worse massacres than the Bolshevik 'red terror'.

The Russian revolutionaries attracted Lukács precisely because they rejected any compromise with forces hostile to socialism: 'The fascinating power of Bolshevism is to be explained by the liberation that results from abolishing such compromise.' (He also refers to the 'spell' of this potential for liberation.) There can be no doubt that Lukács was himself 'fascinated' and 'spellbound' by the Bolsheviks' revolutionary purity and socialist rigour.[133] The references we have been discussing here became a kind of guide on the path that would soon bring him to the Hungarian Communist Party. But first he had to solve the central problem of the relationship between ethical ends and immoral means; and he had to do so by going beyond the abstract, frozen neo-Kantian dualism of 'good' and 'evil'.

Of course, this kind of ethical scruple was not confined to Lukács; it was typical of a whole layer of radicalized intellectuals who hesitated to leap on to the Bolshevik locomotive of history then mercilessly sweeping away all the obstacles in its path. We must now examine the reasoning by which Lukács finally crossed the threshold and threw himself, body and soul, into the torrent of revolution.

In his memoirs, the communist writer József Lengyel – whose solid 'materialism' set him poles apart from Lukács – recounts an anecdote that goes a long way in explaining the trajectory of a whole group of Communist Party members around Lukács. Lengyel tells us that he was 'literally dumbfounded' on learning of the problems Lukács and other party leaders used to discuss in their residential House of the Soviet at the height of the 1919 revolution: 'One of these problems – we communists should take the sins of the world upon ourselves, so that we may be capable of saving the world. And why should we take the sins of the world upon us? Once again there was a very "clear" answer, one taken from Hebbel's *Judith*. . . . Just as God could order Judith to kill Holophernes – that is, to commit a sin – so may he order the communists to destroy the bourgeoisie, both metaphorically and physically. . . . In support of their argument, they also used to refer to Dostoevsky's "Grand Inquisitor".'[134]

[133] In *Gelebtes Denken* (1971), p. 28. Lukács describes his attitude to the Russian Revolution as 'a contradictory fascination, with moments of back-sliding'.

[134] J. Lengyee, *Visegrader Strasse*, Berlin, 1959, pp. 244–5. See the passage in which the

There is something touching, at once bizarre and grandiose, in the fact that communist leaders should have been concerned with such ethico-metaphysical problems in the middle of the revolutionary storm of 1919. All these strange discussions, however, did have a number of political implications. Thus, another witness relates that, after long arguments among Lukács, Sinkó, Ottó Korvin (the 'red security' chief), and others concerning Bolshevism, Dostoevsky, Hebbel, and the Gospels, the friends of Lukács drew the following conclusion: 'During the dictatorship of the proletariat, it is necessary to use all means, even those contrary to the spirit and morality of communist man. This is a sacrifice, a daily but indispensable sacrifice.'[135]

Lukács's first article as a Bolshevik – 'Tactics and Ethics', which is still deeply imbued with fervent moralism – formulates this problematic precisely and succinctly. There are tragic situations, he argues, in which one cannot act without committing a fault, without taking a sin upon oneself. It is then necessary to choose the most just way of being guilty: to *sacrifice* the ethic of one's ego on the higher altar of a universal historical mission. The article ends with the following passage: 'In one of his novels, Ropschin (Boris Savinkov), the leader of the terrorist group during the Russian Revolution from 1904 to 1906, put the problem of individual terror in the following terms: murder is not allowed, it is an absolute and unpardonable sin; it "may" not, but yet it "must" be committed. Elsewhere in the same book he sees, not the justification (that is impossible) but the ultimate moral basis of the terrorist's act as the sacrifice for his brethren, not only of his life, but also of his purity, his morals, his very soul. In other words, only he who acknowledges unflinchingly and without any reservations that murder is under no circumstances to be sanctioned can commit the murderous deed that is truly – and tragically – moral. To express this sense of the most profound human tragedy in the incomparably beautiful words of Hebbel's Judith: "Even if God had placed sin between me and the deed enjoined upon me – who am I to be able to escape it?"'[136]

This passage wonderfully captures the distress with which the ethical-

Grand Inquisitor says to Christ: 'And we who, for their happiness, have taken their sins upon ourselves, we shall stand before you and say, "Judge us if you can and if you dare."' (*The Brothers Karamazov*, p. 305.)

[135] Árpád Szelpál, *Les 133 jours de Bela Kun*, Paris, 1959, p. 200.

[136] Lukács, 'Tactics and Ethics', in *Political Writings, 1919–1929*, op. cit., pp. 10–11.

pacifist, Tolstoyan socialist actually changed into a Bolshevik. Not without reason did Lukács say in his 1967 preface that this article reveals the 'inner human motivations' behind his crucial decision to join the Communist Party.[137] Several accounts confirm that between 1919 and 1920 this problematic was an almost constant obsession of Lukács and his friends in the Hungarian Communist Party (the so-called 'ethical' group). In the words of Ilona Duczynska, clearly referring to Lukács, whom she knew very well, 'a typical theoretician and perhaps the only brain behind Hungarian communism once said to me: "The highest duty for communist ethics is to accept the need to act immorally. This is the greatest sacrifice that the revolution demands of us."'[138]

Even after the defeat of the Hungarian Commune, this same problem continued to haunt Lukács and his comrades in their Viennese exile. The diary of Béla Balázs, to which we referred earlier, contains a note on the discussions that took place in this Vienna circle: 'On these Sundays the only topic we discuss is communism and the place and significance of our ethical individualism and artistic and philosophical "Platonism". . . . Individual ethics (Kierkegaard), our line of development so far, has taken us to the point where we identify ourselves with a movement that excludes individual ethics. . . . If we renounce our ethics, this will be our most "ethical" deed.'[139]

It is significant that, in his 'autobiographical testament', *Gelebtes Denken*, Lukács once more returns to the ethical implications of his joining the Hungarian Communist Party in 1918. He now stresses that 'this key decision for my world view' (*weltanschauliche Entscheidung*) brought about 'a change in the whole way of life. . . . Ethics (behaviour) no longer involved a ban on everything our own ethics condemned as sinful or abstentionist, but established a dynamic equilibrium of praxis in which sin (in its particularity) could sometimes be an integral and inescapable part of the right action, whereas ethical limits (if regarded as universally valid) could sometimes be an obstacle to the right action. Opposition: complex:

[137] Lukács, 'Preface' (1967), p. xi.
[138] I. Duczynska, 'Zum Zerfall der KPU', *Unser Weg* (ed. Paul Levi), 1 May, 1922, p. 99.
[139] Béla Balázs, 'Notes from a Diary', p. 128. N. Tertulian is one of the few critics to have noticed the importance of this theme in Lukács's early development: 'The ethical antinomies which may confront the professional revolutionary, and which appear in Lukács's thought under the influence of Dostoevsky or supporters of Russian terrorism like Savinkov, then found their solution in a revealing apology for the act of *sacrifice*.' ('L'Evolution de la pensée de Georg Lukács', *L'Homme et la Société*, no. 20, p. 26.)

universal (ethical) principles *versus* practical requirements of the right action.'[140]

We can now see why this problem of the means, tactics, or 'sins' lying on the road to the socialist goal – occupied such an important place in Lukács's thought during the period when he was moving towards communism. His tragic world view contained only the Either-Or: absolute opposition, without shade or gradation, between virtue and crime, 'good' and 'evil'; 'the mutually exclusive opposites . . . are separated from each other sharply and definitively.'[141] By contrast, his passage to revolutionary politics and concrete political practice required a completely different, *dialectical* understanding of the relationship between 'good' and 'evil'. In order to become a Bolshevik, Lukács had to move from his tragic Kantian position (rigid opposition of the Ought and the Is) to the dialectical position of Marxism, in which 'good' and 'evil' are contradictory yet united, 'good' is sometimes mediated by its opposite, and an ethically 'pure' end sometimes requires the use of 'impure' and intrinsically blameworthy means. The Tolstoyan Lukács of 1918 appears to have regarded killing a human being as the supreme 'fault'. Indeed, according to another account of those years, he was literally *tormented* by the question: 'Is it permissible to kill one's fellow-being?'[142] He could not become a Bolshevik until he had understood that the revolutionary is under a tragic compulsion to kill on the field of battle in order to achieve the final emancipation of the proletariat. Only through this crucial mediation was he able to move from the position of a tragic spectator to that of a committed actor, from abstract, metaphysical moralism to a more realistic political ethic.[143]

This passage to communism had profound philosophical implications. Lucien Goldmann has rightly observed that the Faustian dialectic of good and evil, 'the idea of a pact with the Devil as the only way which leads to

[140] *Gelebtes Denken*, p. 29.

[141] Lukács, *Soul and Form*, p. 31. In his 1917 and 1918 essays on Béla Balázs, Lukács still explained his enthusiasm for the poet by remarking that his work exhibited 'the triumph of dramatic decisions over opportunistic accommodation, the triumph of living in the spirit of "either-or" over the philosophy of "one could have it both ways"'. (Quoted in I. Mészáros, *Lukács' Concept of Dialectic*, London, 1972, pp. 125–6.)

[142] A. Szelpál, p. 199.

[143] According to Ilona Duczynska, 'the Hungarian communist theoretician' (Lukács) once said to her: 'The true communist has the conviction that Evil (*Böse*) will be transformed into its opposite, Good, through the dialectic of historical development. . . . This dialectical theory of Evil . . . spread like a secret doctrine . . . until it was finally considered as the quintessence of real communism.' (I. Duczynska, p. 99.)

God (the ruse of reason in Hegelian philosophy)' is *one of the crucial points which separate the tragic attitude of* (for example) *Pascal from dialectical thought*. Goethe, Hegel, and Marx, being thinkers within the compass of the dialectical world view, 'all admit that the "ruse of reason", the March of history, will transform individual evil into the very vehicle of progress which will bring about the good as a whole. Mephisto describes himself as the person who "always strives after evil but always achieves the good", and it is he – against his own wish, of course – who allows Faust to find God and to reach Heaven.'[144]

By December 1918, then, Lukács had passed not only from Dostoevskian Tolstoyism to Bolshevism, but also from Kantianism to Marxism, from tragic thought to dialectical thought: *from one world view to another*. This passage could not have been completed without a solution to the ethical antinomy of ends and means – hence the cardinal and almost obsessional importance Lukács attached to this solution during his first period as a communist (1919–20).

Now, the great 'qualitative leap' of 1918, at once political, moral, and philosophical in content, had in reality been prepared by the slow wartime process of gestation. Already in a number of 1915 letters to Paul Ernst, Lukács had used Savinkov's writings to discuss the ethical problem of terrorism in terms similar to those of 1919.[145] In all likelihood, this change was due to the war itself, whose huge-scale massacres gave a new moral relativity to the 'crimes' of terrorists fighting against the Tsar and the imperialist regimes responsible for the carnage of war. In 1915, however, Lukács did no more than pose the problem and try to understand it. In 1918–19, he would be forced to take a position by siding with the 'cruel political realism' of the revolutionaries.

We must lastly examine that crucial week in December 1918 when, 'from one Sunday to the next', Lukács decided to join the Communist Party.

One of the very few documents in which Lukács tries to explain the

[144] L. Goldmann, *The Hidden God*, London, 1964, pp. 174–6. Lukács himself refers to the Faustian 'dialectic of good and evil' in *Goethe and His Age*, London, 1968, pp. 197–8.

[145] 'I see in him [Savinkov] a new form of the old conflict between the first ethic (duty to institutions) and the second (commandments of the soul). The order of priorities is always uniquely dialectical in the case of politicians and revolutionaries, whose soul is turned not inward but out towards humanity. In this case, the soul has to be sacrificed in order to save the soul; basing oneself on a mystical morality, one has to become a cruel political realist and break the absolute commandment . . . "Thou shalt not kill!"' (*Paul Ernst und Georg Lukács*, p. 74.)

immediate background to his 'conversion' is the unpublished 1941 autobiography to be found in the Lukács Archives in Budapest. The section dealing with this period runs as follows: 'The seemingly effortless triumph [of the October 1918 Hungarian Revolution], the seemingly bloodless collapse of the Habsburg monarchy in Hungary, sowed in me the illusion that a non-violent road could also lead in the future to the complete victory of democracy and even socialism. (See my article in the review *Free Thought*.) The events of the first weeks of bourgeois democracy, and in particular its inability to defend itself against the reactionary forces then organizing more and more energetically, led me rapidly to correct my views. I regularly went to rallies held by the newly-founded Hungarian CP. I read its newspapers and periodical reviews, and above all I read Lenin's *State and Revolution*, which was then available in German. Influenced by these events and by my reading, I understood that the communists alone had a way out of the situation and were determined to follow their course through to the end. Acting on these considerations, I joined the HCP in December 1918.'[146] The review *Free Thought* to which Lukács refers is *Szabad-Gondolat*, and the article he wrote for it is 'Bolshevism as a Moral Problem'. As to the activities of the counter-revolution, the head of the October 1918 democratic government, Count Károlyi, admits in his memoirs that reactionary imperial army officers, under the leadership of Julius Gombos (Horthy's future prime minister, who collaborated with the Nazis), were then setting up illegal military detachments. According to Károlyi, Gombos offered him support against the socialists, but the proposal was rejected. Károlyi, in fact, complains that the strengthening of the counter-revolution between December 1918 and January 1919 smoothed the way for 'communist propaganda'.[147]

This important document confirms that the question of violence was at the heart of Lukács's preoccupations, forming the moral-ideological Rubicon he had to cross in order to become a communist. The main theme of Lenin's pamphlet, we should remember, was precisely that proletarian violence is an unavoidable necessity if one wishes to destroy the bourgeois state and open the way to the final goal: a world in which there is no longer violence between men.

Another event which may have influenced Lukács's decision was his first meeting with Béla Kún in late November or early December 1918[148]

[146] Lukács, *Autobiography*, Lukács Archivum, p. 1.
[147] Cf. Michael Károlyi, *Faith without Illusion*, London, 1956, pp. 150–1.
[148] See Lukács's letter to David Kettler in Kettler, p. 68.

– a meeting arranged by Ernö Seidler, who had come from Soviet Russia with Béla Kún and had been elected to the HCP's Central Committee in November. (Ernö was the brother of Lukács's intimate friend Irma Seidler, who had committed suicide in 1911.) The fact that Lukács became a staunch opponent of Kún after 1921 does not diminish the importance of this meeting for his December 1918 ideological crisis (indeed, according to an interview he gave in 1969, he at first had 'very good personal relations' with Kún).[149] Since both the protagonists of this historic discussion are no longer alive, we are reduced to the dangerous game of guessing its content. In our view, it may well have centred on the problem of red terror and revolutionary violence (Béla Kún having just arrived from Russia, where he took an active part in the civil war). As a former soldier in the Austrian imperial army, Kún perhaps referred to the crucial fact that the October revolutionaries, by signing the peace treaty, had saved hundreds of thousands of lives from the carnage of imperialist war.[150] He may also have used the following arguments, as he did on another occasion: 'If you want our revolution to avoid bloodshed, to cost only the minimum of sacrifice, and to be as humane as possible – although for us there is no supra-class "humanity" – then it is necessary to act in such a way that the dictatorship is exercised with the utmost firmness and vigour. . . . Unless we annihilate the counter-revolution, unless we wipe out those who rise up with guns against us, then it will be they who will murder us, massacre the proletariat, and leave us with no future at all.'[151]

Quite possibly, this first meeting with a flesh-and-blood revolutionary armed with an implacably realistic logic played a role in Lukács's decision to set aside Tolstoyan ethics and join the ranks of the proletarian revolution. This does not mean that he and his friends entirely abandoned their moral scruples. In his most naïve political article, the April 1919

[149] See the interview with András Kovács in Lukács, *L'Uomo e la rivoluzione*, p. 49. Lukács here mentions his 'private conversations' with Béla Kún and says that he joined the party about four weeks after its foundation.

[150] Lukács tackles this question in his first article as a Bolshevik, *Tactics and Ethics*, which dates from about January 1919. There he stresses that every communist should hold himself individually responsible for each human life sacrificed in the struggle. At the same time, 'all those who ally themselves to the other side, the defence of capitalism, must bear the same individual responsibility for the destruction entailed in the new imperialist revanchist wars which are surely imminent' (p. 8). This forecast would be strictly realized twenty years later. Of course, Lukács is implicitly referring to the responsibility of the bourgeoisie and the Social Democrats for the massacres of the First World War.

[151] Béla Kún, *La république hongroise des conseils, Discours et articles choisis*, Budapest, 1962, pp. 175–211.

'Party and Class', Lukács extolled the superiority of the Hungarian over the Russian revolution, on the grounds that it had ensured a proletarian seizure of power 'without bloodshed'.[132] We also know that, in May 1919, Lukács protested against the taking of bourgeois hostages. His friend Ervin Sinkó, a writer from a Tolstoyan Christian background, went even further: after the June 24 rebellion of cadets from the Budapest Military Academy, he successfully argued that they should not be executed for treason but required to attend a seminar on Marxism under his personal supervision.[153] Even Ottó Korvin, head of the Commune's political police, was not insensitive to 'ethical-communist' doubts about the conflict between ends and means, the political cause and the methods employed.[154]

These scruples are entirely to the credit of the 1919 Hungarian revolutionaries, expressing as they do the gulf between the revolutionary ethic then held by the communists and the sordid Machiavellianism of the Stalinist epoch, the 'personality cult', and the Moscow Trials. The fact that Lukács could endorse the subsequent degeneration of the communist movement suggests that he went much too far in his Faustian pact with the devil. As a great Bolshevik leader once put it: 'When we say that the end justifies the means, then for us the conclusion follows that the great revolutionary end spurns those base means and ways which set one part of the working class against other parts, or attempt to make the masses happy without their participation; or lower the faith of the masses in themselves and their organization, replacing it by worship for the "leaders".'[155]

The global significance of the transition through which Lukács passed in 1918–19 is very well expressed by a phrase in 'Tactics and Ethics' (1919): *changing the transcendent objective into an immanent one.* This obviously implies a certain change in the content of the end itself: 'The Marxist theory of class struggle, which in this respect is wholly derived from Hegel's conceptual system, changes the transcendent objective into an immanent one; the class struggle of the proletariat is at once the objective itself and its realization.'[156] This passage clearly goes beyond the neo-

[152] Lukács, 'Party and Class', in *Political Writings*, p. 29.
[153] R. Tökés, p. 153. A characteristic detail is that the seminar revolved around a reading and discussion of Dostoevsky's 'Grand Inquisitor'. Cf. J. Lengyel, *Prenn Drifting*, London, 1966, p. 205.
[154] See Lengyel's irritated account in *Visegrader Strasse*, p. 246.
[155] Trotsky, *Their Morals and Ours*, London, 1974, p. 37.
[156] Lukács, 'Tactics and Ethics', p. 5.

Kantian dualist conception of the essay 'Bolshevism as a Moral Problem', which criticized 'Marx's Hegelianism' and counterposed the transcendent socialist objective to the proletariat's class struggle in defence of its interests. We now find *in nuce* Lukács's 'qualitative leap' of November 1918–January 1919 towards both a dialectical world view and the Hungarian Communist Party.

The relationship between the communist Lukács of 1919 and the pro-Marxist Lukács can be understood only in terms of the dialectical category of *Aufhebung*: at once preservation, negation, and transcendence. It is a relationship involving both continuity and a break, in which the two stages are joined to each other by internal consistency rather than logical necessity.[157]

Before 1918, Lukács's thought bore the marks of a tragic antinomy between values and reality, culture and capitalism, human personality and economic reification. This antinomy was accompanied by a deep longing for totality, harmony, universality, and authenticity – in other words, for that unity of the subjective and the objective, essence and existence, individual and community, which supposedly existed in Greece and the Middle Ages only to have been torn apart in the separation and discord of capitalist development. In 1918–19, Lukács came to understand that the proletariat had the capacity to resolve the antinomy by destroying capitalist reality, suppressing reification, realizing authentic values, and bringing a new culture into existence. Thus, Lukács's fervent messianism of 1919 was theoretically grounded on the view that the proletariat bears a new harmony, a rediscovered totality, a universality made real, and a reconstituted unity of subject and object, ethics and praxis, individuality and collectivity. Here, tragic nostalgia for a mythical golden age of the past is transformed into passionate hope in the future – hope that the proletariat, as the messiah-class of history, will secure the world's redemption through the path of revolution.[158]

In another sense, Lukács's decision to join the Hungarian Communist

---

[157] Cf. Meszáros, p. 18; and P. Breines, 'Notes on G. Lukács's *The Old Culture and the New Culture*', *Telos* no. 5, 1970, p. 12.

[158] A. Feenberg compares the role of the Greek epic community in *The Theory of the Novel* with the role of the proletariat in *History and Class Consciousness*. The main difference is that the totality is directly given in pre-classical Greece, whereas it is a goal to be attained by the proletariat through revolutionary action. (A. Feenberg, 'The Antinomies of Socialist Thought', *Telos*, no. 10, winter 1971, pp. 98–9.) See also Raddatz, *Lukács Rowohlt*, 1972, p. 41: 'Lukács carries his ideal of classical harmony – that is, his aesthetic conceptions – into his political ideas themselves.'

Party may be seen as a form of *Pascal's wager*: a risk or 'game' involving the possibility of defeat and the hope of success, in which one's own life is staked for a trans-individual value.[159] Far from being the result of a 'scientific' analysis, Lukács's passage to communism would then depend on an ethico-political *act of faith*. Now, Ervin Sinkó's autobiographical novel about the year 1919, *The Optimists*, contains an interesting presentation of Lukács's views seen in this light. According to Sinkó, Lukács (who appears under the name Vertes) gave the following explanation for his joining the party: 'Hamlet cannot act because he merely knows and does not believe. . . . In order to think along the right lines, a correct theory is enough. But faith is needed if a man who knows good and evil is to be capable of living and fighting.'[160]

It is easy to sneer at the young Lukács's 'eschatology' and 'chiliasm', as so many commentators do today. However, Lukács's dreams become more understandable if we consider that world revolution was very widely expected during this period (1918–19), and that such expectations corresponded, in a far from arbitrary way, to an *objective possibility* of the time. Nor can it be denied that, if the revolution had spread to Europe and the rest of the world in 1919, the resulting proletarian regime would have been much closer to the historical ideal of socialism than the pale bureaucratic caricature that was progressively established on the ebbing revolutionary tide.

The continuity of Lukács's thought and the *Aufhebung* involved in his passage to communism find remarkable expression in an article of his published in June 1919, 'The Old Culture and the New Culture'. A number of writers have already pointed out the importance of this article, as well as its intimate link with Lukács's pre-Marxist writings.[161] In it we discover the conflict between culture and civilization; immanent (ethical and aesthetic) values and market values; the nostalgia for old cultures (Greece, the Renaissance) in 'organic' harmony with social being, and the hope of a new, authentic culture to be established through proletarian revolution, whose basic precept will be the idea of 'man as an end in himself' inherited from nineteenth-century classical philosophy.[162] We

[159] This interpretation of 'Pascal's wager' follows that contained in L. Goldmann, *The Hidden God*, pp. 285–9.
[160] E. Sinkó, *Optimisták*, Budapest, 1953–55, vol. 2, pp. 290–1.
[161] Cf. Kettler, pp. 85–92; and P. Breines, passim.
[162] Lukács, 'The Old Culture and the New Culture', in *Marxism and Human Liberation*, pp. 4–6, 17–19.

144

may therefore summarize Lukács's passage to communism as a 'growing-over' of aesthetics into politics, of a cultural critique of capitalism into the revolutionary praxis of the proletariat. We should also stress, however, that behind the aesthetics of the young Lukács lay an implicit ethic (sometimes actually made explicit) *which was the very bridge or transition* enabling him to pass over to Bolshevism. As he himself pointed out, this ethic was the *theoretical key* to his process of development and change. Thus, in the 1967 preface to *History and Class Consciousness*, Lukács states that his thought during this period of transition was marked by confusion, but not by chaos. There was, despite everything, a general tendency: 'My ethics tended in the direction of praxis, action and hence towards politics.'[163]

Still, the tragic, mystical ethics of the period before 1918 could be transformed into revolutionary politics only through a process of *dialectical awakening*. And in this respect, the Faustian problematic of ends and means played a key role in enabling him to make the 'qualitative leap' from a frozen dualism to the social-practical mediation (*Vermittlung*) of *Sein* and *Sollen*, Is and Ought.

[163] Lukács, 'Preface' (1967), p. xi.

III
Lukács's Leftist Period
(1919–21)

> Alyosha was . . . honest by nature, demanding truth, seeking it, believing in it, and, believing in it, demanding to serve it with all the strength of his soul, yearning for an immediate act of heroism and wishing to sacrifice everything, even life itself, for that act . . . he quite naturally said to himself: 'I want to live for immortality, and I won't accept any compromise.'
>
> DOSTOEVSKY, *The Brothers Karamazov*.

Lukács's decision to join the Hungarian Communist Party in December 1918 was only the first step in his passage from a tragic world view to revolutionary dialectical thought. The process would be gradually completed during the years from 1919 to 1921. His early communism was characterized both by its 'leftism' and by its highly contradictory, unstable, and changing character. In the 1967 preface, he speaks of himself as having then been inhabited by two souls: 'the acquisition of Marxism and political activism on the one hand'; and 'intensification of my purely idealistic ethical preoccupations on the other'.[1]

This contradiction is already apparent in the list of writers who influenced him in the 1918–19 period: Fichte, Hegel, Marx, Dostoevsky, Sorel, Luxemburg, Pannekoek, Roland-Holst, Lenin, and so on. Of course, Lukács had a dialectical relationship with these 'sources': they were *aufgehoben* in an original synthesis peculiar to himself. But Ervin Szabó probably had the decisive political influence over him at this time: 'His syndicalist writings imparted a strongly ethical and abstract-subjectivist coloration to my historico-philosophical efforts.'[2] Thus, in an article published in 1920 Lukács remarked that the attractive power of

---

[1] Lukács, 'Preface' (1967) to *History and Class Consciousness*, London, 1971, p. x.

[2] Lukács, 'Mein Weg zu Marx' (1933), in *G. Lukács, Zum 70. Geburtstag*, Berlin, 1955, p. 324.

146

revolutionary syndicalism lay in its *ethical rejection* of the old Social Democratic parties.[3] What Lukács derived from Szabó, then, was above all an intransigent revolutionary-ethical opposition to the parliamentary compromises and vulgar materialist ideology of the reformist workers' parties.

In 1919, starting from but going beyond these influences, Lukács developed his 'purely idealist' ethical-communist problematic: a fervent and sophisticated blend of utopian messianism, eschatological beliefs, revolutionary moralism, absolute ethics, and neo-Hegelian idealism. This problematic was shared by a whole group of Hungarian Communist Party intellectuals around Lukács. A rather hostile witness has described the group as follows: 'The third type of Bolshevist experimentalist was a complete contrast to the other two [orthodox Leninists and left Social Democrats]. Its representatives were primarily religious, even mystics, numbers of them were nurtured upon German idealism, and ethically set themselves a rigorous standard; but they saw no way of release from the sins and enormities of capitalism and war except through ruthless force. Their attitude was Messianic.'[4]

This ethical rigorism was precisely the bridge between Lukács's 1908–16 tragic vision of the world and his political leftism of the 1919–21 period – just as his 'left ethics' had been the bridge from aesthetics to communism. The young Lukács's tragic world view actually combined two structures of meaning: a) the 'either-or' principle of absolute opposition between the authentic and the everyday, good and evil, the ethical ideal and the existing world's 'total sinfulness' (*vollendete Sündhaftigkeit*); and b) despair, lack of perspectives, the impossibility of attaining values in the world, and the non-existence of a social force capable of 'changing life'.

When in 1917–18 Lukács discovered the revolutionary proletariat as 'a messiah-class, the redeemer of the world', this second component

<hr />

[3] Lukács, 'The Moral Mission of the Communist party', in *Political Writings 1919–1929*, London, NLB, 1972, p. 67.

[4] O. Jaszi, quoted in David Kettler, 'Culture and Revolution: Lukács in the Hungarian Revolution of 1918/19', *Telos*, no. 10, winter 1971, p. 73. The *avant-garde* intellectual Lajos Kassák gives similar testimony: 'They were philosophers, poets and aesthetes who stepped into the healthy storm of revolution. . . . Dangers abounded outside, but they gathered . . . in the Soviet House and the endless bitter debates began. There was György Lukács, the former Heidelberg philosopher, József Révai, former bank clerk and aesthete . . . Ervin Sinkó, the young Christian Tolstoyan writer. . . . Quotations from Hegel, Marx, Kierkegaard, Fichte, Weber, Jean Paul, Hölderlin and Novalis were flying in the air' (in Tökés, p. 197).

disappeared from his ideological universe. But the first remained active during a period of transition (1919–21), colouring the whole of Lukács's political thought with ethical rigorism.[5] The leftism of the young Lukács was therefore rooted in a sharp, absolute opposition between the revolutionary proletariat as bearer of authentic ethical values, and the corrupt and corrupting world of bourgeois society. No compromise was possible between the two. Such *a priori* rejection of compromises and tactical concessions is, of course, the very essence of ultra-leftist politics, and above all of its most extreme and consistent manifestations. As with the 'true life' and the 'impure life' of 'The Metaphysics of Tragedy', the new 'mutually exclusive opposites', socialism and capitalism, have to be 'separated from one another sharply and definitively'. Opportunism and political compromise are the new form of the 'anarchy of light and dark' denounced in *Soul and Form* – that ordinary life governed by the *sowohl/als-auch*, or that drab mediocrity ('neither warm nor cold') spewed out by the New Testament. The Communist Party, considered as a clear, unambiguous structure ('a crystal palace') whose goal is to storm heaven (the 'Tower of Babel'), cannot ground its practice in anything other than total rejection of the capitalist world and all its institutions. Thus, even participation in elections or parliament is already 'to accept the forms of capitalist society'.[6]

Now, we by no means underestimate the importance of Lukács's transcendence of the tragic world view in 1919, nor the profound upheaval involved in his decision to join the revolutionary workers' movement. It seems undeniable, however, that his early political positions still bore the imprint of his pre-Marxist *Weltanschauung*. From a sociological point of view, Lukács's ultra-leftism corresponded to the ethical, abstract, and radical character of intellectual anti-capitalism; while from a historical point of view, it was bound up with a period in which the socialist revolution was an *immediate* or *imminent* reality in Europe.

Lukács's leftism of the period 1919–21 may be divided into three stages – ethical ultra-leftism, political ultra-leftism and left Bolshevism – which together constitute an evolution towards Leninism.

---

[5] Cf. Peter Ludz, 'Der Begriff der "demokratischen Diktatur" in der politischen Philosophie von Georg Lukács', in Lukács, *Schriften zur Ideologie und Politik*, Neuwied, 1967, pp. xxviii–xl.

[6] Lukács, 'Party and Class' (April 1919), in *Political Writings*, p. 32.

1. Ethical Ultra-Leftism: 1919

The most radical and moralist form of leftism appeared in Lukács's first writings as a communist, dating from the period before the establishment of the Hungarian Soviet Republic (January to March 1919). The main text of this stage in Lukács's politico-philosophical development was the pamphlet *Tactics and Ethics*, which, though published only in May 1919, contains essays mostly written before March. Lukács here maintains that 'the class struggle of the proletariat is not merely a class struggle'; 'if it were, it would indeed be governed simply by *Realpolitik*'; but in reality, it is 'a means whereby humanity liberates itself, a means to the true beginning of *human* history'. Consequently, 'every compromise . . . is fatal to the achievement of this true ultimate objective . . . despite all its possible, short-term . . . advantages.'[7] In the name of supreme humanist values, of which the proletarian struggle is but the mediation, Lukács therefore rejects *a priori*, on principle, any compromise whatsoever.

He then vainly tries to marry this ethical-leftist ideology with the real practice of the Bolshevik movement to which he had just adhered. One particularly striking example is his curious 'interpretation' of the Bolshevik stand against German imperialism at Brest-Litovsk: 'Lenin and Trotsky, as truly orthodox, dialectical Marxists, paid little attention to the so-called "facts". They were blind to the "fact" that the Germans had won and had secured for themselves the military opportunity to march into Petrograd at any time, to occupy the Ukraine, and so on. Lenin and Trotsky understood the true reality, the necessary materialization of the world revolution; it was to this reality, not to the "facts", that they adjusted their actions.'[8] This essay, which is the first version of the famous section 1 of *History and Class Consciousness*, ends with a proud and fervent statement that orthodox Marxism should declare 'with the words of Fichte, one of the greatest of classical German philosophers: "So much the worse for the facts."'[9]

It is hardly necessary to point out that the Bolsheviks, far from sharing this neo-Fichtean, idealist contempt for the 'facts', actually took them very seriously indeed. The politics of Lenin and Trotsky consisted not in moralistic rejection of compromise, but in a dialectical recognition of both

---

[7] Lukács, 'Tactics and Ethics', in *Political Writings*, p. 6.
[8] Lukács, 'What is Orthodox Marxism?' in *Political Writings*, p. 26.
[9] Ibid., p. 27.

'the brute facts' (German military superiority) and the deep-rooted tendencies of historical reality (imminence of the revolution in Europe). The Brest Litovsk treaty itself issued from this dialectical viewpoint, and is the classical example of a compromise that in no way sacrifices the interests of the revolution. In his clumsy attempt to identify himself with the politics of Lenin and Trotsky, Lukács merely threw a still sharper light on the difference between his ethical idealism and the revolutionary realism of the Bolsheviks.

Unfortunately, we have only very scanty information about Lukács's activity immediately following his decision to join the Hungarian Communist Party. Between December 1918 and February 1919, together with his disciple Béla Fogarasi, he took part in a number of public discussions organized by the Communist Party at Budapest University, speaking about various ethical aspects of the revolution and the international class struggle. (One of his talks was called 'Terror as a Source of Law'.)

On 20 February 1919, the coalition government of Social Democrats and bourgeois radicals arrested Béla Kún and the other main Communist leaders. A second Central Committee was then formed clandestinely, under the leadership of Szamuely, Révai, Bettelheim, Bolgár, and Lukács. For the next month, this group of intellectuals steered the party on a distinctly ultra-leftist – or to be more precise, putschist – course, making intensive preparations to launch an insurrection in May. Béla Kún was not informed of these plans for a general strike, the seizure of power by red guards of workers, soldiers, and sailors, and the establishment of a proletarian republic.[10]

Lukács's most important article of this period is entitled '"Law and Order" and Violence' – a work characterized above all by 'complete confidence' and 'unshakeable faith' (almost religious, we might add) in 'the process of the world's salvation' (*Erlösungsprozess der Welt*), a morally-tinged conviction that 'the truth . . . will conquer over all self-deception, slander and violence'.[11]

In March 1919 the ruling coalition plunged into crisis and the Social Democrats were forced to appeal to the Communists. After negotiations between the two parties, Béla Kún and his comrades went straight from

[10] Cf. Tökés, pp. 108, 149. It is true that this tactic corresponded to a favourable situation in which the Communist Party's influence was growing and the Budapest workers were becoming more radical. Cf. R. Baudy, *La Commune de Budapest*, Paris, 1973, pp. 70, 82.

[11] Lukács, '"Law and Order" and Violence', in *Political Writings*, pp. 47, 44.

prison to assume power. The Hungarian Soviet Republic was proclaimed. The two parties resolved to fuse on the programmatic basis of the Third International. Lukács celebrated these historic events in an article full of enthusiasm and naiveté ('Party and Class'), which cheerfully announced: 'The parties have ceased to exist – now there is a unified proletariat.'[12]

During the 133 days of the Hungarian Commune, Lukács held the post of Deputy People's Commissar for Education and Culture. Although the commissar was the Social Democrat Zsigmond Kunfi, Lukács seems to have been the dominant force and to have put his own stamp on the commissariat's activities.[13] The period during which he exercised political power certainly strikes one's imagination, irresistibly recalling the dictatorship of philosophers preached by Plato. Only here something else was involved: philosophy was at the service of the dictatorship of the proletariat.

It is not the purpose of this study to present a historical account of Lukács's activity as deputy people's commissar.[14] He himself conceived of his task as a truly grandiose undertaking.[15] And even Oscar Jaszi, a declared opponent of the Hungarian Commune, recognizes that the cultural policy of Lukács and the Bolsheviks was 'the creation of a new spirit of brotherhood, mass faith and a new morality'.[16] The cultural measures taken by Lukács at the People's Commissariat add up to a remarkable combination of classicism and revolutionary boldness. On the one hand, he and his colleagues opened up the theatre to the workers, and encouraged performances for the masses of works by Lessing, Gogol, Calderón, Molière, Ibsen, Hauptmann, Shaw, and so on.[17] On the other

[12] Lukács, 'Party and Class', in *Political Writings*, p. 36. Lukács made a self-criticism of this article in 1920: 'Önkritika', *Proletár*, no. 7, August 1920, p. 13.

[13] On the reasons for Lukács's dominant role, see David Kettler, p. 77.

[14] See the excellent summary in Kettler, pp. 77–92.

[15] See the article 'Revolutionizing Souls', *Faklya*, 20 April 1919.

[16] O. Jaszi, *Magyarens Schuld, Ungarns Sühne*, Munich, 1923, p. 150. (Quoted in V. Zitta, *Georg Lukács' Marxism*, The Hague, 1964, p. 100.) In another text, Jaszi writes: 'Unquestionably there was a certain greatness . . . in the seriousness and the enthusiasm with which the proletarian dictatorship took in hand the things of the spirit.' (*Revolution and Counter-Revolution in Hungary*, London, 1924, p. 144.)

[17] See Kettler, p. 81. Typical of this 'revolutionary classicism' is Lukács's well-known 'Statement' on behalf of the People's Commissariat in April 1919 – a text that shows the lack of bureaucratic constraints over cultural life in the Hungarian Soviet Republic:

'The People's Commissariat for Education will not accord official support to the literature of any particular current or party. The cultural programme of the *communists* distinguishes only between good and bad literature, and refuses to spurn Shakespeare or Goethe on the grounds that they were not socialist writers. . . . The cultural programme of the *communists* is

hand, they launched an explosive sex-education programme which had to be stopped after arousing heated discussions. The bourgeois fury and indignation at Lukács's profoundly *subversive* cultural policy has recently found an echo in the writings of one Victor Zitta. Portraying Lukács as a 'fanatic . . . bent on destroying the established social order', Zitta argues that education became 'something perverse' under Lukács's guidance: 'Special lectures were organized in schools and literature printed and distributed to "instruct" children about free love, about the nature of sexual intercourse, about the archaic nature of the bourgeois family codes, about the outdatedness of monogamy, and the irrelevance of religion, which deprives man of all pleasure. Children urged thus to reject and deride paternal authority and the authority of the Church, and to ignore precepts of morality, easily and spontaneously turned into delinquents with whom only the police could cope. . . . This call to rebellion addressed to children was matched by a call to rebellion addressed to Hungarian women. Among the numerous curious pamphlets published under Lukács's auspices in the Commissariat of Education and Culture, one is singularly interesting, if not typical of Lukács's cultural endeavours. Written by Zsófia Dénes, it deals with "Women in the Communist Social System". . . . Zsófia claimed that in bourgeois society the mistreatment of women was shocking. . . . In her deliciously queer and hilarious pamphlet, Zsófia calls upon women the world over to unite and overthrow the chains

---

to offer the proletariat the purest and most elevated art; we shall not allow its taste to be corrupted by slogan-poetry debased to the level of a political instrument. Politics is only a means; culture is the goal.

'Whatever its origin, anything with real literary value will find the support of the People's Commissar; naturally enough, he will above all support art which grows on proletarian soil, to the extent that it really is art.

'The programme of the People's Commissariat for Education is *to put the fate of literature back into the hands of writers.*

'The Commissariat does not want an official art, and nor does it seek party dictatorship in the arts.' (*Vörös Újság*, 18 April 1919, in *Nouvelles Etudes Hongroises*, vols. 4–5, 1969–70, p. 121.)

It is important to emphasize this aspect of Lukács activity as people's commissar, since a number of conservative and anti-communist historians have denounced Lukács's 'cultural terrorism' (e.g., Eugen Szatmari, *Das Rote Ungarn, Der Bolschevismus in Budapest*, Leipzig, 1920; Victor Zitta, *George Lukács' Marxism*, The Hague, 1964). The unserious nature of these works is illustrated by one of Zitta's passages on the year 1919: 'The Communists had no poet, but Lukács contrived somehow to drag Endre Ady to a ceremony before the House of Parliament on March 1, and proclaimed the dismayed and hopelessly protesting poet, on his death-bed from a venereal disease, "The Saint" of the Commune.' (Zitta, pp. 101–2.) Ady, it so happens, had died on 19 January 1919!

imposed upon them by exploitative bourgeois-spirited males.'[18]

During the last battles of the Soviet Republic, Lukács was a political commissar attached to the Fifth Division of the Hungarian Red Army. According to some accounts, he then showed courage bordering on recklessness, using the piles of earth placed in front of the trenches in order to walk about in a glittering display of 'military leftism'. In his autobiographical novel *Prenn Drifting*, József Lengyel takes Lukács as the model for a character Nándor Benzy (an amusing and quite transparent pseudonym: Benzine = Naphta.). This is how Lengyel, who can hardly be suspected of having sympathy for Lukács, describes his behaviour at the time:

'One day, in the cold dawn, Nándor Benzy appeared in the entrenchment, accompanied by several students.

'The early morning sun threw long, sharp shadows. First thing the newcomer did, was to take a walk along the entrenchment's parapet. . . . Shoulders slightly hunched, spectacles glinting in the pristine sun, he moved deliberately slowly, challengingly, unarmed. . . .

'Sniping started from the Czech entrenchments. Bullets whined over the parapet. Soon machine-guns were heard, another, from near by, barking back in short bursts. . . .

'The students, and everybody else, stared speechless at Benzy, who was still stumbling along the edge of the high parapet. Firing increased.

'With a sudden leap the man from Isonzo, grabbing him by the feet, brought him tumbling down into the entrenchment. . . .

'Prenn, the medical student, some miners and some students were standing around Benzy, who proceeded to wipe his spectacles with an impeccably clean white handkerchief. . . . He showed no sign of fear.'

Lengyel goes on to describe a meeting called by Benzy and his followers that evening in order to explain his irrational gesture: 'We must take on ourselves full responsibility for the blood that is to be shed. And we must provide opportunity for our blood to be shed. This was the practical meaning of my behaviour this morning, so to say: *argumentatio ad*

[18] Zitta, pp. 106–7. Other writers of the counter-revolution also complain about Lukács's role in the People's Commissariat: he has variously been described as 'a fanatical dilettante' (F. Herczeg); 'a supporter of the wildest kind of Bolshevism' (A. Berzeviczy); 'the most bizarre figure in the dictatorship of the proletariat' (G. Gratz); whose thought was 'the unordered and undisciplined quintessence of a whole set of immature, unfinished, confused and obscure ideas' (E. Csaszar). (Cf. Tibor Hanak, *Lukács war anders*, Meisenheim-am-Glan, 1973, p. 38.)

hominem. For there must be no rift between theory and practice.'[19]

In another chapter, Lengyel describes a conversation between Ottó Korvin and Béla Kún in which the head of Red Security says half in jest, half in earnest: 'Benzy, as known to all, is a hero. He has been on the front for three days and legends are being told of his courage. To be quite truthful, I'd add, not without foundation in fact.' In the ensuing discussion, Korvin criticizes the mystical theories of 'Benzy' and 'Sutka', but is interrupted by Béla Kún, taking the side of Lukács: 'Let me say that Benzy does excellent work in Public Education.' Szamuely, People's Commissar for the Armed Forces, expresses some doubt on the matter, but eventually admits that 'in many ways Benzy is doing the right things'. Korvin himself, after making some ironic remarks about the metaphysical discussions among 'Benzy', 'Sutka', and their friends at the House of Soviets, recognizes with a blush and an embarrassed smile: 'I go there myself at times, because I'm interested to hear what they are saying. There are moments when I think they've got something there.'[20]

Lengyel's account confirms that the Lukács of 1919 was still closer to 'the ethic of conviction' than to 'the ethic of responsibility' – in other words, that the consistency of his practice with certain politico-moral precepts ('theory') was more important for him than its consistency with the impact of his actions on objective reality. Lengyel also brings out the reservations the leaders of the 1919 Commune had about Lukács, as well as that certain 'fascination' he exercised over them. All the same, Lukács's experience in political power made a deep impression upon him: his political thought became richer, more practical and concrete. He started to go beyond ethical ultra-leftism and reluctantly to admit that compromises were inescapable. This reluctance and this sense of necessity are both reflected in Lukács's speech of June 1919 to the Congress of Young Workers: 'In the interests of our ultimate objective we are continually forced to compromise. We cannot afford to be particular about the means

[19] Another aspect of Lukács's 'military leftism' is described by the correspondent of an American revolutionary paper who met him in the trenches of the Hungarian Red Army: 'I found Lukács and the others supremely confident of military success. They smile at the suggestion that the small governments surrounding them might defeat the Red Army. The power of the Entente to crush them they acknowledge, but they have a sure and smiling faith that the workers of the Entente countries will prevent this. All these young leaders live in confident hope of new revolutions.' (*The Liberator*, August 1919, p. 6.)

[20] J. Lengyel, *Prenn Drifting*, London, 1966, pp. 152–3, 160, 205–6. Those people who had died at the time of writing appear in the novel under their real names. According to Ilona Duczynska, both the episode in the trenches and the conversations among leaders of the Soviet Republic are 'quite authentic'. (Letter to the author, 3 April 1974.)

we adopt. . . . You, on the other hand [i.e., the youth], are not directly involved in this struggle. Your role is to wage a political struggle free from compromise and to set a moral standard for the wider struggle. For there must be a point in the struggle for the interests of the proletariat, where the flame burns absolutely clearly, where the struggle is uncompromising, completely pure, immaculate. This point is to be found in the spirit of our youth.'[21] This very fine passage reveals the difficulty and distress with which Lukács made the transition from ethical rigorism to a more realist view of political struggle.

After the defeat of the Hungarian Commune (July 1919), Lukács remained underground in Budapest for two months trying to recrganize the party: 'After the fall of the Soviet Republic, Ottó Korvin and I were charged with leading the illegal movement in Hungary. Korvin was soon arrested. I then lost contact with the organization and was forced to emigrate to Austria.'[22] The way in which Lukács speaks of this dangerous and delicate mission confirms both his personal temerity and the trust he had gained from the communist leaders of the time. It shows that the Hungarian Bolsheviks were far from considering him to be a *littérateur*, a head-in-the-clouds philosopher, or a utopian moralist. Several of his 'Sunday Circle' friends (Charles de Tolnay, Karl Mannheim) helped him to hide in Budapest; and at one point, he apparently took refuge in a monastery disguised as a monk![23]

2. Political Leftism: 1920

In 1920, having joined the majority of Hungarian communist cadres in their Vienna exile, Lukács became not only the foremost party theoretician but also its most influential *political* leader. For the first and last time in his life, he was precipitated into the top leadership of his party: in the words of Ilona Duczynska, he was then 'Number-One'.[24] In what

[21] Lukács, 'Speech at the Young Workers' Congress', in *Political Writings*, p. 40.

[22] Lukács, *Autobiographie*, German typescript, Lukács Archivum, Budapest, p. 2.

[23] Y. Bourdet, *Figures de Lukács*, Paris, 1972, p. 44. According to Bourdet, 'after nearly two months of such underground life, Lukács thought it wise to go into exile. . . . It was lucky for him that he did, since his companion in the underground struggle . . . Ottó Korvin, was soon captured and hanged'. This account, which places Lukács in rather a dishonourable light, does not square with the facts. Korvin was arrested in August 1919, and Lukács left Budapest only in September – that is, *after* his comrade had been arrested.

[24] 'Lukács's position in Vienna before factions were formed in the HCP (i.e., in autumn

direction did he steer the party during this brief period? In an article published in 1922, at a time when she was a supporter of the 'Levi current' (after the expelled German Communist Party leader, Paul Levi), Ilona Duczynska made a very harsh appraisal of this 'Lukácsian' intermezzo in Hungarian communism: 'Under the influence of Georg Lukács, theoretical arrogance and a corresponding political practice alien to the masses and the world assumed quite uncontrollable proportions within the HCP.'[25]

Lukács also exerted some international influence. In 1920 and 1921 he was a member of the editorial committee of *Kommunismus*, the Comintern organ for the countries of Southeast Europe.

Lukács's leftism took on a new complexion, becoming less moralist, more political, and in some respects closer to the positions of the communist 'ultra-left' of Pannekoek and Bordiga. During the period from 1919 to 1921, this ultra-left current developed in Western Europe around a number of circles and organizations: a) the Dutch 'Tribune' group, which, expelled from Social Democracy in 1909 as its left-wing, became Communist in 1920 (Anton Pannekoek, M. Gorter, Henriette Roland-Holst, and others);[26] b) the English feminist-oriented Workers Socialist Federation, under the leadership of Sylvia Pankhurst; c) the current around the journal *Il Soviet*, founded by militants from the left wing of the Italian Socialist Party (A. Bordiga); and d) the KAPD (Communist Workers Party of Germany), a group that had split from the Communist Party of Germany (KPD) on the leftist positions of Wolfheim, Lauffenberg, Otto Rühle, Pfemfert, Schröder, and others. Of all such groups, the KAPD was by far the largest, having a working-class base of tens of thousands.

Most of these groups had the following positions in common: rejection of any compromise with national or international bourgeois legality (the Treaty of Versailles), and of any agreement or united front with reformist or centrist parties; opposition *in principle* to working in the trade unions

---

1920) was the most important from the point of view not only of theory, but also of *organization*. I know this because when I returned from Moscow to Vienna in September 1920 on an official party mission, I was ordered to present myself at Lukács's home, 20 Laudongasse, Vienna VIII. At that time he was "Number-One".' (Letter to the author, 6 January 1974.)

[25] I. Duczynska, 'Zum Verfall der KPU', *Unser Weg*, 1922, p. 102.

[26] Back in 1918, under the influence of Ervin Szabó, Lukács had made a study of the writings of Pannekoek and Roland-Holst on the general strike.

and parliament; criticism of the political, trade-union or parliamentary 'chiefs' of the Communist movement. In some cases – for example, the 'national-Bolshevist' Wolfheim and Lauffenberg – the struggle against the Versailles Treaty brought on a drift into 'patriotic' positions. In others (e.g., Otto Rühle), the critique of 'chiefs' and centralism led to a rejection of the revolutionary party and to *rapprochement* with anarcho-syndicalism.[27]

The ultra-left phenomenon embraced numbers of intellectuals: Pannekoek was an astronomer and philosopher, Otto Rühle and Schröde were doctors of philosophy, Pfemfert a writer and Gorter a poet; several artists collaborated with Pfemfert on the journal *Die Aktion*. But for a brief period, the ultra-left also involved a significant current within the working class, above all in Germany. However, these two social components could not hold together for any length of time, and after the expulsion of Rühle and Pfemfert (1920–21) a split occurred in the KAPD in 1922. The working-class base favoured a turn towards struggles around wages, whereas the party intellectuals like Gorter founded an ephemeral Communist Workers International, a much more moralist and sectarian grouping.[28]

In the space between this 'leftist' tendency and the orientation of the Comintern majority lay a number of other currents. Willy Munzenberg had already opposed the KPD leadership in 1919 over the question of participating in elections, and he was now ideologically associated with the leadership of the Communist Youth International. A 'New Left' within the KPD, whose main representatives were Ruth Fischer, Arkadi Maslow, and Paul Fröhlich, criticized Paul Levi's orientation as 'opportunist' and succeeded in winning the party leadership early in 1921. The review *Kommunismus*,[29] under the direction of Ruth Fischer's brother, the Austrian communist Gerhart Eisler, gave its support not only to the German 'semi-leftists' (Fischer, Maslow, et al.) but also to such genuinely ultra-left figures as Pannekoek and Roland-Holst (who defended the KAPD in the columns of the review). However, the tone was set above all by the Hungarian Communists exiled in Vienna: Béla Kún, L. Rudas, E. Varga, and E. Bettelheim, as well as Lukács and his 'disciples' J. Révai and

[27] These two 'deviations' were expelled from the KAPD in 1920.
[28] Cf. Denis Authier, 'Pour l'histoire du mouvement communiste en Allemagne de 1918 à 1921', in *La gauche allemande*, Paris, 1973, p. 124.
[29] Organ of the Communist International for the countries of Southeast Europe.

B. Fogarasi.[30] The fact that such a review could appear in the name of the Communist International, including points of view in complete contradiction with the 'official line', shows how far the early Comintern was from being a monolithic and 'unanimous' body.

In his 1967 preface to *History and Class Consciousness*, Lukács describes *Kommunismus* as the mouthpiece of a 'messianic-utopian sectarianism', taking care to distinguish this from Stalinist-type bureaucratic sectarianism. At the time, he says, he was in favour of 'a total break with every institution and mode of life stemming from the bourgeois world'.[31] His thought was still characterized, although in a milder form, by that sharp opposition between the authentic and the corrupt which dominated his earlier ethical rigorism. Only now it involved not *a priori* rejection of any compromise, but aversion, hostility, and resistance to the participation of revolutionaries in bourgeois institutions.

Highly typical of this problematic is Lukács's little-known article 'Organizational Questions of the Third International'. The illegality to which the Communists are condemned is, he argues, 'the necessary result of the fact that *all their tactics* place them outside the framework of bourgeois society'. The situation in which a Communist Party can function legally (like that of the Italian party in 1920) is never a 'normal' situation but only a passing phase.[32] Lukács's strange conclusion is that, as far as the Comintern is concerned, 'the Second International forms of congresses and central bureaux are already excluded by the technical and organizational conditions of illegality'.[33] Furthermore, he conceives of the Communist International as a *moral entity* rather than a concrete structure: 'the Third International is a normative idea for the action of the proletariat'; it has an 'ought-character' (*Sollenscharakter*), a 'teleological

---

[30] In 1920, Révai published in *Kommunismus* one of his most brilliant essays: 'Das Problem der Taktik'. In his opinion, tactics are based on the opposition between subjective wish and reality, 'a tragic structure if understood conceptually'. Nevertheless, 'in history there is no tragic dimension: whereas for the human soul the necessary exactly coincides with the "unrealizable", in history the necessary is identical with the "realizable" (*Verwirklichbaren*).' (J. Révai, 'Das Problem der Taktik', *Kommunismus*, 1920, vol. 2, p. 1676.) We can see here clearly the passage from the tragic world-view to a historicist-political conception.

[31] 'Preface' (1967), pp. xiii–xiv.

[32] Lukács, 'Organisationsfragen der dritten Internationale', *Kommunismus*, nos. 8–9, March 1920, p. 239. Cf. p. 245: 'The essential illegality of their work must be reflected in their principled illegality.'

[33] Ibid., p. 246.

158

nature' (*Zielartige*), an 'ideal being' (*Ideenhafte*).[34] We need hardly point out the ethico-idealist character of this article's extreme leftism; it no doubt explains why Lukács preferred not to publish it in the 1968 Luchterhand edition of his early writings.

During the same month of March 1920, *Kommunismus* published another article by Lukács – one that was less moralist and less confused, but still based on the leftist premiss of a break between the bourgeois universe and the (proletarian) world of the authentic. This article was his well-known essay on parliamentarism. The rather curious structure of this article reveals how Lukács's thought was then torn between two positions. He accepted the principle of working in parliament, but hedged it with so many qualifications that he ended up virtually rejecting it: a) parliamentarism can only be a defensive weapon of the proletariat (the defensive is defined in a very imprecise manner: 'so long as the process of capitalist disintegration has not begun'); b) every electoral campaign tends to obscure class consciousness and entails opportunist concessions for the sake of winning votes; c) wherever soviets are possible, parliamentarism is superfluous.[35] In March 1920, then, Lukács's position lay half-way between that of the Bolsheviks and that of the 'abstentionists' (Bordiga, the KAPD, and so on).

This article probably had a certain impact. (Indeed, it is still one of the 'classics' of leftist anti-parliamentarism – witness the numerous pirate editions brought out in Germany in the last few years.) And this impact explains why Lenin's article on *Kommunismus*, which mainly attacks Béla Kún's theory of an 'active boycott' of parliament, also contains a paragraph criticizing Lukács's views.[36] At the same time Lenin issued his pamphlet '*Left-Wing' Communism: An Infantile Disorder*, attacking the general positions of the ultra-left current within the European Communist movement. According to Lukács's 1967 preface, Lenin's criticism, 'which I immediately saw to be correct, forced me to adjust my historical perspectives to everyday tactics in a subtler and more mediated manner;

[34] Ibid., p. 238.
[35] Lukács, *Werke*, vol. 2, Neuwied, 1968, pp. 97, 101, 104.
[36] 'G.L.'s article is very left-wing and very poor. Its Marxism is purely verbal; its distinction between "defensive" and "offensive" tactics is artificial; it gives no concrete analysis of precise and definite historical situations; it takes no account of what is most essential (the need to take over and to learn to take over, all fields of work and all institutions in which the bourgeoisie exerts its influence over the masses, etc.).' (Lenin, *Collected Works*, vol. 31, Moscow, 1972, p. 165.)

and in this respect, it was the beginning of a change in my views.'[37]

This change first became apparent in July 1920, when Lukács wrote the essay 'Legality and Illegality' for *Kommunismus*. Reprinted in *History and Class Consciousness*, this too was to become a classic text on the problem. (Even today it is studied by illegal revolutionary groups, in Latin America, for example – a fact that illustrates Lukács's outstanding capacity to formulate each of his positions with rigour and depth.) This article, explicitly going beyond the leftism of 1919–early 1920, constituted a first, highly important step towards the political universe of *History and Class Consciousness*. Rejecting both legal cretinism and the romanticism of illegality, Lukács now moved towards their dialectical *Aufhebung* in the indifference of inner detachment, 'the communist spirit of independence with regard to the law'. Established law, for Lukács at this time, should be regarded simply as an empirical reality, and the question of legality or illegality should become a question of purely momentary tactics, a 'wholly unprincipled solution'.[38] In discussing the ideological inconsistency of the romanticism of illegality, Lukács pointed to the case of Boris Savinkov, the literary ideologist (and active leader) of Russian terrorism who sided with the Polish Whites in 1920 against Soviet Russia. Lukács's choice of this example is indicative of his break with the problematic of 1919. For in 'Tactics and Ethics', Savinkov had been portrayed as the revolutionary hero *par excellence*. Still more significant is the way Lukács now viewed the negotiations at Brest Litovsk: 'Even though Lenin's judgment of the *actual power relationships* was notable for its supreme intelligence and *realistic toughness*, his negotiators were instructed to address themselves to the proletariat of the world and primarily to the proletariat of the Central Powers.'[39] Quite clearly, this analysis is poles apart from the naive idealism of 'Tactics and Ethics', in which Brest-Litovsk was supposed to have proven the Bolsheviks' contempt for the 'facts'.[40]

[37] 'Preface' (1967), p. xiv.
[38] Lukács, 'Legality and Illegality', in *History and Class Consciousness*, pp. 263–4.
[39] Ibid., p. 269; emphasis added.
[40] Another interesting article from this period is 'Opportunism and Putschism' (*Kommunismus*, 17 August 1920), which contrasts the two contradictory deviations with the *revolutionary realism* (a term used here by Lukács for the first time) of double-edged communist tactics: 'On the one hand, they must never lose sight of the oneness and the totality of the revolutionary process. On the other hand, they must always view this same totality from the standpoint of the "demands of the day" . . .' ('Opportunism and Putschism', in *Political Writings*, p. 75.)

3. Left Bolshevism: 1921

Although the change expressed in 'Legality and Illegality' was of great significance, it would be wrong to conclude that Lukács had fully shaken off his ultra-leftism. In the 1967 preface, he points out that his turn after June 1920 'took place within the framework of an essentially sectarian outlook. This became evident a year later when, uncritically, and in the spirit of sectarianism, I gave my approval to the March Action, even though I was critical of a number of tactical errors.'[41]

The story of the events of March 1921 is well known. In reply to a strike mobilization developing in the Mansfeld region, the Saxony government sent in the police and army to repress the strikers. Self-defence was organized locally, and the 'left-inclined' KPD leadership of Fischer, Maslow, Brandler, Thalheimer, and others decided that the moment had come for a 'generalized offensive'. On 24 March, the Communist Party launched slogans for a general strike and the arming of the workers. The strike call was followed by only a minority of workers – between 200,000 and 500,000, according to some sources. On 31 March, faced with the defeat of the 'offensive', the party called an end to these actions. The results were catastrophic: thousands of Communist militants were arrested, and thousands of strikers were sacked; the party's membership fell from 350,000 to 150,000.

In the German Communist Party a stormy debate ensued between the leadership responsible for the March Action and an opposition headed by Paul Levi, Clara Zetkin, Däumig, and others, which condemned the 'putschist adventurism' of the party's orientation. Paul Levi brought out a pamphlet lambasting the KPD leadership and was expelled from the party on account of this 'treasonable' act. The discussion then spread to the Russian Communist Party itself: Zinoviev, Bukharin, and Radek came out in support of the German leadership, whereas Lenin, Trotsky, and Kamenev were more open to the arguments of the 'Levi' opposition. The matter was finally settled at the Third Congress of the Comintern, which met in Moscow in July 1921. Lenin and Trotsky, however, were far from assured of victory: supporting the 'theory of the offensive' were not only the majority of German delegates, but also the Hungarians (led by Béla Kún, who had travelled to Germany in February and was one of those behind the March Action), the Italians, and a number of other delegations. Trotsky later recalled his discussions with Lenin about what would have

[41] 'Preface' (1967), p. xiv.

to be done if the Congress voted against them. In his speech to the delegates Trotsky stated: 'If you, the Congress, adopt a decision against us, I trust you will leave us a sufficient framework in which to defend our point of view in the future.'[42] This is another striking example of the way the Comintern functioned when real democratic debates could still take place – when, despite the undeniable bureaucratic deformations, it was still a living organism. In the end, a compromise was reached: the Congress approved a document that, while recognizing that the March Action had been 'a step forward', expressed clear reservations about the course of the German party.[43]

In his April-May articles in *Kommunismus* and *Die Internationale* (the KPD theoretical journal), Lukács unconditionally supported the 'offensive' tactics of the German Communist Party. However, his own leftism, like that of the KPD leadership, was now situated within a Bolshevik framework, no longer having anything in common with the positions of the KAPD ultra-left. An ethical element continued to underlie his views, although it was now more highly mediated than before; thus, 'the offensive' appeared as the only way to eliminate the gap between 'ought' and 'is'.

In his article 'Spontaneity of the Masses, Activity of the Party', Lukács sought to defend the March Action against its critics on the 'right' wing of the German Communist Party (Paul Levi, Clara Zetkin). He denied that the action had been a putsch, since it had not aimed at the seizure of power; rather it had been an attempt to break 'the Menshevistic lethargy of the proletariat' through an independent party initiative, an attempt 'to sever the knot of the ideological crisis of the proletariat with the sword of action'. Flying in the face of all evidence, he stated that this goal had been attained, and that through the March Action 'we have at last begun to move along the road which will lead the German proletariat to real revolutionary action'.[44]

---

[42] L. Trotsky, *The Stalin School of Falsification*, New York, 1971, p. 34. See also Pierre Broué, *Révolution en Allemagne (1917–1923)*, Paris, 1973, chapters 25–27.

[43] 'The KPD made a number of mistakes of which the most important was that it did not clearly emphasize the defensive character of the struggle, but by the call to an offensive gave the unscrupulous enemies of the proletariat, the bourgeoisie, the SPD, and the USPD, the opportunity to denounce the KPD to the proletariat as a plotter of putsches. This mistake was aggravated by a number of party comrades who represented the offensive as the primary method of struggle for the KPD in the present situation.' ('Theses on Tactics', in Jane Degras (ed.), *The Communist International: Documents*, vol. 1, London, 1971.

[44] Lukács, 'Spontaneity of the Masses, Activity of the Party', in *Political Writings*, pp. 102. 104.

Lukács's articles in *Die Internationale* found a considerable echo. Radek, one of the main supporters of 'left Bolshevism' in the Russian Communist Party leadership, had a particularly high opinion of them. Lukács later recalled a conversation he had with Radek at the start of the Third Congress (although his account should be taken with a pinch of salt): 'I did speak with Radek at some length. He told me that he thought my articles on the March Action in Germany were the best things that had been written on it, and that he approved them completely.'[45]

Even more dubious are the views expressed in Lukács's article 'Organization and Revolutionary Initiative'. Here he put the defeat of the March Action down to the Communist Party's lack of centralization and revolutionary discipline. At the same time, however, he took care to point out that the problem of discipline was not a technical-bureaucratic matter, but an ideological problem, a 'spiritual' (*geistig*), political, and moral question.[46]

Referring to these 1921 'centralist' texts of Lukács, the Italian Social Democratic (neo-Kautskyist) historian Luciano Amodio has put forward the strange hypothesis that 'Stalinism is the child of western extremism . . . a debased, historically (and otherwise) introverted form of extremism upon which a tyranny has been erected'.[47] We can understand how, from a Social Democratic point of view, Stalinism might appear as a form of 'left extremism'. But to argue that Stalinism is the legatee or continuator of western leftism (i.e., of Pannekoek, Roland-Holst, or Lukács and the *Kommunismus* journal) – this is not only to issue a blatant historical falsehood, but also to uphold a thesis that is quite absurd ideologically.

Thus, while it is true that Lukács made a gross blunder in attributing the March 1921 Communist defeat to 'lack of discipline', we should not confuse this mistake with bureaucratic fetishization of Stalinist centralism. In another text written at more or less the same time (May 1921), Lukács insisted that centralism should not become an end in itself, but should be subordinated to political criteria: for example, the autonomy of the Communist movements should not be suppressed in the name of centralism, for such autonomy may prove useful in the struggle against

---

[45] 'Lukács on his Life and Work', *New Left Review*, no. 68, July-August 1971, p. 55.

[46] Lukács, 'Organization and Revolutionary Initiative', in *Political Writings*, pp. 107, 111, 116.

[47] L. Amodio, 'Tra Lenin e Luxemburgo, comentario al periodo "estremistico" di G. Lukács 1919–1921', *Il Corpo*, vol. 2, no. 5, May 1967, p. 422. This thesis is explicitly taken up by G.E. Rusconi, for whom 'Lukács's "left voluntarism" left him open to Stalinism'. See G.E. Rusconi, *La teoria critica della società*, Bologna, 1968, p. 81.

'internal Menshevism' within the Communist parties. And in a more general organizational conclusion quite typical of his problematic, Lukács added: 'With regard to such questions, the exigencies of revolution involve great flexibility in organizational matters. Relations must be structured in such a way that the development leads in the right direction, towards centralization. Yet at the same time, these relations must be kept sufficiently flexible *so that centralism can never be used against the interests of the revolution.* In reality, every organizational form is nothing but a tool of struggle, *an element of that totality which determines and decides everything: the totality of the revolutionary process*'.[48] We need scarcely add that this manner of approaching organizational questions is *the very opposite* of bureaucratic conservatism in its Stalinist and other variants.[49]

A few weeks before the Third Congress, Lukács wrote for the last time about the March Action. Placing KAPD 'leftism' and the opportunism of the KPD right wing (Zetkin) side by side, Lukács argued that both had overlooked the main feature of the Action: its impact on the class consciousness of the proletariat. For him the principal task of the Third Congress should have been to overcome the 'internal Menshevism' that emerged as the party was moving from propaganda to action. Thus, writing on the eve of the congress, Lukács no longer voiced any criticism of the KPD line during the March offensive.[50]

Lukács was a member of the Hungarian Communist Party delegation to the Comintern Congress; and as he points out in his 1967 preface, 'Lenin's criticism had undermined my analysis of the March Action'.[51] Lukács's speech at the Third Congress, recorded in the proceedings, is interesting in a number of respects. It illustrates, once again, the climate of free discussion that reigned in the Comintern in the early twenties. Thus,

[48] Lukács, 'Vor dem dritten Kongress', *Kommunismus*, nos. 17/18, 15 May 1921, p. 594 (emphasis added). In 1920 *Kommunismus* had published an article by the Russian 'left communist' Vladimir Sorin in which he drew attention to the danger of bureaucratization in Soviet Russia.

[49] It is also interesting to note – in view of Lukács's later adherence to Stalin's doctrine of 'socialism in one country' – that he held quite different views in 1921: '. . . the new economic organization of the Soviet Republic is only provisionally limited to the territory of Russia, given the present situation of the world revolution. . . . Socialism means organized world economy.' Lukács, 'Ukrainischer Nationalbolschevismus', *Kommunismus*, nos. 5/6, 1921, p. 187.

[50] 'Vor dem dritten Kongress', pp. 585–6.

[51] 'Preface' (1967), p. xvi. In an interview given in 1970, Lukács recalled that 'Lenin's behaviour at the Third Congress made an enormous impression on me'. ('The Twin Crises', *New Left Review*, no. 60, March/April 1970, p. 42.)

Lukács spoke as an official representative of the 'Hungarian CP minority faction';[52] and although he accepted the general framework of the theses on the March Action submitted by Lenin and the Bolshevik Party, he was not in the least afraid to criticize them as 'containing sections that might give rise to centrist misinterpretations'. He himself held a nuanced position on the March Action: on the one hand, he defended it as 'a great revolutionary mass movement, an essential step forward'; on the other hand, he took issue with the 'theory of the offensive' developed in relation to it, 'those one-sided, putschist conceptions which had nothing to do with the March Action itself'. By way of example, he quoted the words of Pogony, a member of the Hungarian Communist Party leadership faction: 'The party's watchword can only be: the offensive, the offensive at any cost and by any means, in this situation holding serious chances of victory.' Clearly Lukács was taking advantage of the Third Congress rostrum to settle the internal scores of the Hungarian Communist Party. At this point in his speech, he was interrupted by an ironic shout from Radek (a supporter of the 'left' tendency): 'That's exactly what Lukács himself wrote in his *Die Internationale* article.' Lukács went on un-perturbed and did not answer this spiteful remark. To some extent, however, Radek was right: even though Lukács still did not fully agree with Lenin's draft theses, his own views had changed considerably since he had written the April-May articles.[53]

In effect, Lukács's 'leftist' period came to an end with the Third Congress; he would now move on to the further stage in his development represented by *History and Class Consciousness*. Rudolf Schlesinger and some other critics have argued that the March 1921 events are the main historical backdrop to *History and Class Consciousness*, and that this work expresses the same 'theory of the offensive' to be found in his 1921 articles for *Die Internationale*.[54] However, this view quite simply ignores the fact that the Third Congress opened the way for Lukács to overcome his final 'leftism'.

[52] This faction, which Béla Kún accused of 'bureaucratic adventurism', was led by Lander and supported by Lukács, Rudas, Lengyel, and others.

[53] Cf. *Protokoll des III Kongresses der Kommunistischen Internationale, Moskau 1921*, Hamburg, 1921, pp. 591-2.

[54] R. Schlesinger, 'The Historical Setting of Lukács's *History and Class Consciousness*', in Mészáros (ed.), *Aspects of History and Class Consciousness*, London, 1971, p. 196. A similar interpretation is suggested, less explicitly, in Giaro Daghini, 'Towards a Reconsideration of Lukács' Theory of the Offensive', *Telos*, no. 10, winter 1971, pp. 147-9.

4. The Problematic of the Reign of Freedom

The 'leftist' character of Lukács's 1919–21 writings does not imply that they are devoid of interest. Indeed, they raise a number of extremely important questions, albeit in a one-sided, moralistic, and idealist form. Their weakness, paradoxically, is also their strength: for the other side of their abstraction and detachment from reality is an uncommon grandeur of vision and breadth of perspective. This is true especially when they discuss the problematic of 'the realm of freedom', the ultimate goals of socialism, and communist morality.

Basing himself on certain positions of Marx, Lenin, and Luxemburg, Lukács maintains that the 'natural laws' of the economy determine the outbreak, but not the outcome, of crises. It depends on the proletariat itself whether it will be victorious or whether all the contending classes will go down together in a return to barbarism. The liberating revolution is not a gift of fate, but the product of a free decision of the working class. As Engels pointed out, it thereby marks the beginning of a leap into the 'realm of freedom'.[55] After the proletariat seizes power, the development of society is no longer determined by blind economic forces, but by the conscious decision of the proletariat, its moral and spiritual capacity, its powers of judgement and self-sacrifice: 'It depends on the proletariat whether or not "the pre-history of man", the power of the economy over man, of institutions and compulsion over morality, will now come to an end. It depends on the proletariat whether or not the real history of mankind is beginning: that is, the power of morality over institutions and economy.'[56]

These passionate lines were written at the height of the 1919 Hungarian Soviet Republic, in an article significantly entitled 'The Role of Morality in Communist Production', devoted to the problem of labour discipline. The same theme is taken up and elaborated in several articles that Lukács wrote during this period of 'revolutionary power'. Thus, in his June 1919 speech to the working youth, Lukács said that the ultimate aim of socialism is 'to do away with the iniquitous and disastrous autonomy of economic life, to make the economy, production, serve the needs of

[55] Lukács, 'The Role of Morality in Communist Production', in *Political Writings*, p. 50. Through its spirit of self-discipline, fraternity, solidarity, and self-sacrifice, the Communist Party is seen as the prefiguration or initial embodiment of the future reign of freedom.

[56] Ibid., p. 52.

166

mankind, humanitarian ideas and culture'.[57] In other words, the reign of
freedom entails above all the liberation of men from domination by the
economy, exchange-value, and the blind laws of the market. Socialist
organization of production will establish human motivation rather than
commercial requirements as the dominant force in the life of society.[58]

The transition from the old society to the new, from dependence and
reification to freedom and humanity, requires above all else objective
changes of an economic and political nature. However, the transition is not
only economic and institutional in character; it also involves a *moral
change*. Once power has been seized at the *institutional* level, everything
hinges on whether a truly communist *spirit* informs the soviet institutions,
or whether they become occupied by the inescapable legacy of capitalist
society (bureaucracy, corruption, and so on).[59] For Lukács, this spirit is
expressed in the 'communist Saturdays' (voluntary labour performed by
party militants) 'which are in no sense institutional measures of the Soviet
government, but moral actions of the Communist Party'.[60]

The communist man appearing in such actions is, in the last analysis, a
materialization of Lukács's old dream of a 'new man', which he first
discovered in the works of Tolstoy and Dostoevsky. This new man will
leave behind egotism and individualist isolation by advancing to genuine
solidarity and community; through his freely creative activity, he will
produce a new, harmonious culture comparable to those of ancient Greece
and the Renaissance.[61]

In our view, Lukács's problematic of the realm of freedom is of very
great interest indeed, since it touches on key questions almost entirely
absent from standard Marxist literature. Of course, it covers very sensitive
ground, littered with the dangerously attractive mines of utopianism. And
in 1919–20, Lukács obviously did not escape the danger: his thought was
tinged with messianism, inasmuch as he did not understand the realm of
freedom as a long historical process of *transition to socialism*, as a step-by-

[57] Lukács, 'Speech at the Young Workers' Congress', *Political Writings*, p. 39.

[58] Lukács, 'The Old Culture and the New Culture', in *Marxism and Human Liberation*,
New York, 1973, pp. 12–18.

[59] Lukács, 'The Moral Mission of the Communist Party', *Political Writings*, pp. 68–9. In a
footnote, Lukács refers to the article by the Russian Communist Vladimir Sorin, 'Die
Kommunistische Partei und Sowjetinstitutionen', *Kommunismus*, nos. 8/9, March 1920.
Sorin had pointed out the danger of 'conservatism . . . resulting from the material situation of
the growing army of Soviet bureaucrats' (p. 283).

[60] Lukács, *Political Writings*, p. 65.

[61] 'The Old Culture and the New Culture', pp. 10–18.

step struggle between conscious planning and blind economic laws. Instead of envisaging a prolonged process of *liberation*, of *becoming* free, Lukács articulated the idealist vision of a miraculous transformation at lightning speed. In 1921, however, Lukács began to correct this utopian immediatism, writing as follows in a *Kommunismus* article: 'The transition from "necessity" to "freedom" cannot under any circumstances be a once-for-all, sudden and unmediated act, but can only be a *process*, the revolutionary, crisis-prone character of which Engels pinpointed with the word "leap".'[62]

In the development of his thought between his 1918 decision to join the Hungarian Communist Party and the end of his 'leftist' period in 1921, Lukács appears as an idealist intellectual suddenly plunged into the revolutionary torrent, whose moralist fever is gradually cooled by the icy current of real political struggle. His leftism is but the political continuation of his earlier ethical rigorism, the legitimate offspring of his tragic view of the world. The road from 1918 to the Third Congress of the Comintern in 1921 is therefore a progressive coming-down-to-earth after the mystical flights in search of a moral Absolute. At no point, however, did he abandon what is essential: a revolutionary world-historical outlook and a concern with ultimate human goals.

[62] Lukács, 'Spontaneity of the Masses, Activity of the Party', *Political Writings*, p. 99.

IV
'History and Class Consciousness' (1923)

> Materialist dialectic is a revolutionary
> dialectic. . . . The links between
> theory . . . and the revolution are not
> just arbitrary, nor are they particularly
> tortuous or open to misunderstanding.
> On the contrary . . . theory is essen-
> tially the intellectual expression of the
> revolutionary process itself.[1]

We need hardly stress the truly *historic* importance of *History and Class Consciousness*, regarded by many as the greatest twentieth-century work of Marxist philosophy.[2] It is not possible here, given the limitations of space and subject-matter, to study Lukács's *magnum opus* systematically. We shall therefore simply draw out its main politico-philosophical theme, and try to locate it within the evolution of Lukács's thought.

The impact of *History and Class Consciousness* should be measured first of all in terms of its influence on such diverse writers as Révai, Bloch, Mannheim, Horkheimer, Adorno, Benjamin, Sartre, Merleau-Ponty, Lefebvre, Goldmann, Marcuse, Jakubowsky, Adam Schaff, and Karel Košik. But the controversy surrounding the book is also of major importance in gauging its overall impact. A host of opponents have directed critical thunderbolts against this work: 1) Kautsky, who attacked it in the name of the old Social Democratic 'Marxist' orthodoxy; 2) Comintern leaders like Bukharin and especially Zinoviev, who charged from the rostrum of the Fifth Congress that Lukács and Korsch formed

---

[1] Lukács, *History and Class Consciousness*, London 1971, pp. 2–3; cited hereafter as *HCC*.
[2] In our view, József Révai's 1925 evaluation remains true more than fifty years later: 'Lukács's book is far deeper than all those works that have previously dealt with the philosophical principles of Marxism as a special problem: it has a far richer content and greater capacity to verify general and, in appearance, "purely" philosophical propositions within concrete individual problems.' (J. Revai, 'Lukács' *Geschichte und Klassenbewusstsein*', in *Achiv für die Geschichte des Sozialismus und der Arbeiterbewegung*, vol. 11, 1925, p. 227.)

'an extreme left tendency growing into theoretical revisionism';[3] 3) Hungarian Communist Party leaders Rudas and Béla Kún; 4) *Pravda* itself, in a famous article of 25 July 1924; 5) KPD ideologues like Hermann Duncker, who denounced it as idealist;[4] 6) A. Deborin and other 'official' Soviet philosophers.

Without going into detail, we may note that the two best-known critiques, those by Rudas and Deborin, stood squarely on the ground of pre-dialectical materialism. Deborin used copious quotations from Plekhanov to show that Marxism stems from the very 'naturalist materialism' criticized by Lukács; whereas Rudas compared the Marxist laws of society with Darwin's law of evolution, and drew the surprising conclusion that Marxism is 'a pure science of nature'.[5]

The discussion continues to this day, fuelled by the various translations and reprints published in the sixties. Althusser, in particular, sparked it off again by hurling the old 1923 anathema of 'theoretical leftism'. Although the various polemics are otherwise clearly different in content, most of them draw on a single reservoir of vulgar materialism, positivist scientism, and dogmatic orthodoxy; they may be said to constitute a proof *a contrario* of the dialectical character of Lukács's work. In any case, the continuity of interest and debate confirms the extraordinary richness of *History and Class Consciousness*.

For ten years Lukács kept silent in the face of this philosophical barrage; it was an enigmatic silence which requires explanation, although we ourselves do not know of an adequate one. Finally, in 1933, Lukács began a long series of self-criticisms which, together forming a near-total renunciation of the book, were to a large extent sincere and authentic. (In this respect, they differ from those he wrote on, for example, the Blum Theses.) The harshest, most astonishing, and most unjust of these self-criticisms was the one delivered in 1934 to the philosophical section of the Soviet Academy of Sciences. Lukács had no hesitation in declaring that 'the front of idealism is the front of the fascist counter-revolution and its

---

[3] *Fifth Congress of the Communist International*, London, 1924, p. 17.

[4] *Die Rote Fahne*, 27 May 1923. For a survey of these polemics, see M. Watnick, 'Relativism and Class Consciousness: Georg Lukács', in L. Labedz (ed.), *Revisionism*, London, 1962, pp. 145–6; and P. Breines, 'Praxis and its Theorists: The Impact of Lukács and Korsch in the 1920s', *Telos*, no. 11, spring 1972.

[5] Cf. A. Deborin, 'Lukács und seine Kritik des Marxismus', *Arbeiterliteratur*, no. 9, 1924, reprinted in *Geschichte und Klassenbewusstsein Heute*, Amsterdam, 1971, pp. 101–3; and L. Rudas, 'Die Klassenbewusstseinstheorie von Lukács', *Arbeiterliteratur*, nos. 10–11, 1924, ibid., p. 117.

social-fascist accomplices. Any concession to idealism, even on a quite minor question, is a danger to the proletarian revolution. I have therefore come to grasp not only the theoretical falsity but also the practical danger of the book I wrote twelve years ago; and I have ceaselessly fought in the German mass movement against this or any other idealist tendency.'[6] This text should be understood (but not excused) in the light of the ideological shock the victory of German Nazism represented for Lukács. In a highly dubious line of argument, which he would develop at length in *The Destruction of Reason* (1954), Lukács consigned to the philosophical hell-fire of proto-fascism the entire German idealist-romantic tradition from which he himself had emerged.[7]

In the 1967 preface, the last balance-sheet he wrote before his death, Lukács gave a much fairer assessment of *History and Class Consciousness*. After pointing out that it was 'the most radical attempt to restore the revolutionary nature of Marx's theories by renovating and extending Hegel's dialectic and method', Lukács further recognized that it had played an important role in the struggle against Bernstein and Kautsky's revisionism and scientism and that it had won a large number of young intellectuals to the communist movement. Nevertheless, in 1967 he still thought that the work deserved criticism for its 'overriding subjectivism' and 'messianic utopianism'.[8] Unfortunately, for reasons which should one day be clarified, much of the discussion about *History and Class Consciousness* has been side-tracked into a byzantine, metaphysical dispute over the dialectics of nature. Those most responsible have forgotten that Lukács merely wished to underline the obvious difference between *two types of dialectic*: 'the merely objective dialectics of nature' and the 'dialectics of society' in which 'the subject is included in the reciprocal

[6] Lukács, 'Die Bedeutung von *Materialismus und Empiriokritizismus* für die Bolschevisierung der Kommunistischen Parteien – Selbstkritik zu *Geschichte und Klassenbewusstsein*', *Pod Znamenem Marksizma*, no. 4, 1934, in *Geschichte und Klassenbewusstsein Heute*, p. 261. In this text Lukács lumps together as idealist (and therefore close to 'the fascist ideological front') various 'leftist' currents (Pannekoek, Gorter, Korsch), 'counter-revolutionary Trotskyism', left Social Democracy, and 'social-fascism' (Social Democracy).

[7] Cf. ibid., p. 256. In one breathtakingly short paragraph, Lukács passes from the idealism of Rickert and Dilthey to the official fascist philosophers Rosenberg and Beimler. This interpretation of recent philosophy in Germany was developed at length in a work of 1933–34 which combines the best and the worst in Lukács's thought of the time: *Zur Entstehungsgeschichte der faschistischen Philosophie in Deutschland*, Lukács Archivum, Budapest. To a certain extent, this unpublished manuscript may be regarded as a first draft of *Die Zerstörung der Vernunft* (1954).

[8] 'Preface' (1967) to *HCC*, pp. xviii, xxi, xxii, xxv.

relation in which theory and practice become dialectical with reference to each other'.[9] But even more important, they have forgotten that *History and Class Consciousness* is, perhaps above all, a *political* work, the central problem of which is *the proletarian revolution against capitalist reification*. In our view, it is precisely this aspect that accounts for the interest and *topicality* of the book – however questionable may be its all-too-Hegelian paradoxes, one-sided arguments, and meanderings.

If seen in this way as a revolutionary politico-philosophical work, *History and Class Consciousness* remains a masterpiece without equal in Marxist theory. For it achieves a quite remarkable dialectical synthesis (*Aufhebung*) of Ought and Is, values and reality, ethics and politics, underlying tendencies and empirical facts, final goal and immediate circumstances, will and material conditions, future and present, subject and object. This coherent, harmonious unity, which is not just a 'happy mean' but a *transcendence* of opposites, forms the structure of meaning of the whole book, establishing its superiority over Lukács's earlier and subsequent writings.

In *The Theory of the Novel*, with its tragic view of the world, Lukács had spoken of 'the unbridgeable chasm between the reality that is and the ideal that should be'.[10] But in *History and Class Consciousness*, this inflexible opposition (inspired by ethical rigorism) is finally abolished – or *aufgehoben* – in the new conception of *revolutionary realism*. In this sense, it marks the highest point in his development, the final stage of his ideological path from the tragic world view to Leninism. József Révai, one of the very few writers to have grasped the kernel of the work, wrote as follows in his 1925 review: '[Lukács] places the future on the ground of revolutionary dialectics, not as a teleological finality or an "ought" of natural law, but as an active reality informing and determining the present. He thereby goes beyond mere contemplation of history, creating the objective possibility that the object may be transformed through the emergence of class consciousness in the proletariat.'[11]

This *revolutionary realism* – the central shaft around which *History and Class Consciousness* revolves – should not be understood as lying 'half-way' between 'leftist' utopianism and 'right' opportunism. Although it tries to go beyond both these tendencies, it is humanly, morally, and *politically*

[9] *HCC*, p. 207.

[10] Lukács, *The Theory of the Novel*, London, 1971, p. 78.

[11] Révai, p. 233. The fact that in 1949 Révai became a mediocre Stalinist censor of Lukács in no way detracts from the value of his early writings.

much closer to Pannekoek than to Kautsky, to Ernst Bloch than to Friedrich Ebert (to mention but a few 'exemplary' figures). So much is implicit in *History and Class Consciousness*, but it emerges quite clearly, although indirectly, from a short article by Lukács published in 1922 in the KPD daily, *Die Rote Fahne*. He is here discussing literary matters apparently a thousand miles removed from revolutionary politics: the works of Lessing and Goethe. He sees in Goethe's *Tasso* 'a depressing and woefully complete capitulation by the bourgeois intelligentsia before the powers of the feudal-absolutist epoch'; whereas Lessing, in his *Nathan*, turns his back on German wretchedness and counterposes to 'that merely empirical, merely existing (*daseiende*) reality' 'the more authentic, even if more utopian, reality of the true man ... the Kingdom of Humanity (*Menschlichkeit*)'. '*Tasso*', continues Lukács, 'involves reconciliation (*Versöhnung*) with reality. Goethe ... takes the trifling poverty (*Erbärmlichkeit*) of his age and dresses it up in the moderately passionate wonder of his verse.' Lukács concludes this immoderately heated essay by explicitly proclaiming the superiority of even utopian revolt over 'reconciliation': 'We should see as an ever-recurring tragedy for Germany the fact that every ideological or politico-social option has so far been a victory for the spirit of compromise and philistinism: for Luther over Münzer, Goethe over Lessing, Bismarck over 1848.'[12] And, he might have added, for Ebert over Luxemburg.

It is hardly necessary to spell out the political implications of this position, which precisely locates Lukács's *Aufhebung* in relation to the two tendencies that it negates/preserves/transcends. Perhaps it would be of interest to compare these views on Goethe with those of the 'later Lukács'. Thus, in a 1940 essay he wrote: 'The point here is to show that Goethe and Hegel's progressivism is closely bound up with such "reconciliation", that this source of Marxism would not otherwise have appeared in the given historical circumstances.'[13] In the next chapter we shall return to the philosophico-political implications of this change – or rather reversal – in Lukács's orientation.

A number of critics, occasionally even the older Lukács himself, have presented *History and Class Consciousness* as the 'condensation' or 'continuation' of his 1919–21 writings. And the fact that its various

---

[12] Lukács, 'Nathan und Tasso', *Die Rote Fahne*, 13 August 1922. As far as I am aware, this 'forgotten' work is not mentioned in any bibliography.

[13] Lukács, *Ecrits de Moscou*, Paris, 1974, p. 188.

chapters are dated between 1919 and 1922 tends to reinforce this illusion. In our view, however, the work opens a *new* theoretical universe, one that abolishes/transcends the utopian tendencies of 1919-20. Not only were three chapters written in 1922 ('Reification and the Consciousness of the Proletariat'; 'Critical Observations on Rosa Luxemburg's "Critique of the Russian Revolution"'; 'Towards a Methodology of the Problem of Organization'), but most of those dated 1919 or 1920 were *thoroughly* reworked in 1922. In the 1967 preface, Lukács writes that only two of the pre-1922 articles were left unchanged: 'Legality and Illegality' (1920) and 'The Marxism of Rosa Luxemburg' (1921). The former, as we have already pointed out, marked the beginning of Lukács's break with leftism and, to some extent therefore, prefigured the positions of *History and Class Consciousness*; the latter introduced a discordant note precisely insofar as it uncritically accepted Luxemburg's theory of the party ('Rosa Luxemburg perceived at a very early stage that the organization is much more likely to be the effect than the cause of the revolutionary process'[14] – a one-sided position explicitly criticized in the final two chapters of the book. This being said, it is true that the inclusion of these articles points to a certain continuity between the periods 1922–23 and 1920–21. But the break with the 1919–20 period thereby appears all the more profound. The real 'watershed' came in the middle of 1920, about the time Lenin's pamphlet *'Left-Wing' Communism, An Infantile Disorder* was published (July).

In his 1922 preface to *History and Class Consciousness*, Lukács said that he had 'partially reworked' some of the articles, not wishing 'radically to recast them'. Yet at least two major essays had indeed been *radically* altered – a fact which, rather surprisingly, has not been pointed out in any of the numerous studies of Lukács we have consulted. In fact, it will prove highly instructive to compare the original with the 1922 version. For we shall then be able to grasp the *specificity* or *novelty* of the book in comparison to Lukács's previous writings.

The most heavily revised essay, *What is Orthodox Marxism?*, was virtually *rewritten* from beginning to end. The date 'March 1919' which appears at the end of the 1922 chapter is therefore rather misleading. As we have seen, the earlier version bore all the marks of the most stringent and naive ethical leftism: it rigidly and sharply counterposed 'the true, underlying reality' to 'the facts'; and it criticized the vulgar Marxists who, 'judging their actions only by the "facts"', change 'their tactics after every

[14] *HCC*, p. 41.

victory or every defeat'.[15] For the Lukács of 1919, it would seem, genuinely revolutionary politics require that *the same tactics* always be employed, with sovereign disdain for such minor 'facts' as victory and defeat! Lukács's Fichtean leftism here reached its apogee of radicalism and lack of realism.

In the 1922 version, these passages are completely replaced with the following argument: 'Every attempt to rescue the "ultimate goal" or the "essence" of the proletariat from every impure contact with (capitalist) existence leads ultimately to the same remoteness from reality, from "practical, critical activity", and to the same relapse into the utopian dualism of subject and object, of theory and practice to which Revisionism has succumbed.'[16] Lukács adds in a footnote, leaving no doubt about the political significance of his change: 'Cf. . . . Lenin's book, *"Left-Wing" Communism, An Infantile Disorder.*'[17] In reality, Lukács was here criticizing, or rather self-criticizing, the inner core of his leftism of 1919: ethical rigorism, that dualism whereby 'you create a gulf between the subject of an action and the milieu of the "facts" in which the action unfolds, so that they stand opposed to one another as harsh, irreconcilable principles'.[18]

Lukács's new perspective, expressed in these added pages of 1922, went beyond both vulgar empiricism and idealist voluntarism: 'It then becomes impossible to impose the subjective will, wish or decision upon the facts or to discover in them any directive for action.' Revolutionary action is correct which is grounded upon a dialectical knowledge of reality, which discovers the tendencies pointing towards the ultimate objective not in isolated facts, but in the dynamic totality. However, 'this ultimate goal is not an abstract ideal opposed to the process, but an aspect of truth and reality. It is the concrete meaning of each stage reached and an integral part of the concrete moment'.[19]

This 'ideological shift' from his 1919 positions was clearly greater than that involved in his revision of the 1920 essay 'Class Consciousness'. In the latter case, Lukács did not eliminate any of the earlier material, although he did make considerable additions. Taken as a whole, these new sections

[15] Lukács, 'What is Orthodox Marxism?' in *Political Writings, 1919–1929*, London, NLB, 1972, p. 26.
[16] *HCC*, p. 22.
[17] *HCC*, p. 26.
[18] *HCC*, p. 23.
[19] *HCC*, p. 23.

sketch out a theory of class consciousness that goes beyond his former counterposition of opportunism and utopianism.

Opportunism, Lukács argued, is aware only of the 'given situation', the immediate interests of the proletariat, the partial objectives of struggle; it sees class consciousness as the workers' psychologically observable and inevitably passive spectator-consciousness, for which the movement of things is subject to independent laws. Opportunism therefore leads to a vulgar-empiricist practice, a petty-minded and blinkered *Realpolitik*. Utopianism, by contrast, is concerned only with the 'desirable' state of affairs, the abstractly conceived final goal, and looks with an arrogant eye on the momentary interests and petty struggles of the class. In this optic, consciousness is a moral 'ought', or a power capable of moulding the course of things to its own will; it moves from the beyond towards society in order to make it leave the false track hitherto pursued.

Revolutionary dialectics is the *Aufhebung* of these opposite poles, both characterized by a dualist counterposition between the movement of society and the consciousness of that movement. The dialectical conception starts out from the given situation and the immediate interests in order to change and surpass them on the road towards the final goal. Here class consciousness appears as an *objective possibility*, the rational expression of the proletariat's historical interests; it is not a 'beyond' but a product of the historical development and real praxis of the class.[20] It is precisely by defining class consciousness as an objective possibility that Lukács escapes both empiricism and idealist subjectivism.

The concept of 'possible' or 'ascribed' (*zugerechnet*) class consciousness[21] is a favourite target for every critic of *History and Class Consciousness*. One of the most common reproaches, heard from writers as

[20] *HCC*, pp. 73–9. Many commentators have attributed Lukács's use of the concept 'objective possibility' to the influence of Max Weber. While they might be right, we should not forget that this is a category of dialectics – one appearing both in Hegel (who opposes *real possibility* to Kant's formal possibility) and in some of Marx's early writings.

[21] Lukács defines *zugerechnetes Bewusstsein* as 'the sense, become conscious, of the historical role of the class', or 'the thoughts . . . which men *would have* in a particular situation if they were *able* to assess both it and the interests arising from it in their impact on the immediate action and on the whole structure of society' (*HCC*, pp. 73, 51). He further emphasizes that such class consciousness is 'neither the sum nor the average of what is thought . . . by the single individuals who make up the class' (p. 51). [We have here translated the term '*zugerechnetes Bewusstsein*' or '*conscience adjugée*' by 'ascribed consciousness' – a version more frequently employed in English-language studies of Lukács than the 'imputed consciousness' preferred by the translator of *History and Class Consciousness*. Translator's note.]

different as László Rudas and the structuralist Marxists, is that Lukács
was here guilty of *idealism*. Thus, according to Gareth Stedman Jones, this
concept is 'idealist' because, for Lukács, 'the emergence of true proletarian
class consciousness is itself tantamount to the overthrow of the bourgeoisie'.[22] As 'proof', Stedman Jones quotes the following sentence from
Lukács: 'To become conscious is synonymous with the possibility of
taking over society.'[23] But in reality, this sentence means precisely that
consciousness is not 'tantamount' to the seizure of power, but its condition
of *possibility*. The same writer also maintains that Lukács's idealism led
him to ignore the existence of an 'uneven and impure' consciousness:
'Short of full "ascribed" consciousness, [the proletariat] is condemned to
no consciousness at all.'[24] However, we cordially invite Lukács's
Althusserian critic to open *History and Class Consciousness* at the page
where Lukács discusses the *gradations* of class consciousness, which 'are
not merely national and "social" stages . . . but also gradations within the
class consciousness of workers in the same strata. . . . They indicate
degrees of distance between the psychological class consciousness and the
adequate understanding of the total situation'.[25]

More generally, critics of the concept of *zugerechnetes Bewusstsein* may
be divided into two symetrically opposed categories; they level strictly
contradictory accusations against Lukács.

1. The 'empiricist' critics, normally Social Democratic in complexion,
who follow the classical argument first used by Siegfried Marck in his 1924
article in *Die Gesellschaft* (the theoretical journal of the SPD). Marck
maintained that Lukács, in distinguishing between true proletarian class
consciousness and the empirical-psychological consciousness of the class,
was really seeking to provide a theoretical foundation for communist
'vanguard' dictatorship.[26] Rather more subtle is Adam Schaff's variant,
according to which Lukács *underestimated* the role of the existing,
empirical-psychological consciousness of the working class, 'the real views

---

[22] G. Stedman Jones, 'The Marxism of the Early Lukács', in *Western Marxism: A Critical Reader*, London, NLB, 1978, p. 44. (In spite of everything, this is an extremely interesting article.)

[23] Ibid.,

[24] Ibid., p. 42.

[25] *HCC*, pp. 78–9.

[26] Siegfried Marck, 'Neukritizistische und Neuhegelsche Auffassung der marxistischen Dialektik', *Die Gesellschaft*, vol. 1, 1924, in *Geschichte und Klassenbewusstsein Heute*, p. 56. Marck concludes his review of *History and Class Consciousness* with an apologia for the 'critical, anti-dogmatic theory and practice' of the Second International.

and attitudes of the working masses'. As a result, he allegedly fell into 'vanguardist sectarianism' and 'subjectivist voluntarism', attaching importance only to Marxist ideology, revolutionary theory, and the consciousness that *ought to exist*.[27]

We find the same story, tinged with empiricist triumphalism, in the comment of the sociologist Tom Bottomore: 'We have long since passed out of the era in which the real consciousness of social groups, expressed in their beliefs and actions, could be discussed as mere "psychological", "false" consciousness, and be contrasted with the "rational consciousness" enshrined in the ideology of a Communist Party.'[28]

2. For the 'theoreticist' critics of 'orthodox CP' bent – of whom Louis Althusser is the most striking example – the young Lukács and Korsch made the mistake of putting Marx's doctrine 'into a directly *expressive* relationship with the working class'. In Althusser's view, this was 'an idealist and voluntarist interpretation of Marxism as the exclusive product and expression of proletarian practice. . . . Kautsky's and Lenin's thesis that Marxist theory is produced by a specific theoretical practice, *outside* the proletariat, and that Marxist theory must be "imported" into the proletariat, was absolutely rejected – and all the themes of spontaneism rushed into Marxism through this open breach.'[29]

To sum up, Lukács has been accused now of vanguardism, now of spontaneism: for some he underestimated the spontaneous empirical consciousness of the class; for others he ignored the specific relationship between Marxist theory and proletarian practice! When all is said and done, these antipodean critiques may be said to cancel each other out.

In *History and Class Consciousness*, 'ascribed' class consciousness is not at all the 'direct' or 'exclusive' expression of the empirical practice of the proletariat; nor is it an ideology 'imported from outside' into the workers' movement (Kautsky's old thesis which Lenin supported in *What is to be Done?* but discarded in 1905). Neither of these one-sided, mechanical conceptions is capable of defining the complex relationship between 'psychological' consciousness and 'possible' consciousness. As for Lukács,

[27] A. Schaff, 'The Consciousness of a Class and Class Consciousness', *The Philosophical Forum*, vol. 3, nos. 3–4, spring-summer 1972, pp. 344, 354–6.

[28] T. Bottomore, 'Class Structure and Social Consciousness', in I. Mészáros (ed.), *Aspects of History and Class Consciousness*, London, 1971, p. 62. In an incisive critique, Dick Howard rightly characterizes this position as 'liberal empiricism': *Telos*, no. 11, p. 155.

[29] L. Althusser, *Reading Capital*, London, NLB, 1977, pp. 140–1.

he conceived of the relationship not as a rigid metaphysical duality but as a historical *process* through which the class, assisted by its vanguard, rises to *zugerechnetes Bewusstsein* through its own experience of struggle.

Lucien Goldmann is one of the very few writers to have not only understood but also employed and creatively developed the concept of 'possible consciousness'. With reference to the social sciences, he has underlined the importance of distinguishing between two sets of elements in the consciousness of a class: those bound up with a particular conjuncture and those which correspond to the *very nature* of a social class (the 'maximum possible consciousness'). Used in this way, Lukács's concept becomes a tool for criticizing and surpassing bourgeois empirical sociology, with its superficial descriptive 'investigations'.[30]

Let us now turn very briefly to the third revised article, 'The Changing Function of Historical Materialism'. In the original version – a June 1919 speech delivered at the opening of the Research Institute for the Development of Historical Materialism – the text contains several expressions of glaringly utopian, neo-Hegelian idealism: 'The transition to socialism means . . . that ideological factors, human ideas prevail in the work of construction, and that economic life will become a simple function of the idea. . . . The dictatorship of the proletariat rests on a transition period in which the objective spirit – society, the state, the judicial system . . . the armed organization of the proletariat, etc. – still holds undivided sway. . . . However, the objective spirit is no longer a function of economy, but a function of the absolute spirit, of human ideas.'[31] But even though this essay was reworked, Lukács recognized in his 1922 preface that it introduces an 'outmoded' element into the work: an echo of 'those exaggeratedly sanguine hopes that many of us cherished concerning the duration and tempo of the revolution'.[32] Lukács was probably referring to

[30] Cf. Lucien Goldmann, *Cultural Creation in Modern Society*, Oxford, 1977, p. 39: 'To be scientific, sociologists must ask not merely what some member of a social group thinks today about refrigerators and gadgets or about marriage and sexual life, but what is the field of consciousness within which some group can vary its ways of thinking about all these problems without modifying its structure. In short, the inquiry concerns the horizons which a group's consciousness of reality cannot overcome without a profound social transformation.'

[31] Lukács, 'A történelmi materializmus funkcioltozasa', *Internationale* (Budapest 1919), nos. 8–9, p. 17, quoted in Jörg Kammler, *Politische Theorie von Georg Lukács*, Neuwied, 1974, p. 89. Of course, these and similar passages from 1919 disappear in *History and Class Consciousness*, which contains added quotations from Lenin's *'Left-Wing' Communism* (1920) and other works.

[32] *HCC*, p. xli.

those passages which deal with a typical theme of all his 1919 writings: 'the economy . . . is to be the servant of a consciously directed society; it is to lose its self-contained autonomy (*Eigengesetzlichkeit*) . . . ; as an economy it is to be annulled (*aufgehoben*).'[33] It is quite natural that Lukács, in the NEP era of 1922, should have considered this perspective to be 'exaggeratedly sanguine'.

The chapter 'Reification and the Consciousness of the Proletariat', composed in the year 1922, takes up and develops the problematic outlined in these three 'revised and corrected' articles. Lukács criticizes the rigid, inseparable duality between 'is' and 'ought', between acceptance of the existing social structure and the abstract, purely subjective will to change it. However, he also shows that fetishism and utopianism may become complementary: in Tolstoy's work, for example, empirical reality is left to its fact-like existence according to the principle 'resist not evil', while at the same time man is conceived in utopian fashion as a 'saint' having inwardly to transcend an unchangeable external reality.[34] Lukács's critique of Tolstoy is a highly indicative 'ideological symptom' of the road he had travelled since his 'Tolstoyan ethical socialism' of 1918.

The dialectical solution to these antinomies lies in the standpoint of the revolutionary proletariat. Only the proletariat has the capacity 'to see the immanent meaning of history . . . to raise its positive side to consciousness and to put it into practice'. History objectively tends towards the collapse of capitalism, even though it is not able to bring this about through its dynamic. Reality will be transformed only by the action of the conscious proletariat, the 'identical subject-object of history'.[35]

In this chapter, Lukács develops his famous theory of reification: of man's subjection to a world of things (commodities) governed by 'natural' laws independent of the human will. Since this aspect of his work is sufficiently well known,[36] we shall merely point out that it revives, within a new theoretical framework, the pre-war concern of Lukács and the German sociologists (Tönnies, Simmel) with the processes of quantification, hypostatization, and depersonalization characteristic of modern society. In 1923, however, Lukács analysed reification in strictly Marxist terms as an aspect of the capitalist mode of production rather than as a

[33] *HCC*, p. 251. Cf. the German text in *Werke*, vol. 2, p. 429.

[34] *HCC*, pp. 160, 161, 191.

[35] *HCC*, p. 197.

[36] Cf. L. Goldmann, 'La réification', in *Recherches dialectiques*, Paris, 1959; and A. Arato, 'Lukács' Theory of Reification', *Telos*, no. 11, 1972.

'tragic destiny' of culture. Above all, he saw in the proletariat a class that tends, by its very condition, to rebel against reification and to reject its own commodity-like status.

Now, various Marxist writers, particularly in Italy (Bedeschi, Colletti, Pietro Rossi), maintain that the chapter on reification belongs with the romantic critique of science and industry. According to Colletti, the most interesting and sophisticated of Lukács's critics, 'the focal theme of *History and Class Consciousness* is in the identification of capitalist reification with the "reification" engendered by science.'[37] But in point of fact, Lukács never wrote that reification is 'engendered by science'; he merely argued that, by virtue of reification, *human relations* take the form of laws of nature, *the form of objectivity* of natural-scientific concepts.[38] Colletti admits that Lukács was not simply a neo-romantic: for he explicitly dissociated himself from the reactionary struggle waged against reification by German romanticism, the historical school of jurisprudence, Carlyle, Ruskin, and so on; and he distinguished between the application of a natural-scientific epistemological ideal to nature itself (which can only 'further the progress of science') and its application to the evolution of society (which is 'an ideological weapon of the bourgeoisie').[39] Nonetheless, Colletti detects elements of a romantic critique in *History and Class Consciousness*: for example, where Lukács brackets together 'the growth of mechanization, dehumanization and reification', or where he refers approvingly to Tönnies, Simmel, or Rickert. For Lukács, he argues, the problem is not the use to which capitalists put machines, but the very use of machinery itself.[40]

These arguments are unacceptable for two reasons. First, Lukács was not a continuator of Tönnies or Simmel: he carried through an *Aufhebung* of their views within an essentially Marxist problematic. His association with such thinkers should not, in any case, be used as if it were a crushing argument against him. For, as some of his followers have suggested, it could rather stimulate us to re-examine the relationship between Marxism and romanticism, and to make a fresh assessment of the whole romantic tradition.[41] Second, it is by no means clear that Lukács's critique of

[37] L. Colletti, *Marxism and Hegel*, London, NLB, 1979, p. 179.

[38] *HCC*, pp. 130–1.

[39] Colletti, p. 179; and *HCC*, p. 10. Cf. *HCC*, p. 136.

[40] Colletti, p. 184.

[41] Cf. Tito Perlini, *Utopia e prospettiva in György Lukács*, Bari, 1968; and Paul Piccone, 'Dialectic and Materialism in Lukács', *Telos*, no. 11, p. 131.

mechanization, Taylorism, and the modern factory division of labour can be explained in terms of 'romanticism'. After all, there is a powerful Marxist tradition, running from *Capital* to Andre Gorz and Ernest Mandel, which denounces the workings of capitalism at the very heart of the technical process of production and labour.

In a sudden flash of irony, Colletti writes that Lukács went into the factory armed not with *Capital* but with Bergson's *Essai sur les données immédiates de la conscience*. This is suggested to Colletti by the fact that Lukács attacks the reduction of qualitative to quantitative time in the mechanized labour of the capitalist factory. But contrary to Colletti's assertion, the incriminating passage from *History and Class Consciousness* revolves not around nostalgia for Bergson's *durée vécue*, but around a Marxist critique of man's subordination to the machine directly inspired by *The Poverty of Philosophy* and *Capital* itself.[42]

In his struggle against 'the thing', and in his desire to reduce everything to a 'process' – the 'light-and-shade of Heraclitean becoming' – Colletti's Lukács refers beyond the Heidelberg School (Rickert, Simmel) to Hegel's critique of the Kantian understanding. Thus, Colletti situates his polemic with Lukács in the general theoretical framework of 'freeing' Marxism from Hegel, or even Marx from his own Hegelianism. This kind of approach, which is not altogether unlike that of Althusser, has two inevitable results: 1. An attempt to replace Hegel with another 'precursor' of Marxism – Spinoza for Althusser, Kant for Colletti – which in turn involves replacing 'Hegelian' dialectics with ('Spinozist') mechanical materialism or ('Kantian') analytical thought.[43] 2. A consequent rejection of Marx's own insistence on Hegel's place in the genesis of his work and the nature of his method. Thus, Althusser speaks of 'the theoretical incompleteness of Marx's judgment of himself';[44] and Colletti writes in relation to Marx: 'A thinker makes certain "discoveries" . . . and remains nonetheless unable to clearly account for their genealogy. His conscious-

---

[42] Colletti, p. 184; and *HCC*, pp. 89–90. Cf. Marx, *The Poverty of Philosophy*, Moscow, n.d., p. 59: 'Time is everything, man is nothing; he is at the most the incarnation of time. Quality no longer matters. Quantity alone decides everything: hour for hour, day for day.' See also *Capital*, vol. 1, Harmondsworth, 1976 (p. 469), where Marx criticizes the system of mechanical specialization that compels the worker 'to work with the regularity of a machine', resulting in the deformation of his body, muscles, and bones.

[43] For Colletti, Marx continued 'an entire tradition which has as its modern cornerstone Kant's *Critique of Pure Reason*'. (Colletti, p. 198.)

[44] Althusser, p. 92.

ness fails to give a full account of his being.'[45]

Colletti's critique of Lukács, then, is more than anything else a proof *a contrario* of the *Marxist* (and not 'romantic' or 'Hegelian') character of Lukács's method. For as we see, rejection of that method irreversibly leads to rejection of Marx's position on his own thought and on Hegel. Only within Lukács's philosophical perspective does the contradiction between Marx's 'consciousness' and his theoretical 'being' fall away.

Althusser and his school also level the charge of 'left-wing humanism' against both the theory of reification and *History and Class Consciousness* as a whole.[46] In reality, however, the work's political and philosophical axis is a *revolutionary humanism* defined from the standpoint of the proletariat. Far from backsliding into Hegelian idealism, Lukács's humanism is rigorously located within the problematic of *Capital*. And as in Marx's *magnum opus*, it is constituted around three elements: demystification of reified forms, a critique of the inhuman effects of capitalism, and a perspective of human emancipation through socialist revolution. Let us look at each of these in turn.

1. In his critical exposure of reification, Lukács is primarily concerned to break down the reified social forms into a process among men: that is, to uncover man as the kernel and foundation of hypostatized relations. His starting point, naturally enough, is the chapter of *Capital* that deals with commodity fetishism. However, by critically drawing on such classical bourgeois sociologists as Weber and Simmel, Lukács extends Marx's analysis to the *totality* of the forms of social life. Thus, he identifies the process of *Verdinglichung* at every level of capitalist society: the judicial system, the state apparatus, the bureaucracy, intellectual activity, the sciences, and bourgeois culture, morality, and philosophy. As Goldmann has pointed out on several occasions, Lukács found in *Capital* the problematic of *alienation* lying at the heart of Marx's early writings (which were 'rediscovered' and published only in 1932, long after the appearance of *History and Class Consciousness*).

[45] Colletti, p. 113. In making this comparison, we do not wish to question Colletti's theoretical superiority over Althusser.

[46] Althusser, p. 141. Consistent with his overall approach, Althusser ends up condemning the chapter in *Capital* on commodity fetishism as a 'flagrant' and 'extremely harmful' example of Hegel's influence on Marx. See Althusser, 'Preface to *Capital* Volume One', in *Lenin and Philosophy*, London, NLB, 1977, pp. 91–2.

2. Lukács's critique of the dehumanized and dehumanizing character of capitalism is also fully in line with the approach of *Capital*. However, he does place more emphasis than Marx on the inhuman 'psychic' (intellectual and moral) aspects of capitalist reification. Whereas Marx stressed the worker's material degradation in the capitalist factory, Lukács refers above all to the process whereby he is reduced to the level of a commodity, a pure measurable quantity, a 'thing' appended to the machine – a process in which he is stripped of qualitative, human, and individual properties.[47] Lukács also brings out the impact of capitalism – its 'tyrannical essence destructive of everything human' (*das alles Menschliche vergewaltigende und vertilgende Wesen des Kapitalismus*) – upon non-proletarian and semi-proletarian layers, in particular the intelligentsia. The intellectual becomes a seller of his own hypostatized spiritual faculties: subjectivity itself, knowledge, physical constitution, powers of expression, all become commodities set in motion according to laws independent of their bearer's personality. In Lukács's view, 'this phenomenon can be seen at its most grotesque in journalism. . . . The journalist's "lack of convictions", the prostitution of his experiences and beliefs, is comprehensible only as the apogee of capitalist reification.'[48] In this context, Lukács refers us to the famous *Kommunismus* article on the press written by his follower Béla Fogarasi; but another bench-mark was probably Balzac's lucid and unrelenting analysis in *Lost Illusions*.[49]

3. For both Lukács and Marx, the proletarian revolution puts an end to man's enslavement by reified relations, making it possible for society to exercise conscious control over production. The economy 'is to lose its self-contained autonomy (which was what made it an economy, properly speaking)'.[50] When men rationally master the process of production, placing it at the service of genuinely human needs and values, 'the reign of freedom' will already have begun. As we have seen, this problematic already appeared in Lukács's ethical communism of 1919. Now, however,

---

[47] *HCC*, pp. 87–8, 165–6. Of course, these aspects are already present, or at least implicit, in *Capital*.

[48] *HCC*, p. 100.

[49] Cf. B. Fogarasi, 'Die Aufgaben der kommunistische Presse', *Kommunismus*, vol. 2, nos. 25–6, 15 July 1921, p. 850: 'The laws of reification oblige the journalist, as a mere personification of journalism, to carry out these functions in a mechanical and unconscious fashion. As his ink flows, every intelligible structure *becomes a commodity*.' See also Balzac, *Lost Illusions*, Harmondsworth, 1971, p. 373: '"So you stand by what you have written?" said Vernou in a bantering tone. "But we are vendors of phrases and we live by our trade."'

[50] *HCC*, p. 251.

it has lost its character of utopian immediatism: blind economic necessity cannot be suppressed all at once, but 'step by step it is pushed back in the process of transformation until – after long, arduous struggles – it can be totally eliminated'.[51]

Lukács is careful to distinguish this Marxist humanism from the various forms of anthropological humanism: Marx 'never speaks of man in general, of an abstractly absolutized man: he always thinks of him as a link in a concrete totality, in a society'. Although romantic currents (e.g., the Carlyle of *Past and Present*) may vigorously denounce the inhumanity of capitalism, they are unable to go beyond the dilemma of resigned empiricism or utopianism; in the face of capitalist reality, they confine themselves to abstractly positing 'man' as a moral imperative.[52] Marxist humanism, by contrast, is realist and revolutionary: it starts from the concrete contradictions of bourgeois society and shows how they can be objectively overcome through the emancipating action of the conscious proletariat, the only class capable of realizing the human values capitalism negates and debases.

The theory of the party contained in the next chapter of *History and Class Consciousness* ('Towards a Methodology of the Problem of Organization', 1922) marks a political development in Lukács's theory of class consciousness, being grounded on the same methodological premises of revolutionary realism and the subject-object dialectic.

In Lukács's analysis, the Communist party represents the clear historical form of 'possible' class consciousness, the highest level of consciousness and action made objective at the level of organization.[53] As an authentic community, it requires the active commitment of the entire personality of its members – an aspect sharply differentiating it from bourgeois political or administrative bodies, whose members are wedded to the whole only by abstract parts of their existence.[54]

Some writers have charged that this theory is an 'apologia' for existing Communist Parties. However, Lukács was not at all concerned with a *description* of the parties of that time; rather he was referring to a *model* or

[51] Ibid.
[52] *HCC*, pp. 189–91, 197.
[53] *HCC*, pp. 326–9.
[54] *HCC*, pp. 318–20. Here we find a distant echo of German sociology's counterposition between *Gemeinschaft* and *Gesellschaft* – only now it is at the service of the Leninist conception of the party.

goal that would have to be attained if the party was really to become the vanguard leader of the proletariat. This does not imply that the model is an abstract 'ideal': for the Communist Party to which Lukács refers is an *objective possibility*, just like genuine class consciousness. No doubt, however, the Communist Parties of 1922 were much closer to that model than the post-1924 parties of Stalin's Comintern.

Lukács's 1922 views on organization were to some extent inspired by Rosa Luxemburg. They were, however, firmly situated within the framework of Leninism, and for the first time included explicit reservations about Luxemburg's positions.[55] Unlike many of those who lay claim to Leninism, Lukács did more than dogmatically repeat a few one-sided formulations from *What is to be Done?* – formulations Lenin himself criticized after 1907. It was above all Lenin's post-1914 writings, various documents of the Comintern congresses, and *'Left-Wing' Communism* which provided Lukács with his point of departure. Any reading of Lenin is inevitably selective. And Lukács's has the merit that it focused on Lenin's writings for the international workers' movement, those that express the *universal* element in Bolshevism.

Lukács's theory of the party, like his theory of class consciousness, sought to go beyond the traditional dilemma of fetishist opportunism and sectarian voluntarism. Opportunism wholly absorbs the party in the spontaneous movement of the masses, its 'political realism' being a mode of passive adaptation to the lowest (or, at best, the average) level of class consciousness. Sectarianism, for example in its terrorist or Blanquist form, ascribes to the party the task of acting in place of the 'unconscious' mass; it artificially severs 'correct' class consciousness from the living development and struggle of the class; and it conceives of revolution as an isolated act whereby a 'conscious minority' lays hold of power.[56]

For Lukács, genuinely communist organizational practice must be based on living interaction between the party and the unorganized masses. The

[55] Unfortunately we cannot here go into Lukács's views on Luxemburg. In a first period, from about 1920 to early 1921, he adopted Luxemburg's own positions, stressing for example that organization is not a premiss but a result of the revolutionary struggle. Characteristic in this respect is his 1921 preface to the Hungarian edition of Luxemburg's *The Mass Strike*. (For a French translation of this preface see the French edition of the present work.) After the 1921 March Action, Lukács began to criticize Luxemburg's positions and to give his full support to Bolshevik conceptions. To some extent, however, the theory of the party contained in *History and Class Consciousness* is an attempt to synthesize Leninism and Luxemburgism.

[56] *HCC*, pp. 322, 326, 331–2.

heterogeneity of levels of proletarian class consciousness inevitably results in the separation of the vanguard from the mass. But at the same time, the party's role is precisely to bring about a progressive unification of the class at the highest level possible. The Communist Party must not act, in sect-like fashion, *for* the proletariat, but must seek through its actions to advance the real development of the class consciousness of the masses.[57]

Now, some critics have claimed that the organizational and political conceptions of *History and Class Consciousness* tend to foreshadow those of Stalinism. In the view of Luciano Amodio, for example, the Lukács of 1921–23 was among those 'responsible for the genesis of international Stalinism': 'Speaking with the authority of personal experience, Lukács has indirectly exposed the fact that Stalinism, *as an international phenomenon*, was the offspring of this romantic and subjectivist left wing. Thus, in *The Meaning of Contemporary Realism* . . . , he held Stalinism to blame for both economic subjectivism and revolutionary romanticism (its "aesthetic equivalent", p. 140):[58] the self-criticism of *History and Class Consciousness* contained in *Mein Weg zu Marx* is based on the notion of *ultra-left subjectivist activism*! Paradoxically, the self-criticism of *History and Class Consciousness* became a preventive "Aesopian" self-criticism of Lukács's own proto-Stalinism, of his own responsibility in the genesis of international Stalinism.'[59]

This rather amazing passage, typical of a certain arbitrary and confusionist 'Lukácsology', calls for a number of remarks. First, Lukács's 1957 critique of Stalinism as 'economic subjectivism/revolutionary romanticism' was a superficial, 'rightist' critique inspired by Khrushchev's 'secret speech' to the twentieth congress of the Soviet Communist Party; as such it was quite incapable of challenging the *roots* of Stalinism. However, neither directly nor indirectly, in 1957 or at any time thereafter, did Lukács ever write or imply that the kind of messianic, leftist subjectivism of his early writings was at the origin of international Stalinism. Second, it is quite bizarre – and even this is a euphemism – to quote the 1933 self-criticism of the *orthodox-Stalinist* Lukács (*Mein Weg zu Marx*), which was directed against the so-called 'subjectivist leftism' of *History and Class Consciousness*, as if it were a 'preventive self-criticism of

---

[57] *HCC*, pp. 326–8.

[58] The page-reference is to the Italian edition. See Lukács, *The Meaning of Contemporary Realism*, London, 1963, p. 125.

[59] L. Amodio, 'Tra Lenin e Luxemburgo, comentario al periodo "estremistico" di G. Lukács 1919–1921', *Il Corpo*, May 1967, p. 418.

his own proto-Stalinism'! Third, even the slightest acquaintance with the historical facts is enough to establish that *international* Stalinism is the scion of *Russian* Stalinism. Not only did *History and Class Consciousness* have no 'responsibility' in its genesis, but it has been condemned as heretical, anathematized and prohibited by every Stalinist or proto-Stalinist ideologue of the last fifty years.

The American sociologist Alvin Gouldner has presented us with another contrived attack on the alleged Stalinism of the young Lukács. His argument is in many ways contradictory to that put forward by Amodio: 'The bureaucratic vulnerability of Lukács's tradition of socialism also links up with the importance attributed to the role of consciousness in revolution-making and, in particular, with the cognitive, rational, and shaping character of consciousness that derives ultimately from German idealism. . . . For all his revolutionary Messianism, then, Lukács began with a rationalistic pre-bureaucratic conception of socialism, and it is this, and not only his political defeat, that created in him an inner vulnerability to Stalinism.'[60]

For Amodio, Lukács is 'responsible' for Stalinism because of his romantic messianism; for Gouldner, he suffers from an 'inner vulnerability' to Stalinism despite his messianism, because of his rationalism. It is to say the least surprising to discover that Stalinism is a consequence of 'the importance attributed to the role of consciousness in revolutionary action' or of the excessively rational character of that action. Are we then to assume that the essence of Stalinism is conscious and rational revolutionary action?

A number of other writers, particularly those of the American Lukács school grouped around the outstanding journal *Telos*, use considerably more sophisticated arguments in speaking of Lukács's supposed proto-Stalinism of 1923. In general, these critics start from the well-known thesis (itself based on Luxemburg's polemic with the Bolsheviks) that Lenin's theory of the vanguard party led inevitably to Stalin. We refer the reader to an article by Andrew Feenberg, another collaborator on *Telos*, which criticizes this thesis by bringing out the anti-Stalinist character of Lukács's early Marxism and his specific relationship to Lenin and Rosa Luxemburg.[61]

---

[60] A. Gouldner, 'Comments on *History and Class Consciousness*', in *For Sociology*, Harmondsworth, 1975, pp. 418–9.

[61] A. Feenberg, 'Lukács and the Critique of "Orthodox" Marxism', *The Philosophical Forum*, vol. 3, nos. 3–4, spring-summer 1972.

188

Far from 'foreshadowing Stalinism', Lukács's organizational conceptions in *History and Class Consciousness* involve the most radical and profound critique of the bureaucratic type of party. In Lukács's view, what characterizes bourgeois and reformist workers' parties is 'the voluntaristic overestimation of the active importance of the individual (the leader) and the fatalistic underestimation of the importance of the class (the masses)'. Such parties are 'divided into an active and passive group in which the latter is only occasionally brought into play and then only at the behest of the former'.[62] Lukács could hardly have come closer to envisaging the 'personality cult' of the 'Stalinist' parties and their conversion into 'opportunist workers' parties'. And in another passage he correctly grasps the link between such a mode of organization and party *bureaucracy*: 'If the party consists merely of a hierarchy of officials isolated from the mass of ordinary members who are normally given the role of passive onlookers . . . then this will provoke in the members a certain indifference composed equally of blind trust and apathy with regard to the day-to-day actions of the leadership.'[63]

We should note that these are not abstract formulae, but observations based on Lukács's *concrete experience* in the Hungarian Communist Party. About 1921 or 1922, in fact, he began to detect the first symptoms of the bureaucratic disease that would eventually engulf the party. In his 1922 article 'Yet Again the Politics of Illusion', published in Vienna in a collection of texts by the HCP opposition,[64] Lukács denounced the huge bureaucratic apparatus of the party-in-exile: it was, he said, an 'empty and soulless' apparatus organized just like any office (*Amt*), with its 'superiors' and 'inferiors', its artificial cult of authority, and its rules for blind, servile obedience; its life depended much more on Moscow (whose support it tried to gain through promises, illusions, and lies) than on the real struggles of the Hungarian proletariat.[65]

Thus, the Lukács of 1922, with his Leninist conception of the revolutionary party, actually made a rigorous and explicit critique of those phenomena that 'foreshadowed Stalinism'. When he came to accept Stalinism in 1926, he could do so only by breaking (implicitly or explicitly)

[62] *HCC*, pp. 318–9.
[63] *HCC*, pp. 336–7.
[64] L. Rudas (ed.), *Abentuerer und Liquidatorentum, Die Politik Béla Kúns und die Krise der KPU*, Vienna, 1922.
[65] Lukács, 'Noch einmal Illusionspolitik', *Werke*, vol. 2, pp. 156–9. This article was first published in December 1921 in the Vienna journal of the HCP opposition, *Vörös Újság*.

with the positions of *History and Class Consciousness.*

From a historical point of view, Lukács's famous book was the expression of a period of revolts, insurrections, general strikes, and workers' councils, a period of revolutionary upsurge throughout Europe. This historical background does not in the least render the work politically obsolete – quite the contrary. For the new generation of the 1960s has been seeking its historical roots in the 1917–23 period of 'original communism', which it considers to be of exemplary value.

Lukács's actuality is also apparent at the level of *methodology*: his subject-object dialectic tends to rise above the dilemma of a contemporary Marxism split between a subjectivist, 'existential' and leftist current (Sartre) and a structuralist tendency close to pre-dialectical materialism and neo-positivism (Althusser). There has been much discussion on whether Lukács's concept of dialectic is Leninist. Unfortunately, this polemic has greatly suffered from the arbitrary freezing of 'Leninism' at the level of a single work: *Materialism and Empirio-Criticism.* Using this approach, Merleau-Ponty has no difficulty in contrasting 'Leninism' with the 'western Marxism' represented by Lukács; while the Soviet philosopher Deborin can just as happily compare Lukács to Bogdanov.[66] *History and Class Consciousness* is a Leninist work insofar as it is a philosophical expression of the revolutionary dialectic informing Lenin's political writings and his 1914 *Philosophical Notebooks.*[67] We therefore agree with the view of Morris Watnick: 'the underlying structure of its argument is unmistakably Leninist to the core. . . . What Lukács' book challenged was not the essential core of Leninist doctrine – quite the contrary! – but the codified Marxism-Leninism which orthodox scholiasts had proceeded to canonize as the state dogma of the Soviet Union.'[68]

Lukács's short study of Lenin, written in 1924, rests on the same basic theoretical premisses as *History and Class Consciousness,*[69] even though it

---

[66] M. Merleau-Ponty, *Adventures of the Dialectic*, Evanston, 1973, p. 64; and Deborin, p. 629.

[67] These notebooks were published only in 1929 and were thus unknown to Lukács during the period in question.

[68] M. Watnick, 'Georg Lukács: An Intellectual Biography', *Survey*, no. 27, January-March 1959, p. 80.

[69] '. . . Lukács interpreted Lenin's *practice* (his strategy and tactics in the Russian Revolution) as the actualization or putting-into-action of the "subject-object" dialectic.' (P. Breines, 'Praxis and its Theorists', p. 87.)

deals with a number of important problems (for instance, Lenin's theory of the state) that are missing from the earlier work. Structuralist Marxists are therefore on extremely shaky ground when they speak of an epistemological break between Lukács's earlier 'historicist idealism' and the 'materialism' of his book on Lenin. Gareth Stedman Jones, for example, argues that the party in Lukács's *Lenin* 'is no longer simply a vanguard that awakens the masses from a slumbering lethargy . . . but a force which listens to the masses and learns from them, in a permanent dialectic between party and class'.[70]

Now, as a matter of fact, in *History and Class Consciousness* Lukács was already laying stress on 'the most intimate internal relation between party and class'. As an example he mentioned that the non-party worker and peasant masses were drawn into the effort to purge the Russian party in 1921: 'Not that the Party was prepared henceforth to accept the judgment of the masses blindly. But it was willing to take their suggestions and rejections into account when eliminating corrupt, bureaucratized and revolutionarily unreliable elements estranged from the masses.'[71]

Both in *Lenin* and in *History and Class Consciousness*, Lukács praises the revolutionary realism of the Bolsheviks (as expressed in the Brest-Litovsk negotiations, the NEP, and so on), which brought compromises and a firm stand on principles into dialectical inter-relation. This he counterposes to the attitude of those 'left communists', who, spurning all compromise, made an abstract and rigid appeal to 'pure' principles. Bolshevik realism, he argues, ultimately stems from the Marxist-dialectical conception of history, according to which men make their own history *but not in conditions of their own choosing*.[72]

The theory of the party contained in *Lenin* is similarly a development of Lukács's 1923 positions. He rejects as one-sided and undialectical both the traditional Kautskyist theory, in which organization is the *prerequisite* for revolutionary action, and Luxemburg's view of organization as the *product* of such action. Instead, he argues, the Communist Party is at once the producer and the product, the prerequisite and the fruit of revolutionary mass movements; it is the result as well as the conscious originator of historical-dialectical development.[73] At one point in this work, Lukács contrasts the life of the professional revolutionary with 'the superficiality

[70] G. Stedman Jones, p. 52.
[71] *HCC*, p. 338.
[72] Lukács, *Lenin*, London, NLB, 1970, pp. 81–2, 85–6.
[73] Ibid., pp. 32, 37.

of ordinary life';[74] and it may seem that this is a distant echo of the counterposition he made in 1910 between authentic and everyday life. However, there is no longer a tragic duality for the Lukács of 1924. lying beneath the surface of everyday life is a deeply-rooted *tendency* towards revolution, which forms the material bedrock of revolutionary activity.

Despite this continuity between his positions of 1923 and 1924, Lukács's study of Lenin does say something new about two important, even crucial, political problems.

1. On the relationship between the democratic and the socialist revolution, he writes: 'The real revolution is the dialectical transformation of the bourgeois revolution into the proletarian revolution.' The bourgeoisie has betrayed its revolutionary traditions; the proletariat is the only class capable of taking the bourgeois revolution to its conclusion, and in so doing necessarily fuses it with the socialist revolution. 'Thus, the proletarian revolution now means at one and the same time the realization and the supersession of the bourgeois revolution.'[75] In 1919, Lukács had discovered in the proletariat the legatee of the cultural and humanist traditions abandoned by the bourgeoisie. By 1924, he understood that, politically too, it was the proletariat's mission to carry out the historic tasks that the now counter-revolutionary bourgeoisie could no longer assume.

2. When he goes on to discuss internationalism, Lukács first notes the key role of the Bolshevik Party within the Soviet state, and then adds: 'Because *the revolution can only be victorious on a world scale*, because *it is only as a world proletariat that the working class can truly become a class*, the party itself is incorporated and subordinated as a section within the highest organ of proletarian revolution, the Communist International.'[76] These two questions – permanent revolution and the primacy of internationalism – were to become the main issues in the split between the left and the right of the Communist movement. The Left Opposition would lay claim to precisely the Leninism espoused by Lukács in 1924. And when Lukács rallied to Stalin in 1926, he would implicitly revise the positions put forward in *Lenin*.

One of the best-known concepts developed in the 1924 study is *the actuality of the revolution*. In our view, however, this problematic is the site of a certain ambiguity in Lukács's thought: at times the actuality of the

[74] Ibid., p. 37.
[75] Ibid., p. 49.
[76] Ibid., pp. 86–7, emphasis in the original.

revolution refers to a *historical period* of revolutionary struggles, at others to a *revolutionary situation* characterized by 'the collapse of the old framework of society'.[77] If Leninism were the theory of the actuality of the revolution in this second sense, then it would cease to be realistic in a situation of capitalist stability such as Lukács refused to envisage in 1924. Thus, Lukács seems to restrict the validity of Leninism to a situation of revolutionary crisis, or to one in which revolution is imminent: 'Had the historical predictions of the Mensheviks been correct, had a relatively quiet period of prosperity and of the slow spread of democracy ensued . . . the professional revolutionaries would have necessarily remained stranded in sectarianism or become mere propaganda clubs . . . the Leninist form of organization is inseparably connected with the ability to foresee the approaching revolution.'[78] It would seem that this ambiguous formulation (what does 'approaching' mean?) may be one of the roots of Lukács's right turn of 1926. Since we have entered a 'relatively quiet period of prosperity', he may have argued, Leninism has become less actual, and the Communist Party can and should adopt a more 'flexible' structure and strategy.

[77] Ibid., p. 29.
[78] Ibid., pp. 26, 29.

V
Lukács and Stalinism

> We shall tell them that we do your
> bidding and rule in your name . . .
> That deception will be our suffering,
> for we shall be forced to lie.
> DOSTOEVSKY, *The Brothers Karamazov*

From 1924, after the death of Lenin, a process of bureaucratization began
in the USSR, in the course of which the Bolshevik Old Guard was
gradually replaced by a conservative layer, of which the most competent
representative and unchallenged leader was Joseph Stalin. One of the
decisive moments in this historic turn came in 1926. It was then that Stalin
published *Questions of Leninism*, the first explicit formulation of the
doctrine of socialism in one country, and that Bukharin exhorted the
kulaks to 'enrich themselves'. This was also the year of the Fifteenth
Congress of the Soviet Communist Party, at which the Left Opposition
(Trotsky, Zinoviev, Kamenev) were removed from the Politburo. Finally,
it was in 1926 that Chiang Kai-shek was elected an 'honorary member' of
the Praesidium of the Communist International and that the Soviet trade
unions formed a joint committee with the right-wing leaders of the
English trade unions, who had just sabotaged the 1926 general strike.
Using the pretext of stabilization in Europe after the great revolutionary
wave of 1917–23, the Stalinist leadership was gradually to replace
revolutionary internationalism with a *Realpolitik* based on the state
interest of the USSR.

In the 1967 preface to *History and Class Consciousness*, Lukács sums up
his response to this transformation in the following terms: 'After 1924 the
Third International correctly defined the position of the capitalist world as
one of "relative stability". These facts meant that I had to re-think my
theoretical position. In the debates of the Russian Party I agreed with
Stalin about the necessity for socialism in one country and this shows very
clearly the start of a new epoch in my thought.'[1] Indeed a decisive re-

---

[1] Lukács, 'Preface' (1967) to *History and Class Consciousness*, London, 1971, pp.
xxvii–xxviii.

orientation in the life and work of Lukács began in 1926, a profound theoretical and political break with all his former revolutionary ideas, and in particular with *History and Class Consciousness*. In a word, after 1926 his writings are characterized by an identification with Stalinism, albeit with many reservations and qualifications.

Just as Lukács's radicalization had initially occurred through aesthetics and ethics, the new turn first took a cultural and philosophical form, before finding explicit political expression in 1928. In an article written in June 1926, 'Art for Art's Sake and Proletarian Poetry', Lukács criticized the *Tendenzkunst* (politically oriented art) of people like Ernst Toller, the poet and leader of the 1919 Soviet Republic of Bavaria, calling it an 'abstract and romantic utopianism'. He gave a general warning about utopian overestimation in the cultural sphere: initially, the proletarian revolution can only contribute 'very little' to the development of art; cultural changes in the USSR were 'much less rapid than a superficial view might have led one to hope'. This utopian superficiality 'explains the "disillusionment" with the Russian revolution felt by many of those intellectuals who had hoped it would provide an immediate solution to their own particular problems'.[2] For Lukács, this article represented a 'self-criticism' of his hopes of 1919 that a cultural revolution would appear in the wake of the socialist revolution.[3] His renunciation of the 'utopia' of a new culture in the USSR meant a return to the bourgeois cultural heritage.

Lukács also published in 1926 an article rightly acclaimed as one of his most stimulating and profound philosophical works: 'Moses Hess and the Problems of Idealist Dialectics'. The essay is usually considered a direct extension of the Hegelian Marxism of *History and Class Consciousness*. In fact, the 'interpretation' of Hegel is not the same in the two works: in 1923 Lukács saw in Hegel the category of totality and the dialectic of subject/object; in 1926 he detected above all the 'realist' thinker. He now saw in Hegel's tendency to 'reconcile' himself with reality (e.g. the Prussian state) the proof of his 'grandiose realism' and his 'rejection of all utopias'. He recognized that Hegel's tendency to stop at the present was politically reactionary, but from the methodological point of view he saw it as the expression of a profound dialectical realism.[4]

[2] 'L'Art pour l'Art und proletarische Dichtung' in *Die Tat* 18/3, June 1926, pp. 220–23.

[3] Cf. Paul Breines, 'Notes on G. Lukács's "The Old Culture and the New Culture"', *Telos*, no. 15, spring 1970, pp. 16–18.

[4] Lukács, 'Moses Hess and the Problems of Idealist Dialectics', in *Political Writings*

The starting point for the ideological radicalization of the young Lukács in 1908–9 had been opposition to Hegel's *Versöhnung* (reconciliation). Now, at the end of his revolutionary period, Lukács fell back into Hegel's 'reconciliation' with reality. The theme of *Versöhnung* was to reappear in many of Lukács's mature writings and indeed became one of the main axes of his thought.[5] Thirty years later, in a work published in 1958, he quoted a passage from Hegel on the *Bildungsroman* in classical German literature, which strikingly pin-pointed his own perspective: 'During his years of apprenticeship the hero is permitted to sow his wild oats; he learns to subordinate his wishes and views to the interests of the society; he then enters that society's hierarchic scheme and finds in it a comfortable niche.' Commenting on this passage, Lukács spoke of the 'youthful dream' and the 'rebellion' of the heroes of the bourgeois novel, who are broken by the 'pressures of society'; reconciliation is thus 'forced' out of them by social pressures.[6] Described in such a way, is this evolution not similar to Lukács's own, his rebellion crushed at the end of what he was later to consider his 'years of apprenticeship'? Adorno, in a review of this work, stressed with some justification that Lukács's 'forced reconciliation' with the 'socialist' reality of the USSR can be compared with that described by Hegel: it was this reconciliation which 'blocked his road back to the utopia of his youth'.[7]

In the 'Moses Hess' essay Lukács contrasted Hegel with the 're-volutionary utopianism' of Fichte, von Cieszowski and Moses Hess. In his opinion, the principle elaborated by Hegel in the preface to the *Philosophy of Right* ('The task of Philosophy is to understand *what is*, because *what is*, is Reason') was closer to the materialist conception of history than all the

---

1919–29, pp. 181–223.

[5] See, for example, in the recently published Moscow Manuscripts, this remark written in about 1939–40: 'With Hegel, the all-embracing appropriation of reality, and the discovery and revelation of contradiction as its motive force, are inseparable from his particular type of idealism and his particular concept of "reconciliation".' (Lukács, *Ecrits de Moscou*, Paris, 1974, p. 229.(Also Lukács, *Der junge Hegel und die Probleme der kapitalistischen Gesellschaft*, Berlin, 1954, ch. 3, sect. 8).

[6] Georg Lukács, *The Meaning of Contemporary Realism*, London 1963, p. 112.

[7] Theodor Adorno, 'Reconciliation under Duress', in *Aesthetics and Politics*, London, NLB, 1977. In his work *The Young Hegel*, Lukács even considers the 'reconciliation' of the mature Hegel positive: 'It was precisely because he moved away from the revolutionary ideals of his youth that Hegel was able to become the culminating figure of German idealism and to understand the necessity of historical development. . . . The further he departed from his juvenile revolutionary ideals, the more resolutely he "reconciled himself" to the domination of bourgeois society . . . the more powerful and conscious Hegel appears as a dialectician.'

moralistic dreams of Fichteanism. As a consequence, Marx's thought was not to be related to Feuerbach, Hess, and the 'left' Hegelians, who constituted what was essentially a neo-Fichtean current: 'methodologically, Marx took over *directly* from Hegel'.[8]

Obviously this argument contains a grain of truth. However, it is extremely one-sided. It leaves out that for Marx 'philosophers have only interpreted the world in different ways; the point is to change it'; and that, therefore, the 'philosophy of practice' of Fichte, von Cieszowski, and Hess is *also* a foundation stone for Marxism, a *necessary* step in the evolution of the young Marx after his break with Hegel in 1842–3. The essence of Marx's revolutionary dialectic lies precisely in that it transcended both the conservative realism of Hegel and revolutionary (moralistic) utopianism of the Fichtean type. Any attempt to trace Marx's thought back in a one-sided fashion to either of these sources alone produces a conservative, pseudo-realist 'Marxism' or an 'ethical' socialism with no objective basis.

Lukács's essay on Moses Hess therefore lacks balance. It tilts towards 'reconciliation' with reality and lacks the dialectical revolutionary harmony of *History and Class Consciousness*. After a utopian-revolutionary stage lasting from 1919 to 1921, and a short but monumental climax of revolutionary realism from 1922 to 1924, from 1926 Lukács drew nearer to realism pure and simple and, as a consequence, politically closer to the non-revolutionary *Realpolitik* of Stalin. His 'Moses Hess' of 1926 had far-reaching political implications: it provided the methodological basis for his support for the Soviet 'Thermidor'.

This hidden, implicit meaning of the philosophical writings of 1926, 'overlooked' by most commentators, was further confirmed by an essay written in 1935, 'Hölderlin's Hyperion', in which Lukács dealt explicitly with Hegel's attitude to Thermidor itself: 'Hegel comes to terms with the post-Thermidorian epoch and the close of the revolutionary period of bourgeois development, and he builds up his philosophy precisely on an understanding of this new turning-point in world history. Hölderlin makes no compromise with the post-Thermidorian reality; he remains faithful to the old revolutionary ideal of renovating "polis" democracy and is broken by a reality which had no place for his ideals, not even on the level of poetry and thought. While Hegel's intellectual accommodation to the post-Thermidorian reality . . . led him into the main current of the ideological development of his class . . . Hölderlin's intransigence ended in

---

[8] 'Moses Hess', *Political Writings*, p. 203.

a tragic impasse. Unknown and unmourned, he fell like a solitary poetic Leonidas for the ideals of the Jacobin period at the Thermopylae of invading Thermidorianism . . . The world historical significance of Hegel's accommodation consists precisely in the fact that he grasped . . . the revolutionary development of the bourgeoisie as a unitary process, one in which the revolutionary Terror as well as Thermidor and Napoleon were necessary phases. The heroic period of the revolutionary bourgeoisie becomes in Hegel . . . something irretrievably past, but a past which was absolutely necessary for the emergence of the unheroic phase of the present considered to be progressive.'[9]

The significance of these remarks in regard to the USSR in 1935 is obvious. One has only to add that in February 1935 Trotsky had just published an essay in which, for the first time, he used the term 'Thermidor' to characterize the evolution of the USSR since 1924.[10] Clearly, the passages quoted above are Lukács's reply to Trotsky, that intransigent Leonidas, tragic and solitary, who rejected Thermidor and was forced into an impasse. Lukács, on the other hand, like Hegel, accepts the end of the revolutionary period and builds his philosophy on an understanding of the new turn in world history.[11] It can be noted in passing, however, that Lukács appears implicitly to accept Trotsky's characterization of Stalin's regime as Thermidorian.

'Hölderlin's Hyperion' is undoubtedly one of the most subtle and intelligent attempts to justify Stalinism as a 'necessary phase', 'prosaic' yet with a 'progressive character', in the revolutionary development of the proletariat seen as a unified whole. There is a certain 'rational kernel' in this argument – which was probably secretly held by many intellectuals and militants who had more or less rallied to Stalinism – but the events of the following years (the Moscow Trials, the German-Soviet Pact, etc.) were to demonstrate, even to Lukács, that this process was not exactly 'unified'. What Lukács failed to understand was that the Stalinist Thermidor was much more harmful for the proletarian revolution than the French Thermidor had been for the bourgeois revolution. The fundamental reason for this, as Lukács had earlier emphasized in *History*

[9] Georg Lukács, 'Hölderlin's Hyperion', in *Goethe and His Age*, London, 1968, pp. 137–9.
[10] Leon Trotsky, *The Workers' State and the Question of Thermidor and Bonapartism*, London, 1968.
[11] Cf. L. Stern, 'Lukács: An Intellectual Portrait', in *Dissent*, spring 1958, p. 172; also the remarkable article on Lukács by Lucien Goldmann in the *Encyclopaedia Universalis*, Paris, 1971.

and Class Consciousness, was that, unlike the bourgeois revolution, the socialist revolution is not a blind, automatic process, but the conscious transformation of society by the workers themselves.[12]

Lukács's turn assumed a direct political form in 1928 with the 'Blum Theses'. Using the pseudonym 'Blum', he drew up these draft theses for the Second Congress of the Hungarian Communist Party. Some writers attribute the political positions of this text to the influence of Bukharin or Otto Bauer.[13] In our opinion, all that lies behind them is an application to Hungary of the right turn of the Comintern; Lukács was only following the 'general line' of 1924–7. Hungary's tardiness stemmed from the unique precedent of the Béla Kún republic, which made it difficult for the Communist Party to draw up a programme that retreated from the gains of 1919, i.e. from the socialist revolution. It was Lukács's misfortune that these Theses were to be the last echo of the right turn, coming as they did at the very beginning of the International's new (sectarian) 'left' turn.

The central argument of the 'Blum Theses' is that the aim of the Hungarian Communist Party should no longer be the re-establishment of a Soviet Republic, but rather, simply, a 'democratic dictatorship of the proletariat and peasantry', whose 'immediate concrete content . . . does not go beyond bourgeois society'. The point was to replace the semi-fascist regime in Hungary by a bourgeois democracy, in which 'the bourgeois class . . . although it maintains its economic exploitation . . . has ceded at least part of its power to the broad masses of the workers'. He therefore gives the Hungarian party the task of leading 'the true struggle for democratic reforms' and fighting the 'nihilism' prevalent among workers in relation to bourgeois democracy.[14]

We have purposely chosen the most 'right-wing' formulations of Lukács's text, by-passing some more 'leftish' passages which were no more than verbal concessions. The 'Blum Theses' as a whole were both a continuation of the line of the years 1924–7 and an augury of the Popular Front strategy of 1934–8. But they came both too late and too early: they ran totally counter to the ultra-sectarian turn of the Third Period (1928–33), which had just begun. As a result, Lukács was immediately

[12] Cf. also Trotsky, p. 57: 'In contrast to capitalism, socialism is not built automatically, but consciously. The march towards socialism cannot be separated from a state power wishing for socialism.' The anti-Stalinist Lukács of later years seems to have a more lucid and less vindicatory view than in 1935, as we shall see.

[13] G. Lichtheim, *Lukács*, London, 1971, pp. 74–5; Y. Bourdet, *Figures de Lukács*, Paris, 1972, pp. 92–3.

[14] Georg Lukács, 'Blum Theses' (1928), *Political Writings*, pp. 243, 248, 250.

treated to a formidable thrashing in the form of an 'Open Letter from the Executive Committee of the Communist International to the Members of the Hungarian Communist Party', which accused the 'liquidationist theses of comrade Blum' of having been written from the point of view of Social Democracy, and of wanting to 'fight fascism on the battleground of bourgeois democracy'.[15]

The Hungarian Communist Party continued to discuss the 'Blum Theses' throughout 1929, but after the intervention of the Executive Committee of the International, it was obvious that Lukács had lost the day. The Béla Kún faction rejected the Theses as totally opportunist, and even Lukács's faction (the old Landler tendency) was somewhat luke-warm.[16] In 1929, fearing he would be expelled from the party, Lukács published a self-criticism, which emphasized the 'opportunist, right-wing' character of his Theses. As Lukács later acknowledged on various occasions, this self-criticism was totally *hypocritical*; in other words, he continued to be deeply and intrinsically convinced of the correctness of the 'Blum Theses', although publicly rejecting them with all the usual ritual attached to this sort of operation.

Why make such an unconditional capitulation? Because of a 'legitimate desire to stay alive', as certain critics suggest?[17] This does not seem a good explanation: in the USSR of 1929, Lukács ran no risks and nobody would have prevented him from going to Germany (as, incidentally, he did in 1931). The justification given by Lukács later on, in 1967, is more plausible: 'I was indeed firmly convinced that I was in the right, but I knew also – e.g. from the fate that had befallen Karl Korsch – that to be expelled from the Party meant that it would no longer be possible to participate actively in the struggle against Fascism. I wrote my self-criticism as an "entry ticket" to such activity.'[18] The trouble with this argument is that in 1929 the Communist Parties were far from leading any effective struggle against fascism. This was the time of the appearance of the infamous Stalinist doctrine that defined Social Democracy as 'social fascism' and, obstinately rejecting the anti-fascist united front of the workers' parties, proclaimed, barely a year before Hitler's triumph, that

[15] 'Offenen Brief des Exekutivkommittees der Kommunistischen Internationale an die Mitglieder der Kommunistischen Partei Ungarns' (1928) in Peter Ludz, *Georg Lukács, Schriften zur Ideologie und Politik*, Neuwied, 1967, pp. 733–4.
[16] Lukács, 'Preface' (1967), p. xxx.
[17] Bourdet, p. 170.
[18] Lukács, 'Preface' (1967), p. xxx.

'the main blow should be aimed at the German Social Democratic Party'.

Lukács obviously totally disagreed with this catastrophic strategy. In 1967 he recalled that in 1928 Stalin's theory of Social Democracy as 'fascism's twin brother' had 'deeply repelled' him.[19] So why capitulation, self-criticism, and passive acceptance of the Comintern's line? In our opinion, the evidence in Victor Serge's *Memoirs* provides some of the elements of an answer to this question, by illustrating Lukács's state of mind at that time: '"Above all", Georgy Lukács told me, as we roamed in the evening beneath the grey spires of the Votive Church, "don't be silly and get yourself deported for nothing, just for the pleasure of voting defiantly. Believe me, insults are not very important to us. Marxist revolutionaries need patience and courage; they do not need pride. The times are bad, and we are at a dark cross-roads. Let us reserve our strength: history will summon us in its time."'[20]

Serge ascribes this conversation to 'Vienna, in or about 1926'. It may seem presumptuous of us to wish to correct Victor Serge's memoirs, but it seems much more likely that these words were spoken by Lukács in Moscow in 1929. First, no one was being deported in 1926 and, as Serge was in Vienna, it is hard to see how the Soviet government could have deported him to Russia. On the other hand, in 1929 Serge was one of the last oppositionists remaining in Moscow, under constant threat of deportation. Lukács's reference to the revolutionary's lack of pride is incomprehensible in 1926; in 1929, at the time of his self-criticism, it is an accurate reflection of his attitude. Similarly, the expression 'the times are bad, and we are at a dark crossroads' conveys precisely Lukács's dilemma when faced with the sectarian turn of the Third Period. The (relative) complicity with Victor Serge that emerges from the conversation can also be understood in the light of the situation in 1929; to a certain extent, Lukács shared the criticisms the Left Opposition (to which Serge belonged) made of the line of 'social-fascism'. But, unlike Serge, he did not dare lead a frontal attack within the Comintern. He was 'reserving his strength', hoping that 'history would summon him in its time'.[21]

In other words, Lukács saw the 'left' turn of the Third Period as an

[19] Lukács, 'Preface' (1967), p. xxviii.

[20] V. Serge, *Memoirs of a Revolutionary*, Oxford, 1963, pp. 191–2.

[21] Lukács's unpublished autobiography, written in 1971, supports the possibility that Serge erred in ascribing this conversation to 1926. Lukács notes that Serge sometimes tended to describe events as having occurred earlier than they did and states that he did so in regard to several of their conversations. (*Gelebtes Denken*, ms, p. 1.)

isolated phenomenon, a temporary aberration, and he was deeply convinced that, sooner or later, the Comintern would return to a more realistic position, close to the one he was defending in the 'Blum Theses'. While he was waiting for this new turn, which would give first priority to the fight against fascism and allow him to play an active role, he sacrificed his pride, through a self-imposed 'slight humiliation', the self-criticism of 1929. Lukács's forecast was not entirely incorrect: what he did not foresee was that the turn would come only when it was too late, after Hitler's victory and the establishment of fascism in the heart of Europe.

The 'Blum Theses' represent the fruition of a tortuous intellectual pilgrimage. They are the culmination of Lukács's political development and the ideological foundation for his intellectual output after 1928. Shocked by his failure, in 1929 Lukács was to abandon the sphere of political theory for the more 'neutral' and less controversial world of aesthetics and culture. However, as he emphasized in 1967, the basic positions of the 'Blum Theses' 'determined from then on all my theoretical and practical activities'. As further proof of this assertion, Lukács, with a certain irony, quotes the ex-pupil who became his main Stalinist critic, Jószef Révai. The latter wrote in 1950: 'Everyone familiar with the history of the Hungarian Communist Party knows that the *literary* views held by Comrade Lukács between 1945 and 1949 belong together with *political* views that he had formulated much earlier, in the context of political trends in Hungary and of the strategy of the Communist Party at the end of the twenties.'[22]

In fact, this applies not just to the period 1945–9, but, as Lukács himself suggests, to the *whole* of his literary and aesthetic output. Even in the Third Period he defended, with the necessary terminological precautions, the (bourgeois) cultural heritage against the 'proletarian

---

[22] Lukács, 'Preface' (1967), p. xxx, and J. Révai, *Literarische Studien*, Berlin, 1956, p. 235. Actually, Lukács's literary writings of 1945–49 also contained some directly political passages. In *Irodalom es demokracia* (Literature and Democracy), a collection of articles published in Budapest in 1947, Lukács wrote that people's democracy 'did not abolish the capitalist character of the productive order and had no intention of doing so'. (Cf. Hanak, p. 91.) The connection with the 'Blum Theses' is rather obvious. Nevertheless, it may be possible to view Lukács's post-war writings differently. According to Agnes Heller, 'Lukács cherished the hope that the victory over fascism would create an entirely new situation; above all, the possibility of a non-Stalinist form of socialism, which he designated with the concept of *direct democracy*'. Heller maintains that this conception was rooted in the ideal of a democratic community of free men as sketched by Lukács in some of his literary writings of the thirties, on G. Keller, Goethe's *Wilhelm Meister*, and so on. (Agnes Heller, letter to the author, 26 September 1974.)

literature' of writers in the German Communist Party (such as Ernst Ottwalt and Willi Bredel).[23] But it was above all after the 'right' turn of the Comintern in 1934 that Lukács could freely express his literary theories. As Isaac Deutscher emphasizes: 'He elevated the Popular Front from the level of tactics to that of ideology; he projected its principle into philosophy, literary history and aesthetic criticism.'

Nothing illustrates this tendency more than Lukács's attitude to Thomas Mann and Bertholt Brecht. For him, Mann represented rationalism, 'patrician dignity', and the respectability of the bourgeois tradition, as opposed to Nazism. Lukács's attempts to forge an ideological united front with Mann were the cultural equivalent of the Comintern's tactic of political coalitions with the non-fascist bourgeoisie (which entailed the renunciation of any class position). Brecht, on the other hand, was rejected outright because: 'Brecht's utter irreverence for the "bourgeois man", his provocatively plebeian sympathies, his extreme artistic unconventionality – so many dialectical counterpoints to Mann's outlook – implicitly conflicted with the mood of the Popular Front and were alien to Lukács.'[24]

We can now see why Lukács enjoys with some justification the reputation of an 'internal opponent' of Stalinism. Pure Stalinism implied uncritical and unconditioned compliance with every twist and turn of the leadership and its international agencies. But Lukács did not automatically follow the 'general line' dictated by Moscow. *He had his own line*, which sometimes coincided with and sometimes clashed with the 'Centre'. While he accepted the fundamental premises of Stalinist politics (socialism in one country, the abandonment of revolutionary internationalism), Lukács was not a blind follower: whatever the circumstances, he refused to give up his own special popular-frontist ideology.

Therefore it is not surprising that Lukács should have been a figure of

[23] Lukács, 'Reportage oder Gestaltung', 'Kritische Bemerkungen anlässlich des Romans von Ottwalt', and 'Aus der Not eine Tugend' in *Die Linkskurve*, 1932. Nevertheless, this defence of the cultural heritage of the past, of Balzac and Goethe, against the sectarian divagations of Third Period neo-Proletkult, did of course have a justifiable side to it; it was, moreover, related to the wing of the KPD that had most reservations about the Stalinist doctrine of 'social-fascism': Heinz Neumann and Willi Münzenberg. In this connection, see Helga Gallas, *Marxistische Literaturtheorie*, Neuwied, 1971, p. 60. To a certain extent, this position of Lukács with respect to traditional culture had affinities with the theses defended by Trotsky in *Literature and Revolution*, when the latter was polemicizing against the Russian partisans of Proletkult.

[24] Isaac Deutscher, 'Lukács as a Critic of Thomas Mann', in *Marxism in our Time*, London, 1972, pp. 291 and 292.

some standing in the political-cultural establishment of the official Communist movement in the years 1934-8 and 1944-8, while being in 'disgrace' in 1929-30, 1941 and 1949-50. It is no accident that, in the explicit criticisms he made of Stalinism after 1956, Lukács denounced in particular the aberrations of the Third Period, the theory of social-fascism, and the 'grotesque' policy of the Comintern between 1939 and 1941 – when the struggle against Nazism and fascism was simply swept under the carpet and replaced by a struggle against the western democracies, accused of being instigators of the war.[25] What Lukács could not accept was Stalinist policy in the so-called 'left' periods, which considered bourgeois democracy (or Social Democracy) to be the prime enemy rather than fascism; any implicit or open compromise with fascism was profoundly repugnant to him. More generally, it might be said that Lukács was in opposition whenever Stalinism was in sharp conflict with western (bourgeois) democracy and culture; which is why he was criticized as a right-opportunist by the Comintern and the Hungarian Communist Party in 1928-30 and why he was arrested in Moscow in 1941.

This arrest merits some comment. Lukács was held for a month or so and it appears that he was accused of having been a 'Trotskyist agent' since the beginning of the twenties.[26] According to Lukács's later reminiscences to his students in Budapest, he was ordered by the NKVD to write his political autobiography. Such a document usually served as a basis for police interrogation of prisoners, which is what happened in his case. In the Lukács Archive in Budapest, there is a three-page political auto-biography in German, covering a period up to April 1941. More than likely this is a copy of a document given to the NKVD by Lukács. The text contains some detailed information about his life as a Communist militant, but includes a bizarre anomaly: there is absolutely no mention of what Lukács always presented as the central axis of his political activity and the reason why he remained loyal to the USSR and the official Communist movement – the struggle against fascism. The very words 'fascism' and 'Nazism' are nowhere to be found in the document, and there is only one fleeting, neutral reference to 'Hitler's rise to power' in 1933. The only possible explanation is that this text was written between April and 22 June 1941 (when the Nazis invaded Russia); i.e. during the time of the

[25] Cf. Lukács, 'Preface' (1967), p. xxviii, and 'The Twin Crises', in NLR 60, 1970, pp. 39-40.
[26] Cf. Istvan Meszáros, *Lukács' Concept of Dialectics*, London, 1971, p. 142.

Molotov-Ribbentrop Pact and German-Soviet 'friendship'. If this is the case, Lukács may well have been arrested because he was considered a potential opponent of Stalin on the question of Nazi Germany – as, in fact, he was, although he took care to hide the fact in his autobiography for the NKVD – and he was released shortly after the German invasion (apparently after Dimitrov had made strong representations on his behalf), when his intellectual services to anti-fascism became useful once more.[27]

Lukács again found himself 'in opposition' in 1949–51, at the peak of the Cold War, and was denounced in Hungary (by Rudas, Révai, Horvath, etc.) as a 'revisionist', 'objectively aiding imperialism', etc. *Pravda* joined in the offensive with a violent attack by Fadyeev and, for a time, Lukács believed he was in danger of being arrested again.[28] This gives us a further insight into the spurious and profoundly insincere nature of his two most notorious self-criticisms of 1929 and 1949 – both, incidentally, rejected by his Stalinist censors as incomplete and unsatisfactory. For Lukács's political and intellectual career from 1928 onwards was coherent: it was a consistent attempt to 'reconcile' Stalinism with bourgeois-democratic culture.

How can Lukács's great turn in 1926–8 and the break from his revolutionary past be explained? Running through his autobiographical writings and interviews of the last few years there is a recurrent theme: 'it was already clear by the nineteen twenties . . . that those very intense hopes with which we followed the Russian Revolution from 1917 on were not to be fulfilled: the wave of world revolution, in which we placed our confidence, did not come to pass.'[29] In 1919 Lukács had fostered a grand messianic vision of an international proletarian revolution which would be the dawn of a new world, the renaissance of humanist culture, and the beginning of the age of freedom. This fervent hope runs through all his writings until 1924, albeit in a more subdued and realistic form. Lukács saw the revolutionary proletariat as the inheritor of all the best traditions of classical philosophy, rationalist humanism, and revolutionary democracy, which had been betrayed, flouted and abandoned by the modern bourgeoisie. The new society and culture founded by the

[27] Evidence on this point is, however, contradictory: cf. Julius Hay, *Geboren 1900*, 1971, pp. 277–8.
[28] Cf. Meszáros, pp. 146–7. This was the time of Rajk's trial and execution.
[29] Lukács, 'The Twin Crises', p. 37.

world-wide socialist revolution would be a dialectical *Aufhebung*, the conservation/negation/transcendence, of this political and cultural heritage.

The ebbing of the revolutionary tide, and the internal changes in the USSR after 1924, caused a profound and distressing disillusionment in Lukács, as in many intellectuals of that era. He refused to return to the fold of the bourgeoisie (as some of those 'disillusioned' intellectuals were to do); his support for the workers' movement was irrevocable. On the other hand, he thought the Left Opposition utopian and unrealistic; a return to the revolutionary principle of 1917–23 seemed impossible. What was he to do? Confronted with the frustration of his great hopes in a new socialist world, the dialectical transcendence of bourgeois humanism, Lukács fell back on a less ambitious and more 'realistic' project: the reconciliation of bourgeois-democratic culture and the Communist movement. Because his ideas were too closely linked to the prospect of the imminent world revolution, he was left ideologically disarmed when faced with the relative stabilization of capitalism. Disoriented by the disappearance of the revolutionary upsurge, Lukács clung to the only two pieces of 'solid' evidence which seemed to him to remain: the USSR and traditional culture. Seeing that the new, transcendent synthesis had failed, he would at least attempt a mediation, a compromise and an alliance between these two different worlds. Lukács's post-1926 writings, despite their intelligence, their undeniable interest, and their theoretical depth, are rather like the glowing embers of a dying furnace.

Much later, in 1956, in common with many cadres, intellectuals, and ordinary militants in the Communist movement, Lukács entered a period of open crisis, a period of questioning and criticism of Stalinism. Explicit criticism, let it be stressed, since veiled objections to Stalinist bureaucracy, expressed in 'Aesopian language', were to be found in some of Lukács's works written well before the Twentieth Congress. For example, in a 1952 essay Leo Kofler, using the pseudonym 'Jules Devérité', pointed out Lukács's criticism of Stalinist bureaucratic optimism in the essay 'People's Tribune or Bureaucrat?', itself written in 1940.[30] However, in this particular text, not only is Lukács's criticism of bureaucracy in the USSR

---

[30] Cf. L. Kofler, 'Das Wesen und die Rolle der Stalinistischen Bürokratie' (1952), in *Stalinismus und Bürokratie*, 1970, p. 63. In a 1969 text Lukács himself welcomed Kofler's essay as objective proof of his opposition to Stalinism before 1953. Cf. Georg Lukács, 'Lénine – Avant-propos', in *Nouvelles Etudes Hongroises*, Budapest, 1973, p. 94.

made in the name of Stalin himself (he claims that 'the elimination of bureaucracy in the USSR is part of the Stalinist programme of the liquidation of the ideological and economic remains of capitalist society'),[31] but, above all, his criticism remains very sketchy and superficial, confining itself to a denunciation of the rhetorical exhortations and feigned optimism of the bureaucrats and their literary spokesmen.

As of 1956, Lukács began to 'settle old scores' with Stalinism – and, to a certain extent, with his own Stalinism. Of course, he welcomed the Twentieth Congress of the CPSU with enthusiasm, and was to consider it a sort of re-run of the Seventh Comintern Congress (1935), which had heralded the turn to the Popular Front.[32] His participation in the ephemeral government of Imre Nagy in 1956, as Minister for Culture, is well known. However, Lukács's post-1956 anti-Stalinism was of a particular type – both incomplete and (to use a convenient label) 'rightist'.

It was incomplete in that Lukács refused to question some of the basic elements of Stalinist policy, such as socialism in one country; because he only condemned the Moscow Trials as 'politically superfluous, since the Opposition had already lost all power', thus implicitly accepting the 'correctness' of Stalin's policies, at the time.[33] A particularly striking example is the 1957 Preface to *The Meaning of Contemporary Realism*, in which Lukács ventures to compare Stalin's mistakes with those of Rosa Luxemburg.[34]

It was 'rightist' in that Lukács inclined towards defining Stalinism as essentially a 'leftist' deviation, a 'sectarian subjectivism'.[35] From the time of his first anti-Stalinist text, the 28 June 1956 speech at the Political Academy of the Hungarian (Communist) Workers' Party, he put forward

[31] Georg Lukács, 'Volkstribun oder Bürokrat?' in *Probleme des Realismus* I, Werke, Band 4 1964. It might be argued that this is a precaution in 'Aesopian' style.

[32] 'If we appear weak, if those forces wishing to show Leninism as Stalinism back to front are to succeed, then the Twentieth Congress will get bogged down, just as in the thirties the grand initiative of the Seventh Comintern Congress did not bear the fruits one might justifiably have expected in 1935'. Lukács, 'Discorso al dibattito filosofico del Circolo Petöfi' (15 June 1956), *Marxismo e Politica Culturale*, Milan, 1972, p. 105.

[33] Georg Lukács, 'Brief an Alberto Carocci' (8 February 1962), in *Marxismus und Stalinismus*, Hamburg, 1970. Cf. also the 1960 Preface to *Existentialisme ou Marxisme?*, Paris, 1961, p. 7: 'Since Khrushchev's speech in 1956, I know that the great trials of 1938 were unnecessary.' In the main part of the work, written in 1947, in a polemic with Simone de Beauvoir, Lukács was still defending the absurd argument that the Moscow Trials had 'increased the chances of a Russian victory at Stalingrad', ibid., p. 168.

[34] Lukács, 'Preface' (1957), in *The Meaning of Contemporary Realism*, p. 10.

[35] In *The Meaning of Contemporary Realism*, written in September 1956, he sees Stalinism as a combination of 'economic subjectivism' and 'revolutionary romanticism'.

the argument that the main mistake of the past had been excessive loyalty to the 'truths of 1917'. According to Lukács, 'innumerable errors in strategy made by our party can be traced to the fact that we simply carried over the truths of 1917 and of the revolutionary period immediately following 1917 . . . with no criticism at all, and without examining the new situation, into a period in which the main strategic problem was not the struggle for socialism, but a trial of strength between fascism and anti-fascism'.[36] It is not necessary to spell out the close link between this vision of the past and the problematic of the 'Blum Theses'. Not surprisingly, the Stalinist period he criticizes most vigorously is 1928–33. The orientation of the USSR between 1948 and 1953 seemed to him, in the last analysis, to be a relapse into the same basic errors.

Lukács aimed the same type of criticism at Stalin's domestic policy: he accused him of having used 'methods of government from the Civil War period, in a situation of peaceful internal consolidation'; 'everything which is objectively inevitable in an intense revolutionary situation . . . was transformed by Stalin into the foundation of everyday Soviet life'.[37] In other words, not only does Lukács make no distinction between the USSR under Lenin (1917–20 was relatively the most democratic and 'pluralist' period in the history of Russia) and the USSR of Stalin, but his criticism of Stalinism is precisely that it 'artificially' maintained the politics, attitude, and orientation of Lenin's time. This position is nothing more than a logical extension of Lukács's 'popular frontist' perspective, which dates back to the twenties. His post-1956 anti-Stalinism was fundamentally the rendering explicit of his criticisms of the USSR and the Comintern which had remained implicit and unarticulated before the Twentieth Congress.

Thus it is not surprising that Lukács totally supported 'Khrushchevism', both in its internal aspects (partial criticism of Stalinism) and its external ones (peaceful co-existence as the international strategy of the Communist movement). He even went so far as to maintain for a time – even though he had always fought economism – that 'in the last analysis' economic competition between different systems 'determines . . . who will emerge victorious from co-existence in the international class struggle'. For 'it is clear that economic competition between systems . . . is, in the last resort . . . the decisive ground on which to determine whether

[36] Georg Lukács, 'Der Kampf des Fortshritts und der Reaktion in der heutigen Kultur' (1956), in *Marxismus und Stalinismus*, p. 139.
[37] Lukács, 'Brief an Alberto Carocci', p. 185 and 'Zur Debatte zwischen China und der Sowjetunion, theoretische-philosophische Bemerkungen' (1963), ibid., p. 211.

the people of one system will choose their own, or a rival system. . . . *Economic development itself is the most effective propaganda in this competition.*[38] It is clear that because of these Krushchevist premises, Lukács was unable to foresee what, from 1963 onwards, was to become a major political phenomenon: the immense powers of attraction of the 'poor' revolutionary states (China, Vietnam, Cuba) for young people; these states are opposed to advanced capitalism, not by 'economic competition', but by a different *model of society* (economic, political, cultural and moral).

Lukács did, however, step outside the narrow confines of the Twentieth Congress and 'Khrushchevism' in his criticism of the 'personality cult'. It seemed absurd to him that the problematic of a period of world-historic importance should be reduced to the individual qualities of one man: one must, he stressed, go beyond the 'person' to the organization, to the 'machine which produced the "personality cult" and then established it by an incessant, extended propagation . . . without the well-oiled operation of such a machine the personality cult would have been only a subjective dream, a product of abnormality'.[39] Around 1966 his views started to become more radical, and he criticized official 'de-Stalinization' as insufficient.[40] However, he never grasped the roots of the Stalinist phenomenon or sought to develop a Marxist analysis of the Soviet bureaucracy, but confined himself to denouncing its 'super-structural' aspects: brutal manipulation, predominance of tactics over theory, etc. At the beginning of 1968 he was still defining Stalinism as a type of 'sectarianism' that wished to 'perpetuate the *belle époque* of the Civil War'.[41]

In 1968, Lukács began to take a new turn towards the 'old Lukács'. At the risk of over-simplification of a contradictory development, this can be characterized as the beginnings of an orientation to the revolutionary Left.

---

[38] Lukács, '*Zur Debatte zwischen China und der Sowjetunion*', pp. 208–9, and 'Probleme der Kulturellen Koexistenz' (1964), ibid., pp. 215–16 (Lukács's own emphasis). In fact this argument was too far removed from Lukács's basic position, too vulgarly economist for him to defend it for long. In 1966–67 he challenged it specifically: 'A rise in the standard of living alone will never be capable of acting as a real pole of attraction for western countries (this was one of Khrushchev's illusions)'. 'Le Grand Octobre 1917 et la littérature', in *L'homme et la Société*, no. 5, July–September 1967, p. 14.

[39] Lukács, 'Brief an Alberto Carocci', p. 172.

[40] Abendroth, Holz, Kofler, *Conversations with Lukács* (1966), Bari, 1968, p. 189.

[41] Georg Lukács, 'Alle Dogmatiker sind Defaitisten', in *Forum*, May 1968.

In his last essays and interviews, elements can be found of a left criticism of Stalinism qualitatively different from that of 1956–67, although there are points of continuity.[42] As in the past, the starting point for this 'left turn' was of course a favoured world-historic year of the twentieth century: 1968 – which, in the space of a few months, experienced the Tet offensive in Vietnam, student revolt on an international scale, the May events in France, the Cultural Revolution in China, the Prague 'spring' and Soviet invasion. Lukács correctly grasped the crucial importance of these events: in an interview in 1969 he stated: 'Today this whole system is facing the initial stages of an extraordinarily profound crisis. . . . I mean by this the Vietnamese War, the radical crisis in the United States . . . the crisis in France, in Germany, in Italy. . . . Looked at in a world-historical perspective, we are at the threshold of a world crisis.'[43] As for Czechoslovakia, in an informal conversation with one of his former Hungarian students, only weeks after the occupation of Prague by Warsaw Pact troops, Lukács clearly showed his anger and stressed the terrible historical implications of the event: 'This is the greatest disaster for the communist movement since the German social-democrats approved the Kaiser's war credits in 1914. That put an end to the first dream of the socialist fraternity of man. Need I say more?'[44] Some young revolutionary students from Western Europe, who visited Lukács in September 1968, were struck by the harshness of his criticism of the USSR and also by his great interest in the May events in France.[45] Lukács understood the dialectical relationship between the two crises, that of Stalinism and that of the bourgeois world, and constantly stressed their interdependence.

At the age of eighty-three, therefore, Lukács entered a new stage in his political-ideological development, which was, to a certain extent, a return to the revolutionary orientation of his youth. Obviously, history cannot be repeated, and the Lukács of 1969–71 can in no way be identified with what he was in 1919–24: the word 'return' is used metaphorically to point out a

---

[42] On a series of issues – Stalin's 'realism' after the decline of the world revolution, self-criticism of the 'messianism' of *History and Class Consciousness*, etc. – Lukács did not totally abandon his former positions.

[43] Lukács, 'The Twin Crises', p. 44.

[44] George Urban, 'A conversation with Lukács', in *Encounter*, October 1971, p. 35. We should add, in passing, that the vote on war credits in August 1914 was viewed by Lenin as the ultimate bankruptcy of the Second International, and thus the beginning of a realization of the need to set up a new international proletarian organization. However, we would be forcing the comparison a bit too far if we attributed such conclusions to Lukács.

[45] Report by C. Urjewicz to the author, September 1974.

certain analogy between two distinct phenomena.

In this sense it is extremely significant that one of the first expressions of his return was a 're-appropriation' of Ady. At the beginning of 1969, Lukács wrote an article on Ady (following a long silence on his favourite poet of the past), which directly linked the work of the great writer, who died in 1919, to the prospect of a deep-rooted change in contemporary Hungary: 'I believe that when Hungary has really passed beyond the Stalinist era and begun to construct a living socialism, founded on a new proletarian democracy, there will be many more people who find that Ady is their favourite poet.'[46] Lukács's strong praise for Ady as a consistently revolutionary poet was closely linked to a new opposition to Hegelian 'realism': 'I have never considered the Hegelian concept of reconciliation with reality (*Versöhnung mit der Wirklichkeit*) to be a valid one. Even during my Hegelian period, my intellectual attitude was dominated by Ady's "the mission to veto" . . .'[47] By contrasting Ady's *Ugocsa non coronat* with Hegel's *Versöhnung*, Lukács returned to the revolutionary problematic of his youth and challenged what, from 1926 to 1968, had formed – implicitly or explicitly – the 'philosophical' basis of his unstable and difficult compromise with Stalinism (and its bureaucratic successors): the idea of reconciliation.

At the end of 1968, this challenge assumed a directly political form in an essay on Lenin and the transitional period, completed after the occupation of Czechoslovakia (only one chapter has been published, in Hungary in 1970). In this essay, Lukács contrasts the socialist democracy of Lenin with Stalinist bureaucratic manipulation. One example he mentions in this connection are the 'Communist Saturdays' of 1919, which were self-activity, freely chosen in the service of the community. It is no accident that, in this context, Lukács quotes his remarkable article of 1919, 'The Moral Mission of the Communist Party'. Of course, he mentions its idealistic limitations; but the problematic of 'the reign of freedom' and the

[46] Lukács, 'The Importance and Significance of Ady', in *New Hungarian Quarterly*, no. 35, vol. X, autumn 1969, p. 60.

[47] Georg Lukács, 'Mon chemin vers Marx' (1969), in *Nouvelles Etudes Hongroises*, 1973, p. 78. See also Lukács's interview with *New Left Review* (no. 68, July 1971, p. 58): 'Ady was a revolutionary who had great admiration for Hegel, but he never accepted this aspect of Hegel, which I myself always rejected, from the beginning: his *Versöhnung mit der Wirklichkeit*.' The formulation 'always rejected' is inexact, as we have seen. (See note 7 above.) In reality, as of 1926 Lukács had accepted – with reservations, of course – 'this aspect of Hegel'. The formulation in the NLR interview may represent an attempt by Lukács to 'reinterpret' his past.

transition to communism have once more begun to interest him.[48]

At the beginning of 1969, Lukács clarified his new position as a revolutionary left critic of Stalinism in an interview: 'So as not to conceal my personal ideas, by socialist democracy I understand democracy in ordinary life, as it appeared in the Workers' Soviets of 1871, 1905 and 1917, as it once existed in the socialist countries, and in which form it must be re-animated.'[49] Nearly all Lukács's interviews in the years 1969–71 contrast workers' soviets with both arbitrary bureaucracy and bourgeois democracy, as a true, authentic democratic system that arises each time the revolutionary proletariat appears on the stage of history.[50] For the first time, Lukács presented the Hungarian Soviet Republic of 1919, in spite of its weaknesses, as an example of socialist democracy – opposed, in every respect (particularly culturally), to the methods of the Stalinist era.[51] One of the most important political consequences of this new revolutionary perspective was Lukács's scepticism towards 'self-reform' by the bureaucracy. He had believed in this for a long while, and expressed himself prudently on so delicate a subject; but in his last interview, just before his death, he was clear and trenchant: 'I have never yet seen a reform carried out by bureaucrats. . . . I do not think there can be a bureaucratic change and, what is more, I do not really think there is any such intention . . . they want to maintain the bureaucratic balance we have today.'[52] Significantly, Lukács went on to mention the events in Poland, the 'explosive strikes' of 1970, adding: 'what happened in Poland can happen today or tomorrow in every socialist country'.

His new orientation was also expressed in relation to the class struggle in the capitalist world, particularly in his attitude towards Vietnam. He emphasized the world-historical implications of the Vietnamese struggle in a striking analogy: 'The defeat of the USA in the Vietnam war is to the "American way of life" rather like what the Lisbon earthquake was to French feudalism. . . . Even if decades were to pass between the Lisbon

[48] Lukács, 'Lenin und die Fragen der Übergangsperiode' (1968), in *Goethepreis, 1970*, pp. 84–5. Cf. on this point Meszáros, p. 151.

[49] Lukács, 'Die Deutschen, eine Nation der Spätentwickler', in *Goethepreis, 1970*, p. 112. One significant detail: Trotsky is mentioned, together with Lenin, as a leader of the October Revolution, both 'having led the movement of the Workers' Soviets'.

[50] Cf. for example, NLR 60, p. 41; NLR 68, p. 50; Y. Bourdet, *Figures de Lukács*, p. 187, etc.

[51] Lukács, 'La Politique Culturelle de la République des Conseils', interview of 1969 in *Action Poétique*, no. 49, 1972, p. 31.

[52] Lukács, Interview with Y. Bourdet in *Figures de Lukács*, p. 186.

earthquake and the fall of the Bastille, history can repeat itself, in the sense that out of movements which are at first completely immature ideologically and based solely on a legitimate feeling of revolt, real movements are formed.'[53] The Lisbon earthquake of 1755 triggered an extraordinary ideological crisis in Europe, particularly in France. The deadly and absurd event (total destruction of the city and 20,000 deaths) challenged Leibniz's optimistic (and conformist) ideology, 'We live in the best of all possible worlds', Alexander Pope's 'What is, is right', as well as the whole concept of divine Providence. Voltaire made his Doctor Pangloss, the philosopher of smug optimism, die in the Lisbon earthquake.[54] Thus, for Lukács, the consequence of the Vietnam war was, by analogy, as follows. First, the end of optimistic illusions in an 'era of peace' on a world scale – illusions he himself had harboured since 1956.[55] Second, the decline of what he called 'cybernetic religion': blind faith in machines, computers, and electronic instruments, omnipotent and provident fetishes, substitutes for the God of the eighteenth century, which were all defeated by the NLF.[56] Last, and above all, the appearance of an enormous crisis of values, a radical challenge to imperialist ideology, which could later erupt in a massive revolutionary upsurge of international dimensions. This is no longer the messianic hope for immediate revolution that Lukács had in 1919; for the first time since the twenties, he was beginning to conceive of world revolution as a real historical prospect, in the present century.

From this standpoint, Lukács began to criticize the reformist workers' parties: Social Democracy, whose politics in Germany for fifty years had been just a 'series of capitulations', and the Communist Parties – 'In Germany, the parties, and unfortunately this includes the Communist Party itself, because of their exclusive orientation to tactical decisions and their loss of a grand historical perspective, no longer act as a pole of attraction for young people.'[57] He began to regard the student movement sympathetically, and with (critical) interest. He refused to label these radicalized youth currents 'ultra-leftist' – a convenient formula used far

---

[53] *Goethepreis, 1970*, p. 108.

[54] Voltaire also wrote a philosophical poem on the event. Cf. L.G. Crocker, 'The Problem of Evil', in J.F. Lively, *The Enlightenment*, London, 1966, p. 159: 'The Lisbon earthquake, which occurred in that most Catholic of cities on All Saints' Day, 1 November 1755, was a *crise de conscience* for the eighteenth century.'

[55] 'We are now entering an era in which peace and co-existence have become possible.' Lukács, *Der Kampf des Fortschritts und der Reaktion* (1956), p. 141.

[56] Interview with Lukács on ORTF, 1971.

[57] *Goethepreis, 1970*, p. 110.

too frequently by the leadership of the traditional Communist Parties. On the contrary he stated: 'Anyone who thinks he can apply a book written by Lenin in 1920 to American youth of 1969 or that Lenin's criticism of Roland-Holst can be made to fit Dutschke would be terribly mistaken.'[58] In radical contrast to the bureaucratic line on the 'adventurist', 'manipulated', or even 'provocative' character of the young 'ultra-leftists', Lukács explicitly stated: 'I think that this student movement which is springing up, not just in Germany, but all over the world, is an exceptionally positive phenomenon' that must be understood as the product of a simultaneous crisis in the two systems that triumphed in the Second World War: Stalinism and the 'American way of life'.[59]

On 4 June 1971 death cut short, at its outset, this astonishing 'return to first principles'; after half a century of 'reconciliation' and 'lost illusions', Lukács had, in the last three years of his life, begun to rediscover the intense hopes, the red flame of the People's Commissar of 1919.

[58] Lukács, 'The Twin Crises', p. 43.
[59] Lukács, *Goethepreis, 1970*, pp. 107–8.

Index